THE ECONOMY
OF IRAQ

THE ECONOMY OF IRAQ

Oil, Wars, Destruction of Development and Prospects, 1950–2010

Abbas Alnasrawi

Contributions in Economics and Economic History, Number 154

Greenwood Press
Westport, Connecticut • London

330.9567
AU5e

Library of Congress Cataloging-in-Publication Data

Alnasrawi, Abbas.
    The economy of Iraq : oil, wars, destruction of development and
prospects, 1950-2010 / Abbas Alnasrawi.
        p.   cm. – (Contributions in economics and economic history,
    ISSN 0084-9235 ; no. 154)
    Includes bibliographical references and index.
    ISBN 0-313-29186-1 (alk. paper)
    1. Petroleum industry and trade – Iraq – History – 20th century.
    2. Petroleum industry and trade – Iraq – Forecasting.   3. Iran-Iraq
    War, 1980-1988 – Economic aspects – Iraq.   4. Persian Gulf War, 1991–
    –Economic aspects – Iraq.   5. Iraq – Economic conditions.   I. Title.
    II. Series.
    HD9576.I72A647   1994
    330.9567'0442 – dc20   93-37510

British Library Cataloguing in Publication Data is available.

Library of Congress Catalog Card Number: 93-37510
ISBN: 0-313-29186-1
ISSN: 0084-9235

First published in 1994

Greenwood Press, 88 Post Road West, Westport, CT 06881
An imprint of Greenwood Publishing Group, Inc.

Printed in the United States of America

∞™

The paper used in this book complies with the
Permanent Paper Standard issued by the National
Information Standards Organization (Z39.48 – 1984).

10 9 8 7 6 5 4 3 2 1

To the Children of Iraq

Contents

Tables

Acknowledgments

It gives me great pleasure to take this opportunity to acknowledge with gratitude the support I received in researching and writing this book.

A sabbatical leave from the University of Vermont helped me to devote my time to work on the manuscript. A small grant from the Graduate College at the University of Vermont helped with the research work which was carried out at the libraries of Harvard University. Discussions with many friends and colleagues in this country, Europe, and the Arab world helped clarify many issues.

At Greenwood Press, I am grateful for the support and guidance I received from Dr. James R. Ice. I owe Sandy Mable and Dottie LaBrie special thanks for their invaluable assistance in the preparation of several drafts of the manuscript.

The constant support and encouragement shown by my family is greatly appreciated.

I alone am responsible for any errors that may remain.

Introduction

In 1960, Iraq's real GDP measured in 1980 prices was $8.7 billion. In 1979 GDP peaked at $54 billion. And by 1993 Iraq's GDP has declined to $10 billion, the equivalent of what it was in 1961. Put another way, these figures inform us that more than three decades of real GDP growth have been erased. But these dismal statistics tell a small part of this unique episode in the history of the second half of this century. This is so because the GDP in 1961 had to support 7 million people; in 1993 it had to support a population that has grown to nearly 21 million. Such a drastic collapse in per capita GDP translates into the nullification of nearly half a century of growth and improvement in the living standards of the population.

To place this change in some international context, Iraq in the years prior to its invasion of Kuwait was at the top of the per capita GDP ladder of developing countries. By 1993, real monthly earnings were lower than the monthly earnings of unskilled agricultural workers in India—one of the poorest countries in the world.

What happened to an economy noted for the wealth of its oil reserves, agricultural potential, water resources, relatively high rates of literacy and skills, vast access to foreign technology and expertise, an enviable balance-of-payments surplus and foreign reserves, and a long history of determined effort to develop and diversify the economy?

Simply stated, the central concern of this work is to find an explanation or explanations of what happened to cause this unprecedented and unparalleled collapse. To this end, the first chapter is devoted to an examination of the critical role of the oil sector in the Iraqi economy. Chapter 2 is devoted to a study of Iraq's development policies under the monarchy and assesses development programs and policies in the

1950s. In the following chapter, the development plans of the republican regime in the period 1958-68 are evaluated. In Chapter 4, the Baath party's economic philosophy, development strategies, and plans are analyzed. The demise of development that started with the outbreak of the Iran-Iraq war of 1980-88 is examined in Chapter 5. In Chapter 6, the economic consequences of the 1990 invasion of Kuwait, including the impact of the United Nations sanctions on the Iraqi economy, are examined. Chapter 7 examines Iraq's changing economic fortunes in the period 1950-93, and the last chapter attempts to shed some light on Iraq's economic future against the background of the economic destruction of the two Gulf wars.

THE ECONOMY
OF IRAQ

CHAPTER 1

The Evolution of Iraq's Oil Industry

One of the most striking features of the world oil map is the concentration of crude oil reserves in a few countries. In the Western Hemisphere, most of the oil reserves are concentrated in the United States, Venezuela, Mexico, and Canada. In the Eastern Hemisphere, they are concentrated in the former Soviet Union, North Africa, and the Middle East. Because of the stage of their economic development, the United States and the former Soviet Union developed their oil industries primarily to meet their countries' own demands for energy. But since other oil-producing countries have a very low indigenous demand for energy, their oil resources were developed to meet world demand for oil—mainly that of the industrialized countries of Western Europe, Japan, and later on the United States.

Foreign capital and technology had to be called upon to develop oil resources since capital requirements for developing, producing, transporting, refining, and finally marketing oil products were well beyond the capabilities of countries like Venezuela, Iraq, Iran, Kuwait, Saudi Arabia, Libya, Indonesia, Nigeria, and Algeria.

The pattern of relationships between Iraq, as well as other oil-producing countries, and the oil companies exploiting oil resources was regulated by concession agreements. According to the provisions of the concession, the foreign-owned oil company obtained an exclusive right to develop and export Iraq's oil; it was the sole determinant of the level of oil output and export; and it alone had the prerogative to set the price of oil. In short the government had no input in the development or the pricing of what became the most important commodity of the national economy. The role of the government was a passive one in that it became a recipient of a fixed sum per unit of export.[1]

OIL CONCESSIONS IN IRAQ AND
THE AGREEMENT OF 1952

The history of foreign capital seeking investment in Iraq oil goes back to the latter part of the nineteenth century when Iraq was still part of the Ottoman Empire.[2] It was not until 1925, however, that the first concession for the exploration and production of oil was granted to the Turkish Petroleum Company (subsequently renamed Iraq Petroleum Company – IPC) for a period of seventy-five years. Oil was first struck in commercial quantities in 1927. Two affiliates of IPC, Mosul Petroleum Company (MPC) and Basra Petroleum Company (BPC), secured additional concessions from the Iraqi Government. MPC was awarded a seventy-five-year concession in 1932; and BPC obtained another seventy-five-year accord in 1938. The three concessions covered the total area of Iraq.[3]

These three companies were owned in equal shares of 23.75 percent by British Petroleum (BP), Shell Petroleum (Shell), Compagnie Français des Petroles (CFP), and Near Eastern Development Corporation, which was owned equally by Standard Oil of New Jersey (Exxon) and Mobil. The remaining 5 percent went to Participation and Exploration Company.

The 1951 nationalization of the oil industry in Iran, the adoption of the principle of profit-sharing between some of the companies and host governments such as Venezuela and Saudi Arabia, and the persistent demand of Iraq for more royalties led to a series of negotiations between IPC, MPC, and BPC and the government. These negotiations culminated in the agreement of 1952[4] – henceforth called the Agreement – the two most important provisions of which are: (1) The hitherto fixed payment per unit of production was replaced by a new formula of profit-sharing according to which the government would receive annually 50 percent of the profits resulting from the operations of the companies in Iraq. Profits were defined as the difference between the posted price of oil exports and the cost of production, and (2) the government was entitled to receive f.o.b. seaboard terminal, as part of its 50 percent share, up to 12.5 percent of the net production. The government had the option to sell this amount at whatever price it could obtain.

THE GROWTH OF OUTPUT AND REVENUE

The Agreement was an important landmark in Iraq's petroleum history and economy in that it ushered in an era of unprecedented growth in the oil sector.

The growth of the oil industry was a response to the worldwide increase in demand for petroleum in the post–World War II period. It resulted from the need to rebuild the shattered economies of Europe, the exceptional increase in military demand for oil in peacetime, mechanization of agriculture in many parts of the world, the emergence of petroleum-based industries, the substitution of oil for coal as a source of energy, the general explosion in the demand of the transportation sector, and general boom conditions which prevailed in the industrialized countries. In addition, it was projected that the United States, which became a net importer in 1948, would rely to an increasing degree upon importing low-cost foreign oil to meet its rising energy requirements.[5]

While the worldwide increase in demand for crude oil helped Iraq to expand its output, the newly introduced profit-sharing principle provided for a much higher revenue per unit of output, which increased to $0.84 per barrel in 1952–59, compared with $0.22 per barrel in 1950.[6]

Under the new contractual arrangements, the level of oil revenue became a function of (1) cost of production, (2) price of crude at the Iraqi border, (3) share of the government in profit, and (4) the level of output. Since (1) and (3) were fixed by the Agreement itself, the determinants of oil revenue become, therefore, output and price, both of which were beyond government control.

OIL OUTPUT

Until the early 1970s, most of the oil outside the United States and the former USSR was produced by a few vertically integrated multinational oil corporations. These international oil firms are Exxon, Shell, BP, Mobil, Texaco, Gulf Oil Corporation (Gulf), Standard Oil of California (Chevron), and CFP.

In 1960, these firms produced 34.1 percent of U.S. oil and 87 percent of Venezuelan oil. The eight companies in the same year produced 92 percent of Middle Eastern oil. In Iraq, as well as in other oil countries, the operating company that produced the crude was owned jointly by more than one of these eight companies. Thus, in one combination or another, a number of or all of the major oil companies owned 100 percent of the operating companies in Kuwait and Saudi Arabia, 94 percent of those in Iran, and 95 percent of those in Iraq. In addition to these joint ventures, five major firms were parties to long-term contracts of the sale and purchase of oil from Kuwait and Iran.[7]

In Iraq, prior to the enactment of the 1972 nationalization measures, oil was produced by IPC and its affiliates on behalf of its shareholders. The volume of output was jointly determined by the shareholders, knowing that Iraq was only one of several sources of supply. An elaborate mechanism was instituted to guide IPC. The 1948 Agreement among IPC shareholders stipulated that each partner must submit its oil requirement for a five-year period five years before the beginning of the period. A shareholder should, for example, submit in 1960 its oil requirements for the period 1965-70. The oil so produced was delivered to the shareholders' terminals at the Mediterranean or the Persian Gulf at cost of production, since IPC was organized as a non-profit production company. This delivery at the cost of production is limited to that part of the owner's requirement that does not exceed its share in IPC capital.[8]

Those who nominated more than their share in the joint ownership had to buy the increment from partners who nominated less than their IPC ownership share. The oil so transacted was priced at a "production cost plus" formula. The cost element was the actual cost of production and delivery. The plus element was half the difference between production cost and the posted price at the terminals. This clause of the Agreement provided, in other words, for equal profit sharing between an underlifter and an overlifter.

It goes without saying that it was to the advantage of any single country that oil be produced at maximum capacity since higher volumes would generate higher revenue at the prevailing price. But such output, however, would have to be at the expense of other sources of supply. Should every country's demand for higher output be met simultaneously, a glut was bound to push prices downward.

To prevent this situation from arising, any single firm was required to regulate its offtake from the various sources, including Iraq, in such a way as to meet the market's demand for oil at a price that would maximize its profits, which in turn would maximize the net integrated return across a wide network of investment around the globe.[9]

THE PRICING OF IRAQ CRUDE OIL TO 1950

Under the oil concession system, the power to determine output and posted prices was vested in the concession holders. The government was a passive recipient of oil revenue. Prior to 1952, as was indicated earlier, such revenue was fixed; while under the provisions of the 1952 Agreement, the revenue varied as it became a function of the difference between cost of production and the posted prices.

The price of Iraqi crude oil, like that of the other producing countries of the Middle East, was set at oil-exporting terminals in the Persian Gulf region and the East Mediterranean. At these two locations, the sellers published (posted) the price at which they were willing to sell the oil at their disposal f.o.b. In the absence of large number of sellers and buyers, since the international oil industry was dominated by a few firms, the determination of posted prices became an administrative decision rather than the outcome of ordinary forces of market supply and demand.

Under these conditions, posted prices were derived directly from a historical pattern in which the prices of oil at the United States Gulf of Mexico (USGM) were the ruling prices.[10] According to this formula, which was the foundation of the oil price structure until 1941, the buyer of crude oil was billed at the ruling prices at USGM, plus the freight charges from USGM to the point of destination, irrespective of the actual source of supply. Moreover this formula had the effect of equalizing the delivered price of oil for any buyer regardless of the location of the seller.

With all other producing centers secondary in importance to the United States, it was not only convenient but also profitable for the suppliers of non-American oil to link their prices to USGM prices, since the latter were based on the higher production cost of the marginal producer.[11] The anomalous nature of this system from the perspective of the consumer may be seen in the case of the Iraqi consumer who was charged prices based upon quotations in USGM, regardless of the facts that (1) the crude oil was produced in Iraq; (2) it was produced at low cost; (3) it was refined in a nearby refinery; and (4) it was marketed by a local company.[12]

This single basing point system came under pressure as the capacity of the Middle East oil industry expanded, and outlets for the increased output had to be found either in the adjacent markets or in markets closer to the United States.[13] In either case the Middle East exporter was faced with two alternatives. The first was to reduce his f.o.b. price in order to displace American oil, and the second was to make freight absorption while continuing to quote the USGM prices.

Given the pattern of the world oil markets and of ownership among the international suppliers, it was only natural to follow the second course of action.[14] But the adoption of this course of action meant that the exporter of Middle East oil would not only have to make freight absorption on the sales he made in the direction of the United States but also have to be content with either the lessening or complete elimination of phantom freight on the sales he made in his vicinity.[15] To put it differently, the Middle East began to emerge as a new production center quoting USGM prices and charging the actual freight costs from its sources of supply.[16]

This development had the effect of establishing a "natural" market area for Middle East oil. The westward limit of this area was the "watershed" where it was to the benefit of the seller to ship Middle Eastern oil rather than Western Hemisphere oil. This "watershed," at the freight rate prevailing then, was in the region of Italy.[17]

However, as the United States began to lose its position as a net oil exporting country and as Middle East oil continued to increase and new markets for it had to be found, a break in the linkage with USGM pricing formula had to be effected.

The adjustment to the new conditions was facilitated when the removal of the price controls by the U.S. Office of Price Administration coincided with a period of oil shortage, thus allowing a series of increases in the prices of American and Venezuelan oils. The Middle East prices were also raised, but not by the same proportion. The differential in f.o.b. prices in the two regions helped the exporter of Middle East oil to push his oil westward beyond the equalization point.[18] By mid-1948, the United Kingdom became the new watershed; and by 1950, this new watershed was pushed further westward to the U.S. Atlantic coast through reductions in Middle East prices to compensate for the region's distance from the new consumption centers in the United States.

With the selection of New York as the new watershed where Middle East and Western Hemisphere oils meet, the wheel had turned full circle from a USGM-plus formula to a U.S. Atlantic coast-minus formula.[19]

This series of developments ended with Middle East prices publicly posted for the first time in 1950. Moreover, this shift to publicly posted prices coincided with the replacement of fixed royalties per unit of output by an income tax that was set to give Iraq 50 percent of the profit. The significance of the new system for the Iraqi economy was that the government acquired, for the first time, a direct interest in crude oil prices.[20]

PRICE DEVELOPMENTS, 1950–1960

When Middle East crude oil prices were posted in 1950, the market consisted of a few sellers producing for their own needs and participating with each other in production enterprises and long-term contracts. If we add to this the fact that the demand was strong and output was carried out at near capacity, we can see no reason why prices should not remain stable. Price stability during this period reflected the close adjustment between supply and demand in crude oil prices, which in turn were reflected in the market prices at which products were sold to consumers.[21]

In an oligopolistic market where there are only a few sellers, a cut in the price initiated by one seller is bound to be followed by his rivals in order to protect their market shares. On the other hand, a rise in the price may not be followed, and thus the price cutter may lose his own share of the market. Once a satisfactory level of prices is reached, the sellers prefer to adhere to it and thus minimize their rivals' reactions rather than attempt a net gain in the volume of their sales by changing the price. But should market forces make a change in the price desirable for the group, then one of the sellers will take the lead in setting a new price which, if acceptable to his rivals, will be adhered to.[22]

Middle East crude prices, which moved parallel with (though below) those in the Western Hemisphere, began to show signs of strain toward the end of this period. This was mainly due to the emergence of excess capacity that manifested itself in the discounting of posted prices. But with the emergence of this excess capacity, the few sellers lost their power to control prices and output, as can be seen in the following paragraphs.

Basically, for every oil firm, especially the integrated ones, spare capacity is unavoidable from time to time. This surplus capacity is important for the firm as an insurance against a variety of embarrassments such as an unexpected high demand, natural disasters, or unexpected interruption of normal trade channels.[23]

However, the surplus capacity that developed during the 1950s was of a different nature. The oil industry committed itself to an expansion of its productive capacity in the hope that the initial high demand would continue. This expectation did not materialize, and surplus capacity began to appear.[24]

This excess capacity would have been worked off if the oil companies were free to lower their prices and import all the oil they wished into the European and American markets. For one thing, coal protectionism in Europe presented a serious problem to any oil firm attempting to cut its prices, for fear that low crude oil price might provoke retaliation in the form of import restrictions.[25] Another reason was that the oil protection policy in the United States acted as a depressant on the attempt to cut prices in order to increase imports. To protect the domestic oil industry from the effect of the cheap Middle Eastern oil, the United States restricted oil imports, first on a voluntary basis in 1957 and then by making the restriction mandatory in 1959.[26]

If we add to these factors the nature of market itself — few sellers jointly involved in oil production ventures and long-term supply contracts — then it should be expected that no seller was in a position to precipitate a downward movement in prices.[27] In a situation like this, nonprice competition had to be intensified. Discounts off the posted prices became an important tool in this competition.

More important, however, was the entry toward the end of the 1950s, of nonintegrated firms into the Middle East oil industry. Their successful entry proved that the height of the barrier to entry was not as prohibitive as it had been earlier. This was illustrated by the entry of such firms as the Japanese Arabian Oil Company, Ente Nazionale Idrocarburi, and other independent companies.[28] The consequences of such entry are clear: the displacement, partially at least, of integrated oil from some markets, increase in surplus capacity, and intensification of pressure on posted prices.

In addition to the entry of independent firms, there was the destabilizing influence of the reentry of Soviet oil exports into the world markets in 1958. These exports were part of a policy of the Soviet oil trust to regain the traditional share of 19 percent of world trade which it had in the early 1930s.[29]

Moreover, a pressure on the prices of crude oil came from the opposite end of the market (i.e., the products' market). The expanding capacity of independent refiners, especially in Europe, and the availability of "distress" oil, made it possible to sell oil products at prices lower than those offered by the integrated firms.[30] This practice helped these refiners to expand sales and market share and eventually bring product prices down.[31] This in turn reacted upon crude prices with further pressure and discounts.[32]

As the number of sellers and buyers increased, transactions outside the integrated network expanded. While the new sellers were in a position to sell to independent buyers at lower than the posted prices, the integrated firms had either to compete and offer their oil at similar prices or to lose their markets. Since they were unable to reduce the postings, discounts off these postings had to be made.

Thus the price of Iraq oil ex-Basra before the Suez Crisis of 1956 was $1.87 per barrel (36° API). However, once the crisis was over, oil companies began to offer their oils at discount. By late 1958, Middle East crudes were estimated to be discounted by 11 to 13 cents per barrel.[34] In February 1959, BP took the lead in reducing the prices of all its Middle East oils by 18 cents a barrel. Thus Iraq oil of 36° API was priced at $1.82 and $2.31 per barrel at Basra and in the east Mediterranean respectively.[33,35] In this move the sellers did no more than take formal note of discounts.[36] In August 1960, there was another round of price cuts ending with pricing Iraq oil at $1.74 and $2.21 per barrel at the above two locations respectively.

This price reduction is significant for two reasons. First, the way in which the prices finally settled at the new levels reflected the strain under which the system was functioning. This strain was reflected in the manner in which the integrated companies differed in their evaluation of the timing and the magnitude of the price cut.[37]

Second, as a direct reaction to this price cut, the oil-producing countries formed the Organization of the Petroleum Exporting Countries (OPEC). One of OPEC's earliest resolutions was the demand that prices be restored to their pre-August 1960 level and that they be stabilized.[38]

NATIONALIZATION AND OIL
PRICE DEVELOPMENTS IN THE OPEC ERA

The erosion of Middle East and Venezuelan oil prices relative to the prices of U.S.-produced oil; the introduction of an oil quota system in the United States; the general downward pressure on prices as the number of sellers increased; and the powerlessness of any one government to legislate a change in its oil output, prices, and income persuaded oil-producing countries to coordinate their positions vis-à-vis the oil companies. The boycott of nationalized Iranian oil in the early 1950s served as a painful reminder of the devastating economic and political consequences of such acts, as well as the dispensibility of any one country's oil in the pattern of international oil supply. Although the nationalization of the Suez Canal by Egypt in 1956 demonstrated a potential for success, it was not until 1960 that the Organization of Petroleum Exporting Countries was created.[39]

While the immediate impetus for the creation of OPEC was the unilateral price reductions by the oil companies, the new organization did not have the power, the means, or the unity of purpose to force the companies to change their pricing policies. Although several resolutions were passed by OPEC calling upon the companies to restore prices to their August 1960 levels, the companies simply ignored such calls. And by 1963 OPEC abandoned the price issue in favor of other means to raise per-barrel revenue for member countries. The price issue remained dormant until 1970 when the Libyan government was successful in negotiating an increase in its posted oil prices and a rise in the tax rate from 50 percent to 54 percent. Following the Libyan settlement, the companies unilaterally announced an increase in Middle East posted prices, as well as an increase in governments' share of the profit to 55 percent, from the traditional 50 percent.

The decade of the 1970s ushered in a number of major changes in the world oil market, international monetary system, the oil concession regime, oil prices, and Iraq's oil revenue. Some of the significant changes in the world oil market include the emergence of the United States as the single most important oil-importing country, the gradual disappearance of excess capacity in oil-producing countries, the interest of the latter in conservation, and the continued rise in the number of independent oil companies willing to offer better terms to producing countries. To preempt demands for higher prices, the companies agreed to enter into OPEC-wide negotiations over prices. These negotiations, which culminated in the February 1971 Tehran price agreement, stabilized tax rates and prices over the next five years. The net result of the changes amounted to an increase in per-barrel revenue for the key 34-degree API Arabian Light crude from 91 cents in 1970 to $1.53 by 1975.

A few months after the conclusion of the Tehran agreement, the international monetary system was thrown into a major crisis when the U.S. government decided in August 1971 to suspend convertibility of the dollar into gold, leading to the dollar's depreciation in terms of other currencies. Since the dollar was the currency in which oil prices were expressed and government revenue was computed, the new crisis prompted OPEC to go back to the companies to seek upward price adjustments to offset the loss in the dollar purchasing power, a loss which the companies offset in part.

Concurrent with these fiscal changes, OPEC sought a change in the concession system that would allow member countries to purchase equity interest in operating companies such as Aramco, KPC, IPC, and others. By the end of 1972, an agreement was reached according to which governments were allowed to acquire a 25 percent interest in 1973, which was to rise to 30 percent in 1978 and then gradually to 51 percent by 1982.

Iraq, however, distinguished itself from other OPEC member countries by its decision in June 1972 to nationalize the IPC concession after twelve years of disputes and negotiations, thus ending a system of foreign control over its oil resources which had been in existence for nearly fifty years.[40]

THE 1973 OIL PRICE REVOLUTION

The forces of change in the international oil industry, the crisis of the international monetary system, and the continued rise in the demand for oil and in prices of petroleum products persuaded many oil-producing countries that the provisions of the Tehran agreement ceased to provide adequate compensation for their depletable national resource — oil. In order to protect member countries' interests, OPEC decided to ask the companies to set higher posted prices. When the negotiations started on October 8, 1973, the price of the Arabian-marker crude oil was about $3 per barrel, yielding government revenue of about $1.76 per barrel. The failure of oil companies to respond to OPEC demand that the price be raised by $2 (they offered 45 cents only) and the continued Arab–Israeli October war, which had already been raging when the negotiations started, prompted the governments to raise prices unilaterally to $5.12 per barrel, thus increasing their revenue by $1.28 per barrel to $3.04 per barrel.[41]

Soon after the October price increase, an oil shortage emerged because of the decision by Arab oil-producing countries (except Iraq) to lower output and impose an embargo on oil exports to the United States in the hope of influencing the outcome of the October war. These measures, which created panic buying, pushed oil prices to new heights. Taking advantage of these conditions, OPEC decided to double the price of oil as of January 1, 1974 when the price of the Arabian marker was raised to $11.65 per barrel, giving the government a per-barrel revenue of $7.[42]

Iraq, whose government nationalized IPC in 1972, was now in a position to receive the entire value of oil exports, giving it a much higher per-barrel revenue. Such revenue was further augmented as the government started the process of nationalizing BPC in 1973. The sharp increase in Iraq's oil revenue in the 1970s may be appreciated from the data in Table 1.1.

The combination of Iraq's own policy and the OPEC price explosions of 1973 and 1974 pushed Iraq's oil revenue from ID 214 million in 1970 to ID 1.7 billion in 1974. Oil revenue increased from 16 percent of Iraq's GNP in 1970 to 57 percent in 1976. Data in Table 1.1 show the evolution of Iraq's oil output and revenue and the rise in the relative importance of the contribution of oil revenue to the economy.

This sudden and sharp rise in oil revenue, together with the newly acquired control over its own oil resources and the availability of considerable reserves to be developed, convinced the government that it would be in the long-term interest of the country to build an integrated oil industry.

Table 1.1
Oil Revenue, Oil Output, Gross Domestic Product, and Population, 1950–1990

Year	Oil Revenue (ID billion)	GDP (ID billion)	Oil Revenue to GDP (Percentage)	Oil Output (Million Barrels per Day)	Population (Million)
1950	.005	.196	3	0.14	5.2
1955	.074	.413	18	0.70	6.1
1960	.095	.601	16	0.97	6.9
1962	.095	.695	14	1.0	7.3
1964	.126	.805	16	1.3	7.8
1966	.140	.941	15	1.4	8.3
1968	.203	1.1	18	1.5	8.9
1970	.214	1.3	16	1.5	9.4
1972	.219	1.5	15	1.5	10.0
1974	1.7	3.4	50	2.0	10.8
1976	3.1	5.4	57	2.4	11.5
1978	3.7	7.2	51	2.6	12.4
1980	8.9	15.8	56	2.6	13.2
1982	3.4	13.1	26	1.0	14.1
1984	3.0	14.8	20	1.2	15.4
1986	2.2	14.9	15	1.9	16.5
1988	3.5	17.4	20	2.7	17.6
1989	4.6	20.0	23	2.8	18.1
1990	2.9	23.9	12	2.1	18.9

Source: Government of Iraq, *Annual Abstracts of Statistics;* OPEC, *Annual Statistical Bulletin;* Central Bank of Iraq, *Annual Report;* International Monetary Fund, *International Financial Statistics Yearbook;* United Nations, *National Accounts Statistics: Analysis of Main Aggregates, 1980–1989,* New York: 1991.

Note: GNP for the period 1950–1955; GDP for 1960–1989. ID, Iraqi Dinar, equals $2.80 between 1950 and 1968; $2.79 in 1969; $2.78 in 1970; $2.96 in 1971 and 1972; $3.38 in 1973–1981; and $3.21 since 1982.

THE EMERGENCE OF IRAQ'S NATIONAL OIL INDUSTRY

The seeds of a national oil industry were planted as far back as 1961 when Law No. 80 was passed. According to the provisions of the law, the government assumed control over all lands that were not actually developed by the oil companies, or 99.5 percent of the areas covered by three concession agreements. The significance of the law was summed up as follows:

Law No. 80, of 1961, constituted the first step towards the strategic objective of the oil policy, namely, freeing oil wealth from foreign domination and exploitation, bringing it back under national control and placing it in the service of people's welfare.[43]

In order to realize this broad national policy objective, the Iraq National Oil Company (INOC) was created in 1964. But the newly created entity was not given the necessary legal and financial resources to develop the reacquired resources. It took another three years and two laws before INOC was given the exclusive rights to exploit the country's oil resources in 1967. In 1972, INOC was successful in producing and marketing oil from fields covered by Law No. 80. In addition to producing oil, Iraq succeeded also in developing other facets of a well-developed national oil industry, including the training of specialized labor force; building of pipelines, refineries, export facilities, and loading terminals; acquisition of oil tankers; and creation of marketing networks at home and abroad. The decision to develop a national oil sector was intended to use the country's oil wealth as the mainstay of the economy: Iraq National Oil Company became responsible for the execution of that part of the national oil policy that aimed at creating and developing a large, solid, and integrated oil industry that would become the mainstay of accelerated economic development.[44]

The inherent weakness and danger in such policy is its equation of national ownership of the oil sector with freedom of action. It is true of course, as was indicated earlier, that by nationalizing its oil sector Iraq could appropriate to itself the entire amount of the rent (i.e., the difference between the cost of production and the price) instead of receiving only a fraction of that rent as was the case under the concession system. It is also true that by taking over the operations of the oil sector Iraq was able to free itself from the uncertainty associated with decisions made by multinational firms over which it had no control. Yet the mere transfer of ownership to a national authority did not by itself free Iraq from the uncertainty of the constantly changing forces of supply and demand of the wider world economy. To put it differently, while Iraq succeeded in increasing its oil income per unit of output and in mapping the size and direction of its oil sector, its dependency on the world economy remained nevertheless unchanged.

Another observation with respect to the new emphasis on the oil sector is in order. The success of the nationalization measures and the rise in oil prices and the stress on developing the oil sector as the "mainstay of accelerated economic development in Iraq" bound rather dangerously Iraq's prospects of economic development to only one sector, the performance of which is ultimately beyond the control of the government. In other words, should the demand for or the price of oil decline or new sources of supply outside Iraq and other OPEC countries emerge, or should Iraq's exporting facilities be disrupted or destroyed, then the entire economy would suffer.

The experience of Iraq in the 1980s and 1990s illustrates this point. When Iraq nationalized IPC in 1972, its oil output was 1.5 million barrels per day (MBD). By 1976, it rose to 2.4 MBD, and by 1979 it was 3.5 MBD. The combination of higher output and higher prices pushed Iraq's oil revenue from ID 219 million in 1972 to-ID 3.1 billion in 1976 and to ID 8.9 billion in 1980. The outbreak of the Iran–Iraq war, which resulted in the destruction of Iraq's exporting facilities in the southern part of the country and the closure of its pipeline across Syria, reduced Iraq's oil output to 1 MBD in 1982, a level of output that had been reached as far back as 1960. As a result of this decline in output and exports and the decline in oil prices after 1981, Iraq's oil revenue plummeted from ID 8.9 billion in 1980 to ID 2.2 billion in 1986.

The impact of what happened in the oil sector on the rest of the economy was immediate and widespread. The government was forced to curtail imports, suspend development projects, introduce austerity measures, and become a major foreign debtor. Although oil production, exports, and revenue increased after the end of the war with Iran in 1988, the 1990 invasion of Kuwait and the consequent embargo on all transactions with Iraq forced the oil industry to produce at less than 10 percent of its capacity to meet the economy's local requirements.

The importance of oil revenue as a source of economic development spending is explored in the following chapters.

NOTES

1. Certain parts in this and the next two chapters draw on Abbas Alnasrawi, *Financing Economic Development in Iraq: The Role of Oil in Middle Eastern Economy* (New York: Praeger, 1967).

2. For the historical development of the oil concessions, see Stephen Hemsly Longrigg, *Oil in the Middle East* (Oxford: Royal Institute of International Affairs, 1961); Benjamin Shwadran, *The Middle East, Oil and the Great Powers* (New York: Council for Middle Eastern Press, 1959); U.S. Congress, Senate, Subcommittee on Monopoly of the Select Committee on Small Business, *Inter-*

national Petroleum Cartel (Washington: 1952) (henceforth cited as *FTC Report*); Charles Issawi and Mohammed Yeganeh, *The Economics of Middle Eastern Oil* (New York: Praeger, 1962); Ian Seymour, *OPEC: Instrument of Change* (London: The Macmillan Press, 1980).

3. In December 1961, the government passed Law No. 80 of 1961 restricting the operations of those companies to the areas where their producing oil fields are located. In other words, since December 12, 1961, the concession areas of these companies have been reduced from 435,780 sq km to 1,938 sq km. See *Petroleum Press Service,* January 1962, p. 7.

4. Iraq Petroleum Company, Mosul Petroleum Company, and Basra Petroleum Company, *Agreement with the Government of Iraq* (Hertford, U.K.: Stephan Austin & Sons, 1952).

5. J. E. Hartshorn, *Politics and World Oil Economics* (New York: Praeger, 1962), p. 37.

6. See *Middle East Economic Survey* (MEES), August 27, 1965, and Seymour, *OPEC,* pp. 13–14.

7. For the details of joint ownership and the long-term contracts, see *FTC Report,* Chapters 4–6; Hartshorn, *Politics,* Chapter 11; Wayne A. Leeman, *The Price of Middle East Oil* (Ithaca: Cornell University Press, 1962), Chapter 2.

8. Hartshorn, *Politics,* pp. 162–163; *FTC Report,* Chapter 4. See also Walter Adams, James W. Brock, and John M. Blair, "Retarding the Development of Iraq's Oil Resources: An Episode in Oleaginous Diplomacy, 1927–1959," *Journal of Economic Issues* 27(1):69–93.

9. Hartshorn, *Politics,* p. 315.

10. P. H. Frankel, "What Price Oil? The International Structure," *Oil Forum,* November 1948.

11. Walter J. Levy, "The Past, Present and Likely Future Price Structure for the International Oil Trade," in U.S. Congress, *The Third World Petroleum Congress, A Report to the Joint Select Committee on Small Business* (Washington: 1952), pp. 21–37.

12. See *FTC Report,* p. 95.

13. It should be mentioned that most of the European and Latin American imports during the 1930s and 1940s from the Western Hemisphere were actually drawn from the Caribbean region (Venezuela). This was achieved by pricing the Venezuelan crude oil f.o.b. Caribbean at the same USGM price for crude oil of comparable quality minus the U.S. import tax. Since the transportation costs from the Caribbean and the USGM to the U.S. eastern seaboard are the same, this has resulted in identical delivered prices for the oil of these two regions. The same prices for the Caribbean oil were also quoted for shipments to other destinations. See Levy, "The Past," p. 25; Hartshorn, *Politics,* p. 133.

14. Hartshorn, *Politics,* p. 136.

15. Arthur Smithies, "Economic Consequences of the Basing Point Decisions," *Harvard Law Review* 62:308–318.

16. Ibid.; Hartshorn, *Politics,* p. 136. It should be noted that the large-scale military operations in the Eastern Hemisphere that stepped up the demand for Middle East oil during World War II, prompted the British Government, as the major buyer of Middle East oil, to question the practice of being billed

for bunker supplies at the Persian Gulf what it would have had to pay for fuel shipped from USGM. A compromise solution was reached, according to which the British Government was to pay for the oil bought in the Persian Gulf region the same f.o.b. price as for oil of comparable quality at the United States Gulf, plus the actual freight costs from the Persian Gulf to the actual destination. See "Adjustment Prices of Bunker Oil Supplies," *Petroleum Times,* May 13, 1944.

17. Hartshorn, *Politics,* p. 137.

18. Ibid.

19. P. H. Frankel, "American Oil in a Changing World," *Oil Forum,* November 1950, p. 449.

20. Hartshorn, *Politics,* p. 138.

21. Shell International Petroleum Company, *Current International Oil Pricing* (London: 1963), p. 8.

22. Crude oil market up to the end of this period had all the features of oligopoly. For pricing under oligopoly, see William Fellner, *Competition among the Few* (New York: Augustus M. Kelly, 1960); Joe S. Bain, *Pricing, Distribution and Employment* (New York: Henry Holt and Co., 1953); William Fellner, "Collusion and Its Limits under Oligopoly," *American Economic Review, Proceedings* 41 (May 1950): 54–62; P. M. Sweezy, "Demand under Conditions of Oligopoly," *Journal of Political Economy* 47 (August 1939): 568–673, reprinted in *Readings in Price Theory,* ed. George J. Stigler and Kenneth E. Boulding, (Homewood: Richard D. Irwin, 1952), pp. 404–409; Bernard F. Haley, "Value and Distribution," in *A Survey of Contemporary Economics,* ed. Howard S. Ellis (Homewood: Richard D. Irwin, 1948); Jacob Weissman, "Is Oligopoly Illegal? A Jurisprudential Approach," *Quarterly Journal of Economics* 74 (August 1960): 437–463, especially p. 459; Kenneth E. Boulding, *Economic Analysis* (New York: Harper and Bros., 1955); K. W. Rothchild, "Price Theory and Oligopoly," in Stigler and Boulding, *Readings in Price Theory,* pp. 440–464.

23. M. A. Adelman, "The World Oil Outlook," in *Natural Resources and International Development,* ed. Marion Clawson (Baltimore: Johns Hopkins Press, 1964), pp. 27–125; Shell, *Current International,* p. 10.

24. A. J. Meyer, "Economic Modernization," in *The United States and the Middle East* (New York: American Assembly, Columbia University, 1964), p. 71.

25. Adelman, "The World Oil Outlook," p. 83.

26. Hartshorn, *Politics,* p. 129.

27. Adelman, "The World Oil Outlook," p. 85.

28. Hartshorn, *Politics,* Chapters 17 and 20.

29. Adelman, "The World Oil Outlook," p. 92.

30. Shell, *Current International,* pp. 9–11.

31. Adelman, "The World Oil Outlook," p. 97.

32. Shell, *Current International,* pp. 9–11.

33. *Oil and Gas Journal,* June 3, 1957.

34. Adelman, "The World Oil Outlook," p. 87.

35. *Petroleum Press Service,* March 1959.

36. Adelman, "The World Oil Outlook."

37. On August 9, 1960, Esso (Exxon) took the lead in cutting the prices of its oil in the Persian Gulf and the East Mediterranean by an amount ranging

from $0.04 to $0.14 per barrel. Iraq oil at the East Mediterranean was priced at $2.17 per barrel, a cut of $0.14, while that at the Persian Gulf was priced at $1.70, a cut of $0.12. The reactions of the rivals to these price changes were not uniform. While Shell followed the example of Esso by cutting both prices by the same amount, BP reduced its price at the East Mediterranean to $2.21, Socony to $2.19, and CFP to $2.23 per barrel of crude oil of the same quality. As to the price of Iraq oil in the Persian Gulf, BP decided to set it at $1.74, and Socony at $1.70 per barrel. It is obvious that a situation like this cannot prevail, and some of the rivals are called upon to make further adjustments. When Shell decided to change sides by revising its price changes to the levels set by BP, Esso (the initiator of the price changes) was forced to abandon its earlier postings and follow Shell in adopting those of BP. Other sellers followed suit. See Hartshorn, *Politics,* Chapter 1, especially p. 21; *Oil and Gas Journal,* August 15 and September 19, 1960.

38. Hartshorn, *Politics,* p. 20; Seymour, *OPEC,* Chapter 2.

39. OPEC was founded by Iraq, Iran, Saudi Arabia, Kuwait, and Venezuela. In addition to these five founding members, eight other countries were admitted to membership between 1961 and 1975. These countries are Qatar in 1961, Indonesia and Libya in 1962, Abu Dhabi (currently part of United Arab Emirates) in 1967, Algeria in 1969, Nigeria in 1971, Ecuador in 1973, and Gabon in 1975.

40. For a detailed treatment of OPEC–company relations in the decades of the 1960s and early 1970s, see Abbas Alnasrawi, "Collective Bargaining Power in OPEC," *Journal of World Trade Law* 7(2):188–207; "The Petrodollar Energy Crisis: An Overview and Interpretation," *Syracuse Journal of International Law and Commerce* 3(2):369–412.

41. For a more comprehensive account of these and related developments, see Seymour, *OPEC,* Chapter 5.

42. Ibid.

43. Iraq National Oil Company, *Iraq National Oil Company and Direct Exploitation of Oil in Iraq* (Baghdad, 1973), p. 5.

44. Ibid., p. 7.

CHAPTER 2

Oil and Development under the Monarchy, 1950–1958

The idea that oil is an exhaustible national resource, producing revenues to be used for investment purposes, goes back to 1927 when the government received its first royalties from oil. It was decided at the time to view such royalties as a budgetary surplus to be used to finance infrastructural projects such as roads, bridges, irrigation, and buildings. The dual budgeting system, distinguishing ordinary and capital expenditures, continued to be in effect until 1950.[1]

The era of development planning in Iraq, which began in earnest in 1950, may be divided into three distinct periods: (1) development planning under the monarchy, which extends from 1950 when the Development Board was created to 1958 when the monarchy was overthrown; (2) development planning in the republican period 1958–68; and (3) development planning since 1968, when the present regime under the rule of the Baath party seized power.

THE DEVELOPMENT BOARD AND ITS PROGRAMS, 1950–1958

The acceleration of Iraq's oil production in the postwar period from .091 million barrel per day (MBD) in 1949 to .697 MBD in 1955, and the increase in oil revenue, which went from ID 31 million to ID 74 million during the same period, prompted the government to embark upon a policy of channeling oil revenue for development purposes. This policy was reinforced by the World Bank which made the granting of a $12.8 million loan to Iraq conditional upon the creation of an autonomous agency for development.[2]

This agency, which came to be known as the Development Board, was established in 1950. The law creating the board stipulated that all revenues from oil be credited to the board's account with the Central Bank of Iraq.[3] The law entrusted the new board with these tasks: (1) presenting a general economic and financial plan for developing the resources of Iraq and raising the standard of living of its people through the implementation of projects in the fields of water storage, flood control, irrigation, drainage, industry, mining, and communications; (2) conducting a survey of the country's exploited and unexploited resources; and (3) handing over the completed projects to the specialized ministries for administration and maintenance.

The General Program for the Development Board's Projects was adopted in the following year for the period 1951/52–1955/56. This five-year program envisaged a total expenditure of ID 66 million and revenues of ID 95 million. The pattern of expenditure allocation and sources of revenues under this new program are shown in Table 2.1.

However, soon after this program was adopted, the 1952 Agreement with oil companies, which increased Iraq's per-barrel revenue considerably, was concluded. The increase affected the newly created Develop-

Table 2.1
General Programs of Development Board's Projects

	First General 1951/52– 1955/56		Second General 1951/52– 1956/57		Third General 1955/56– 1959–60		Fourth General 1955/56– 1960/61	
	ID Millions	(%)	ID Millions	(%)	ID Millions	(%)	ID Millions	(%)
Expenditures								
Agriculture*	30.0	45.7	53.4	34.4	114.4	37.6	168.1	33.6
Industry	--	--	31.0	19.9	43.6	14.3	67.1	13.4
Transport and Communication	15.9	24.2	26.8	17.2	74.2	24.4	124.4	24.6
Buildings and Housing	12.6	19.2	18.0	11.6	60.9	20.0	123.2	24.6
Others	7.2	10.9	26.2	16.9	11.4	3.7	17.3	3.5
Total	65.7	100.0	155.4	100.0	304.3	100.0	500.1	100.0
Revenues								
Oil	91.1	95.8	164.6	97.6	215.0	99.7	385.1	98.7
Non-oil	4.0	4.2	4.1	2.4	0.7	0.3	4.9	1.3
Total	95.1	100.0	168.7	100.0	215.7	100.0	390.0	100.0

Source: Government of Iraq, *Laws Nos. 35 of 1951, 25 of 1952, 43 of 1955, and 54 of 1956.*
*Includes flood control, reservoirs, irrigation and drainage projects, land reclamation, and agriculture proper.

ment Board in two ways. First, instead of channeling all the proceeds from oil to the board, a law was passed allocating 70 percent of the oil revenues to the board with the remaining 30 percent channeled to the ordinary budget. Second, the plan was revised by increasing programmed expenditures to ID 155 million and revenues to ID 169 million while extending the plan period by another year.[4]

No sooner had this new program been adopted than a change in the structure of the development administration was instituted. The new structure entailed the creation of the Ministry of Development which was to serve as the link between the board and the council of ministers, on the one hand, and act as the executive arm of the board, on the other.[5] Once again the existing plan was revised and replaced by a new five-year plan for the period 1955/56–1959/60. The new plan envisaged a total expenditure of ID 304 million and revenues of ID 216 million.[6]

While this program was being implemented, the British economist, Lord Salter, was preparing for the board a report on various aspects of Iraq's economic development policy.[7] This, together with an optimistic projection of oil revenues, led to the adoption of yet a fourth program for the period 1955/56–1960/61, with estimated total expenditures of ID 500 million and revenues of ID 390 million.[8]

During the fourth year of the implementation of this program, the revolution of July 1958 overthrew the monarchy and abolished the Development Board, replacing it by a ministerial committee. The new committee decided to continue the implementation of the program at a slower rate until a new machinery for development could be organized.

PLANNED VERSUS ACTUAL DEVELOPMENT SPENDING, 1951/52–1957/58

Table 2.2 (p. 20) contains a summary of total development expenditure and revenue as well as sectoral performance measured by actual spending relative to planned expenditure for fiscal years 1951/52–1957/58.

One of the striking features of development expenditure is that actual expenditure lagged considerably behind planned expenditures. This is evident in every sector although the performance in some sectors was much worse than that in others. By contrast, actual revenue tended to be very close to planned revenue. Table 2.2 shows that while the board planned to spend ID 312 million during this period actual expenditure was only ID 178 million, or 57 percent of the total. Actual revenue for the period, on the other hand, was close to projected revenue, 93 percent. This means that the Development Board's actual spending amounted to 70 percent of its receipts.

The pattern of allocation and implementation gives rise to several

Table 2.2

Total Planned and Actual Development Expenditures and Revenues,
1951/52-1957/58

		Planned (ID) (Millions)	Actual (ID) (Millions)	Actual:Planned (Percentage)
I.	Expenditure			
	Agriculture	117.8	61.6	51.8
	Industry	51.1	19.1	37.4
	Transportation and Communication	66.6	38.6	58.0
	Building and Housing	38.2	24.1	63.1
	Other	38.6	35.2	91.1
	Total	312.3	178.1	57.0
II.	Revenue			
	Oil	269.4	245.9	91.2
	Total	275.7	256.4	93.0
III.	Actual Expenditure: Actual Revenue			69.5

Source: Calculated from *Law No. 6 of 1952,* schedules A and B; *Law No. 54 of 1956;* Central Bank of Iraq, *Quarterly Bulletin,* selected issues; Ministry of Development, *Annual Report on the Accounts of the Development Board and the Ministry of Development for the Fiscal Year 1954* (Baghdad, 1957); *Annual Abstract of Statistics.*
Note: The fiscal year in Iraq ran from April 1 to March 31. As of January 1, 1976, the fiscal year was changed to coincide with the calendar year. Details may not add up to totals because of rounding.

observations regarding the board's priorities and limitations. It can be seen that while irrigation, roads and bridges, and buildings more than maintained their relative importance in terms of actual versus planned expenditure, the industrial sector, on the other hand, received much less attention in the execution stage. Only 37 percent of the appropriated funds were actually invested in this sector – 11 percent of total actual spending. In addition to the obvious neglect of industry, there was also a serious neglect of the agricultural sector. As the data indicate, the board spent only 52 percent of the funds appropriated to this sector – 35 percent of its total spending.

While it can be argued, and rightly so, that flood control and irrigation projects and other infrastructural projects were necessary, this is not a sufficient explanation for the gross neglect of agriculture and industry. In a country heavily dependent on consumer goods imports where more than three-fourths of its labor force depended on agriculture, the neglect of the two most important goods-producing sectors raises several questions as to the nature and direction of development, as is seen in the following paragraphs.

HIGHLIGHTS OF ALLOCATIONS FOR DEVELOPMENT, 1950–1958

Basically, the essence of planning for economic development is to mobilize national savings into productive investment in order to generate a rate of increase in national output that is higher than the rate of increase in population. The difference between the two growth rates would help increase the standard of living.[9] This task requires also that investment spending be made in such a way as to yield the highest possible rate of growth of output with the least possible waste. This does not explain who would be making the necessary decisions to attain these objectives. While in the industrialized countries the question has long been settled in favor of the private sector and market forces, this was not so in the case of developing economies.

There is general agreement that the numerous imperfections of the market will impede the necessary process that would transform a basically underdeveloped economy like Iraq's into a growing economy. Given this reality, planning becomes a necessary tool to accelerate economic development. In Iraq, the government found it necessary to expand its role in the economy when it decided to utilize oil revenues to finance investment projects and to adopt policies to stimulate the nonoil sectors of the economy.

A comprehensive development program must therefore consist of objectives and aggregate targets in terms of the following: (1) national income and employment; (2) a public investment program for the economy's different sectors; (3) projection of private investment among various major sectors; (4) a combination of fiscal, monetary, and trade policies to stimulate and influence private investment; (5) definition of the role of the private sector; and (6) policies designed to effect basic institutional changes.[10]

Should it prove to be beyond the ability of a country like Iraq to meet these requirements, then the next best thing would be to try to provide for broad targets in terms of income and employment. In other words, the plan must provide a sense of direction for the economy, and national income accounts should help planners determine growth targets. If these aggregates are not used as a basis for development planning, then the plan will be no more than a list of investment projects. This was the case in Iraq during the first decade of its development experiment.

During this period, the concept of development planning in Iraq was understood to mean those government policies that were concerned with capital spending directed and controlled by the Development Board. Economic planning meant the utilization of as much as possible of the revenue from oil to build public investment projects.

The first program, as a matter of fact, did not even mention such concepts as national income, employment targets, and fiscal and monetary policies. There was only a passing mention that the program was intended to raise the standard of living through the development of the country's resources.

The lack of basic understanding of economic planning and its goals is reflected in the meager allocation for agriculture. In a country like Iraq, where agriculture is the most important sector, the first plan allocated only ID 1.5 million to agricultural development proper with the bulk of the ID 30 million earmarked for irrigation projects. This was done at a time when the overall program was drafted with a surplus of ID 29.4 million. This neglect of agriculture was matched by a comparable neglect of the industrial sector. Moreover, the program failed to establish a link between public and private investment. It also failed to anticipate the response of the nonoil sectors of the economy to the injection of new investment funds and to predict the leakage of income in the form of payment for imports. Nor did the plan recognize the impact of its spending on prices and income distribution.

The absence of meaningful planning can also be seen in the collection of projects under the heading "Land Reclamation and Other Projects," which covered an assortment of unrelated projects such as land reclamation, artisian wells, summer resorts, aerial survey, mining survey, telecommunication services, and expansion of the civil airport.[11]

In 1952, only one year after the first plan was adopted, the second plan projected total expenditures of ID 155.4 million or 237 percent of the first plan's total expenditure. This plan followed the path of the first in emphasizing the importance of irrigation, roads, and buildings. Industry and mining, as one sector, was introduced and given 20 percent of the investment funds. A casual look at the allocations for industrial development reveals that such allocations were not divided even at project level. Thus a sum of ID 31 million was allocated to natural gas, cement, fertilizers, sugar, and textile industries.[12]

The third program, adopted in 1955, had total planned expenditure of ID 304.3 million and revenue of ID 215.7 million. This meant that the new program contemplated an annual rate of spending of ID 60 million, compared with only ID 30 million under the previous program. But as with the programs that preceded it, the relative importance of the various sectors in the program did not reveal any basic change in its approach or in its priorities. Irrigation and flood control projects still had a very high priority, receiving 35 percent of total allocation, while allocation for transport and communications and buildings and housing increased to 44 percent, rising from 29 percent in the previous plan. Funds for agricultural development proper were reduced from ID 11.6 million (7 percent of the total in the previous plan) to only ID 6.5 million (2 percent of the total in this plan). Industry, on the other hand, received ID 43.6 million (14 percent of the total) compared with 20 percent previously. But ID 10 million (22 percent of industrial allocation) was earmarked for power stations. Another ID 22 million (50 percent of the total) was allocated to a number of unrelated industries gathered under the heading "other industries," including woolen, cotton, and silk industries, and also industries based on the utilization of natural gas. It is safe to infer that these industries were under study and were not ready for implementation. If we exclude these two headings from what was allocated to industry, we find that what was left represented only 4 percent of the total.

It should also be noted that what was actually spent was spent on projects that did not provide permanent or sizable employment. Nor did the spending show tangible results as measured by national income data. This policy raised a number of questions as to its economic justifications and political consequences.

To help it find guidance to deal with these problems and the various recommendations given by a number of technical advisers, the board commissioned Lord Salter "to give advice as to the timing and balance of the different projects of the Development Board and their co-ordination with action by other authorities, having regard to the impact of each undertaking upon the others and upon the general economy of the Country."[13]

The recommendations presented by Lord Salter, which coincided with the completion of certain studies on housing and drainage, constituted the basis for the adoption of a new (fourth) program in 1956, covering a period of six years. Total spending under the fourth program was projected at ID 500 million and total revenue was estimated at ID 390 million.

Irrigation, to which 31 percent of the total appropriation was allocated, once more continued to "occupy the pride of place among the projects covered by the General Program."[14] Other infrastructure projects received 44 percent of the appropriated funds, and 13.4 percent of the total went to industry, mining, and power stations.

Again, if we exclude the appropriations for mining and power stations and for industries under consideration, the share of industrial development would decline from 13.4 percent to 3 percent of total planned expenditure. Similarly, agricultural development had low priority since its allocation did not exceed 3 percent of the total.

THE DEVELOPMENT BOARD
AND THE AGRICULTURAL SECTOR

When the development programs were launched in the early 1950s, Iraq aside from the oil sector was an agricultural country with about four fifths of its labor force employed in agriculture. This sector's contribution to Iraq's nonoil GDP during the period under consideration ranged between 22 percent and 36 percent. Like other developing countries, Iraq had an agricultural sector that suffered from chronic underemployment and from seasonal unemployment that reached as high as 75 to 80 percent.[15]

It should be stressed that Iraq has always been in the fortunate position of not being overpopulated, with large areas of cultivable land and considerable water resource endowment. In comparison with other underdeveloped countries, the per capita potentially cultivable land in Iraq is 3 to 3.5 acres compared with one-half acre in Asia and less than one-third acre in Egypt.[16]

It is imperative, therefore, that agriculture should be the primary concern of all efforts, in order to increase the rate of economic growth. The development of the agricultural sector is vital to the process of economic development because (1) it releases agricultural labor for nonfarm employment, (2) it helps increase exports and reduce imports, (3) it is expected to meet the inevitable rise in demand for food associated with growing population and higher income, and (4) it generates more savings to finance investment in the agricultural sector and other sectors of the economy.

Any development policy, therefore, should have as its foremost target the reduction, if not the elimination, of the high rate of unemployment. But to achieve this, the industrial sector must also grow in order to provide employment opportunities for the absorption of the surplus farm labor and for the growth in the labor force. To channel the unemployed to the newly created industries requires a rise in the productivity of agriculture in order to meet the rising urban demand for agricultural products. It also requires an increase in the purchasing power of the rural population, thereby increasing the demand for industrial products. It is safe to say that without the simultaneous increase of investment and output in both sectors, the twin goals of a higher standard of living and higher rate of employment would not be attained.

One of the most outstanding and influential features of agriculture in Iraq during this period was the immense concentration of land ownership among a tiny fraction of landholders.

Given Iraq's agricultural population of 2.5 million in the early 1950s, it was found (as noted earlier) that agricultural land per person was several times larger than in Egypt.[17] But the landownership structure was such that most of the land was owned by a relatively few large landowners. According to a 1952–53 agricultural census of six provinces with 14.5 million donums (56 percent of agricultural lands), thirteen proprietors owned between 50,000 and 100,000 donums, twenty-one proprietors owned between 100,000 and 200,000 donums, and two landowners owned more than 1 million donums each.[18]

More important than the structure of landownership was the pattern of the prevailing practices of distribution of agricultural output between landowners and cultivators. Depending on the region of the country, extent of investment by owners, and methods of irrigation, the landlord's share ranged between one-half and five-sevenths of the crop. But the relationships between the landlord and his cultivators went beyond the mere distribution of benefits. The practice of cultivating only one-half of the land and the low productivity of cultivable land not only forced the peasants to accept meager returns for their labor but also ensured that they were never able to pay back the debt they perpetually owed to landlords. The historical evolution of these relationships, which outlined peasant obligations to landlords and were codified by a series of laws, turned cultivators into virtual serfs – with monumental human, social, and economic costs for the entire country.[19]

Such a system of land tenure gave rise to two interrelated problems of income distribution. Within the rural sector, a minority of landlords received most of the output while the majority of rural population lived in conditions of grinding poverty.[20] And since the majority of the population was made up of rural peasantry, with agriculture contributing about one-fourth of the national product, the distribution of national income tended to have another bias in favor of the urban population. This resulted in a pattern of income distribution in which the per capita income of the rural villager was less than one-half of that of the town or city dweller.[21] Such an impoverished rural majority could not be expected to provide the necessary market for expanding local industry, not to mention the ability to generate savings for investment.[22]

Another problem that plagued agriculture in Iraq was the inadequacy of a natural drainage system. Since irrigation water carries some dissolved salts, it becomes necessary to use more water to wash the salt away. However, if the salt to be washed away is below the root levels it is necessary to prevent the water table from rising, since the rising water table may carry the salt to the surface where it is left behind after the water evaporates. To avoid this disastrous outcome, a drainage system becomes a necessity. In many areas, there must be at least as many drainage ditches as there are irrigation ditches; but since the drainage ditches must be deeper, the cost for the construction and maintenance of the drainage system may exceed the cost of irrigation canals.[23]

With these fundamental problems, one would have expected the development programs to include an agricultural development policy that would lead to a better distribution of landownership, better methods of cultivation, and a different system of irrigation and drainage.

The introduction of agrarian reform to solve the land problem was not possible since the very nature of the power structure of the political system was such that the landed class and their political supporters dominated the legislative apparatus and other decision-making bodies.

Schemes for the solution of the other two problems of expanding land under cultivation and drainage were possible to draw up and would have benefited the landowners directly and the peasants indirectly because of the sharecropping system. But judging from the insignificant allocation of funds, neither of these problems received the necessary attention. Instead, a considerable part of the board's resources went to irrigation, which actually included projects for flood control, water storage, and irrigation.

The board's approach to the question of agricultural development seems to have been influenced by two major groups of consultants who presented blueprints for flood control and for the utilization of the stored water. They recommended the building of a series of dams for the storage of water during the flood season and its subsequent use for summer irrigation. These blueprints represented the culmination of the engineer's approach, into which the people of Iraq did not enter except insofar as they provided labor. When the oil money began to flood the board, the plans for spending seemed ready made in the long list of irrigation projects.[24] But bringing new land under cultivation before improving the system of land already under cultivation was unjustifiable since it left the system of exploitation and agricultural backwardness intact.

Given the land tenure system at the time, the benefits from the stored waters had to accrue to the already privileged minority thus raising the value of their land as summer irrigation was made possible by the expenditure of public funds at virtually zero cost to them.

This disparity in the distribution of the benefits of public investment programs, needless to say, gave rise to social, economic, and political consequences that neither the board nor its engineers chose to include or could include in their calculation.

To mitigate this inequality of income distribution, one of two courses could have been followed. One was to institute an agrarian reform; but the possibility of its adoption, as mentioned earlier, was remote. The second was to adopt fiscal measures to capture at least some of the incremental income from land proprietors. But even a moderate measure like this was not possible to adopt in a country where the levers of political and legislative powers were in the hands of land proprietors. In commenting on this kind of spending Lord Salter had this to say:

It is not unnatural that sections of the community should regard it as unjust that one section, already more privileged than others, should now be further enriched to such an extent at the public expense and should resent a policy which would have that effect.

In these circumstances one tempting course is to outflank the problem instead of attacking it directly. There are large areas of Miri Serf land, owned by the Government. With the aid of new irrigation and drainage works this land can be made cultivable. Small settlers can be established without any question of enriching the already rich arising. And in this case, apart from the direct benefits to the new settlers of farming their holdings, either as small owners or as tenants of the State, the existence of such opportunities of new settlements would perhaps, lead to an improvement of the conditions of work of workers on the great estates. It is along this line, the line of least resistance, that the policy has tended to develop.[25]

The difficulty with such a policy of least resistance, however, is that the creation of a new settlement is a much more difficult and complex undertaking than building a dam or opening an irrigation canal since it requires carefully adjusted and intricate actions of many kinds. There must be survey and classification of the land to be settled – much more detailed than the general survey already available – to determine the kind of cultivation suitable and therefore the size of the plots to be distributed. The settlers must be carefully selected, with suitable experience; and equipment and credit facilities must be arranged. Special measures must be taken to reduce health hazards and to ensure that there are houses, schools, hospitals, and essential public services.[26] Even if we assume the government of Iraq of the 1950s had all the determination, the necessary technical expertise and skills, and administrative machinery (which it did not have at the time), this indirect approach to the problem was bound to fail for a number of reasons. First, the pace of implementing this policy proved to be very slow. Up to 1958, only 20,000 families were settled, with another 5,000 families slated for settlement in the next five years.[27] This is a very small number in a country where agriculture absorbed about three-fourths of the labor force. It is highly unrealistic, therefore, to hope that this slow rate of settlement would have benefited a large number of peasants or exercised any beneficial influence on the conditions of those who remained on the privately held land or on the problem of unemployment. Second, a considerable part of the land so distributed found its way to the privileged landlord by virtue of his position as a tribal chief, thus reinforcing the existing pattern of landownership. Third, the government's desire to show fast results led it to start the process of land distribution prior to the completion of the necessary irrigation and drainage networks.

A policy that failed to address the root cause of the stagnation of Iraq's agricultural sector, the land tenure system and the pattern of distribution of benefits that flowed from it, could not be expected to succeed. Suffice it to say that between 1953 and 1958 the area under cultivation for the principal three field crops – wheat, barley, and rice – increased by 20 percent; yet the value of the output of the entire agricultural sector in real terms, 1956 prices, from all sources including field crops, livestock, fishery, fruits, dates, and vegetables increased by only 4.4 percent. And within this sector, the value of field crops – wheat, barley, beans, cotton, and tobacco – actually declined from ID 30.8 million in 1953 to ID 28.5 in 1958. Within the agricultural sector, the share of field crops declined from 39 percent in 1953 to 30 percent in 1958. This decline took place at a time when the population increased from 5.6 million to 6.5 million.[28]

It can be seen from the data that the policies of the Development Board failed to achieve the elementary task of increasing the output of the most important sector of the nonoil economy, a sector that was the source of employment and income for the majority of the population.

This failure was not surprising given the inability and unwillingness of policy makers to tackle the central problem of landownership and its feudal nature, which determined the pattern of relationships between landlords and peasants. In the final analysis, the Development Board policies had to conform to the orientation of the political leadership of the country at the time, a leadership that believed in the benevolence of the land tenure system. Thus, in a 1957 statement, the prime minister, Nuri Al-Said, not only denied the need to change the landownership system but went as far as to assert that the whole problem was a mere communist ploy designed to undermine the social and political system:

The tribal system considers the sheikh of the tribe as the father or the manager of the affairs of the tribe living in his area. . . . The sheikh receives one half of the crop . . . and when he dies his land will be distributed among his sons and other inheritors and so in one generation the large landholdings will become small holdings. But Communism started to incite the tribes against their sheikhs when these sheikhs are working to develop the country and increase production.[29]

It is clear from this position of the country's political leadership that any change in the land tenure system was neither contemplated nor considered beneficial. The change had to await the July 1958 revolution, which overthrew the monarchy and with it the land tenure system.

THE DEVELOPMENT BOARD
AND THE INDUSTRIAL SECTOR

The failure of the board's agricultural development policy, which set Iraq on the path to dependency on food imports, was matched by its failure to invest in the industrial sector. In Iraq, industrialization is important not only as a means to raising income and achieving economic diversification but also because of its contribution to the development of agriculture. As stated earlier, without an expanding industrial sector it would be more difficult to solve the problem of agricultural unemployment and poverty. If agricultural output and productivity increased, a market for the expanding agricultural output would have to be found. This could be accomplished if the expansion of the industrial sector proceeded simultaneously with that of the agricultural sector — this expansion would raise the demand for food and raw materials.

Prior to the creation of the Development Board, government policy of encouraging local industry took two forms. First, certain laws were enacted allowing exemptions from income tax, customs duty, and property tax and permitting use of state land.[30] Second, the state-owned Industrial Bank was authorized to establish industrial enterprises, sponsor and subscribe to the capital of private and public companies, and extend short- and long-term loans.

The Industrial Bank's contribution to industrial development was limited in the size of loans it could grant and the extent to which it could subscribe to the equity capital of industrial enterprises. The bank confined its aid to enterprises that either processed agricultural products or produced building materials, but it failed to play a role in providing technical training or market research or in introducing new industries.[31] In brief, the contribution of the bank to industrial development was modest, limited, and conservative.

With the flow of oil revenue and the creation of the Development Board, the question of industrial development should have taken a new turn; but this was not the case, especially in the early years of development planning. The first program did not allocate any funds for this sector. The second allocated 20 percent of its total budget, while the third and fourth programs allocated 14 percent and 13 percent respectively.

The change in policy manifested in the second plan seems to have been prompted by the World Bank's mission report. The mission found that

conditions . . . are generally favorable to further industrial development . . . an expanding agriculture should provide material for processing . . . and when the standard of living among the rural population is raised there should be a growing domestic market for industrial products. In oil and natural gas the country possesses a cheap source of power and fuel as well as an important source of raw materials.[32]

The mission went on to recommend that government ownership of industry should take place only where absolutely necessary. It then offered the following policy guidance:

Particular care should be taken that government assistance does not foster inefficient industries at the expense of the country's standard of living. This danger is by no means unreal. . . . Iraqi-owned enterprises can qualify for these benefits as long as they primarily use raw materials available in Iraq or produce goods imported in considerable quantities. Neither of these conditions is necessarily relevant to efficient production, and it is therefore suggested that the law be amended to stipulate that in general, such benefits should be accorded only by enterprises which have a reasonable prospect of becoming efficient enough to withstand foreign competition. Industry is also protected in many cases to high import duties and in some cases . . . by import prohibition. In a small country like Iraq, where the limited market affords opportunity for only one or two plants in each field and where the entrepreneurial class is small there is an acute danger of monopoly and attendant high prices. . . . While the Mission recognizes the need for temporary, moderate protection of certain industries, it wishes to emphasize strongly the need for progressive reduction in special assistance.[33]

Professor Carl Iversen, who was commissioned to study Iraq's monetary policy, offered similar advice when he stated that

though in the long run Iraq will have to industrialize, it seems to be in the best interest of Iraq not to force this development but to concentrate on raising the efficiency of agricultural production. . . . Iraq has large comparative advantages in agricultural production, whereas the possibilities of creating new industries able to compete on equal terms with producers abroad are more limited and remote. Inflation should be countered by measures . . . including increased imports of consumer goods.[34]

Lord Salter followed the same line of thinking when he said that the expenditure of money and effort on developing industries that could not compete with foreign manufacturers except in a highly protective domestic market could be wasteful and damaging to Iraq's general progress and prosperity.[35]

Finally, along the same line of thinking, Arthur D. Little, Inc., which was commissioned by Iraq to make a survey of potential industries, stated that

forced industrialization with the aid of tariff protection or government subsidy might lead to inefficiency and waste of economic resources, and no industry has been recommended unless it is anticipated that it will produce at a cost below the landed price of comparable imported goods or raw material before import duty has been levied. If an industry can produce goods in Iraq at a price equal to or lower than the landed price without import duty its establishment is truly economic. . . . In the future it may be desirable to apply a less stringent test.[36]

Broadly speaking, these arguments are based on three lines of reasoning. The first is that since Iraq is an agricultural country with a relative abundance of water and cultivable land, it has a comparative advantage in developing its agriculture. Since world demand for food and agricultural raw materials was expected to grow, Iraq should have no difficulty selling its agricultural products abroad. Another reason behind these recommendations was the fact that Iraq did not have the skilled labor force necessary for a broad program of industrialization. As Lord Salter pointed out, it is wise to go from one stage to another depending on the availability of domestic resources and not jump the stages.[37] A third explanation for this policy recommendation is that the protection the industrial sector receives will tend to further the imbalance in the distribution of income between the rural and the urban sectors of the economy. In other words, an accelerated program of industrialization that will raise the prices of the domestically produced manufactured products will have the effect of lowering rural real incomes relative to urban earnings.

In assessing the relevance of these arguments to Iraq, several observations are in order. The first argument can be criticized on the ground that it was developed in reference to the advanced industrial countries. Moreover, the argument assumes conditions of perfect competition in order to achieve the necessary equalization of opportunity cost and market price, since such equalization is in turn necessary for the determination comparative advantage.[38] But this is not the case in Iraq where market prices, particularly those of the factors of production, form a very imperfect guide to resource allocation because there are fundamental disequilibria reflected in the prevalence of massive unemployment.[39] As an illustration of this imbalance, agriculture in 1953 absorbed about 80 percent of the labor force but contributed only 25 percent of the GDP.

The adoption of such a policy for industrial development would have led to one of two outcomes or to both. First, the increase in rural income would eventually have led, in the absence of domestic industry, to balance-of-payments difficulties; otherwise, the government would have to deal with the problem of inflation. Second, the concentration on the development of agriculture for the world market would have exposed the economy to the consequent instabilities associated with the

inevitable fluctuations in foreign exchange earnings of primary commodities.[40] This, in turn, would have accentuated Iraq's dependency on
foreign trade and led to the unavoidable defeat of the very goal of development policy, which sought to loosen the dependence of the economy
on foreign markets. Furthermore, Iraq was in the unique position
where the supply of capital was abundant. The waste that would have
resulted from industrialization could easily have been absorbed.

The conclusion seems to be that there was no justification in the case
of Iraq to delay industrialization until such time when industry could
stand on its own feet.

The second line of reasoning behind the experts' advice against industrialization, i.e., lack of skilled workers, can be criticized on several
counts. It is true that there will be a waste of economic resources if the
factories are built but are not run efficiently and there will be waste of
resources if workers are trained but there is no work for them. The
ideal solution, of course, is to attempt to do both at the same time. One
solution would have been to adopt a program to import skilled workers
that could be accompanied by a thorough program of training. Moreover, the supply of skilled workers will increase as the process of industrialization gains momentum. To put it differently, the factories, though
not efficiently run, would serve as training centers. Hence the recommendation that Iraq should give special attention to handicraft industries is of only limited advantage.[41] With an abundant supply of
capital, Iraq could afford to follow a policy of rapid economic development, achieved in part through rapid industrialization without restricting consumption. What makes this approach more appealing is the
knowledge at the time that the flow of oil revenue, and consequently
the availability of capital, was assured. This would mean that Iraq
would be better prepared to overcome the critical minimum-effort hur-
dle in the early stage of development.[42] Without this, Iraq could not
hope to accomplish within a few generations a process of industrialization that took the developed countries much longer to achieve.

The third line of reasoning, that the solution must be sought not in
protecting industry but in agrarian reform, can be said to be unrealistic. It is true that the living standard and the distribution of income
could have been improved if an agrarian reform had been instituted;
but as we have seen earlier, such a drastic measure was not and could
not have been contemplated. It may be contended that industrialization would have resulted in redistribution of income in favor of the
urban population at the expense of the rural population. But this problem could have been mitigated by fiscal measures.

The board seems to have subscribed to the advice of the experts.
This is evident not only in the allocation of a small share of its funds to

industrial development but also in its failure to achieve its own modest targets.

In the midst of the Development Board's fourth general program, the July 1958 revolution succeeded in overthrowing the monarchy, and a new era of development planning in Iraq was ushered in.

NOTES

1. See Kathleen M. Langley, *The Industrialization of Iraq* (Cambridge: Harvard University Press, 1962), p. 47; Hisham Mutawali, *The Economy of Iraq* (in Arabic) (Damascus: Center for Economic Studies, 1964), pp. 131–136.

2. It was asserted that the appointment of one U.S. citizen and one British citizen to the membership of the board was another condition the World Bank stipulated for the granting of the loan. See Mohammad Salman Hasan, *Studies in the Iraqi Economy* (in Arabic) (Beirut: Dar al-Taliaa, 1966), p. 229.

3. Government of Iraq, *Law No. 23 of 1950.*

4. Government of Iraq, *Law No. 25 of 1952.*

5. Government of Iraq, *Law No. 35 of 1953.*

6. Government of Iraq, *Law No. 43 of 1955.*

7. Lord Salter, *The Development of Iraq, A Plan for Action* (Baghdad: The Development Board, 1955).

8. Government of Iraq, *Law No. 54 of 1956.*

9. Oskar Lange, "Planning Economic Development," in *Leading Issues in Development Economics,* ed. Gerald M. Meier (New York: Oxford University Press, 1964), p. 487.

10. United Nations, Economic Commission for Asia and the Far East, "The Central Role of Planning," in Meier, *Leading Issues,* pp. 423–425.

11. Government of Iraq, *Law No. 35 of 1951.*

12. *Law No. 25 of 1952,* "Explanatory Note."

13. Salter, *Development of Iraq,* p. 134.

14. Government of Iraq, *Law No. 54 of 1956,* speech by the minister of development upon the presentation of the program to the Parliament.

15. Food and Agricultural Organization Mediterranean Development Project, *Iraq, Country Report* (Rome, 1959), p. 12. Henceforth cited as *FAO Report.*

16. Kathleen M. Langley, "Iraq: Some Aspects of the Economic Scene," *The Middle East Journal* 28 (Spring 1964): 180–188.

17. See Doreen Warriner, *Land Reform and Development in the Middle East: A Study of Egypt, Syria, and Iraq* (London: Royal Institute of International Affairs, 1957), pp. 115, 140.

18. Ibid., pp. 141–142.

19. For a detailed treatment of the evolution of land tenure system in Iraq see Warriner, *Land Reform,* Chapter 4; Hanna Batatu, *The Old Social Classes and the Revolutionary Movements in Iraq: A Study of Iraq's Old Landed and Commercial Classes and of Its Communists, Ba'thists, and Free Officers* (Princeton: Princeton University Press, 1978), Chapters 5 and 6.

20. See Yusif A. Sayigh, *The Economies of the Arab World: Development*

since 1945 (New York: St. Martin's Press, 1978), pp. 27–29.

21. A. J. Meyer, "Economic Modernization" in *The United States and the Middle East* (New York: American Assembly, 1964), p. 59.

22. Ibid.

23. Food and Agricultural Organization, Mediterranean Development Project, *Iraq, Interim Report* (Rome 1957), pp. 20–21.

24. See Warriner, *Land Reform*, p. 120.

25. Salter, *Development of Iraq*, pp. 54–55.

26. Ibid., p. 50.

27. *FAO Report*, p. 48.

28. See Ministry of Planning, *Detailed Framework of the Five-Year Plan for 1965–1969* (in Arabic) (Baghdad: Ministry of Planning, 1969), p. 18.

29. Cited in Ibrahim Kubba, *Feudalism in Iraq between Nuri Al-Said and the "Free World" Experts* (in Arabic) (Baghdad: Al-Maarif Press, 1957), p. 7.

30. International Bank for Reconstruction and Development, *The Economic Development of Iraq* (Baltimore: Johns Hopkins University Press, 1952), p. 40. Henceforth cited as *IBRD Report*.

31. Langley, *Industrialization of Iraq*, pp. 140–163.

32. *IBRD Report*, p. 33.

33. Ibid., pp. 38, 40–41. The benefits referred to in the quotation are provided for by the various laws for the encouragement of industry.

34. Carl Iversen, *Monetary Policy in Iraq* (Baghdad: National Bank of Iraq, 1954), pp. 147, 227.

35. Salter, *Development of Iraq*, p. 73.

36. Arthur D. Little, Inc. *A Plan for Industrial Development in Iraq* (Cambridge, 1956), p. 3.

37. Salter, *Development of Iraq*, pp. 19, 70.

38. Hollis B. Chenery, "Comparative Advantage and Development Policy," *American Economic Review* 51 (March 1961): 18–51.

39. United Nations, Economic Commission for Asia and the Far East, "Survey of Criteria for Allocating Investment Resources," in Meier, *Leading Issues*, p. 234.

40. International Monetary Fund, "Fluctuations in Export Earnings," in Meier, *Leading Issues*, pp. 390–393.

41. Salter, *Development of Iraq*, p. 75.

42. Walter Galenson and Harvey Leibenstein, "Investment Criteria, Productivity, and Economic Development," *Quarterly Journal of Economics* 69 (August 1955): 343–370.

CHAPTER 3

Oil and Development Planning, 1958–1968

The period 1958–68 was characterized by a series of radical political and economic changes that altered the process and the goals of development planning in Iraq. By far the most important change was the success of the July 1958 revolution in overthrowing the monarchy, which had been installed by Britain in 1921, and establishing a republican regime in its place. With the backing of all opposition groups and political parties, the new regime set out to introduce numerous changes to reorient and broaden Iraq's domestic and foreign priorities. These changes included, among other things, undertaking agrarian reform that established ceilings on landownership, introducing more generalized social programs, delinking the Iraqi dinar (ID) from the British pound sterling by leaving the sterling area, establishing (for the first time) economic relations with the Soviet Union and East European countries, stressing the importance of industrial development, and initiating the long process that eventually led to the nationalization of the oil industry and the creation of a national oil sector.

The Abdel Karim Qasim regime, which came to power in July 1958, lasted until February 1963 when it was overthrown by an alliance of a military-politico grouping that ruled the country until November 1963 when the military elements of the alliance ousted their civilian counterparts. The new military-dominated regime remained in power until July 1968 when it was ousted in a coup by another military-politico grouping led by the Baath party, which has remained in power until the present time.

In this chapter, an assessment of development policies in the period 1958–68 is undertaken. Subsequent chapters are devoted to the policies of the regime that has been in power for the last quarter-century.

DEVELOPMENT PLANNING IN THE QASIM ERA, 1958-1963

When the 1958 revolution occurred, the fourth general program for the Development Board's projects, 1955/56-1960/61 was in its fourth year.

The new republican leaders pledged to alter the economic priorities of the previous regime and reorganize the structure of development planning administration since development under the monarchy proved to be a dismal failure. According to these leaders, such failure was unavoidable for several reasons. First, there was an absence of meaningful planning, which in turn led to the plundering of Iraq's resources by foreign and local interests. This is so because the dependency of the economy – especially the sectors of oil, finance, banking, and foreign trade – on foreign imperialism was made worse by the development policy which perpetuated Iraq's status as a market for foreign capital and goods and as an exporter of raw materials and fuel at low prices. Second, the economic structure exhibited all aspects of backwardness and imbalance. Thus agriculture with its feudal base was the predominant sector and industry was insignificant. Balance of payments and the ordinary budget showed deficits. Output, productivity, income, and employment were low. These conditions led in turn to serious inequality in the distribution of income, inflation, internal migration to the capital city, and immigration. Third, the policy in general led to the isolation of Iraq from Arab countries, hence hindering the attainment of economic and political unity. Fourth, although revenues from oil could (and should) have been used in a manner that would have created an independent economy, the policies of the Development Board led to the deepening of the economy's features of dependence outlined above because of (1) the composition of the board itself was such that foreign interests penetrated the board and were in a position to have the final say in the determination of economic policy; (2) the position of the foreign executive members was complemented and supported by a large number of foreign experts, engineers, and consulting and contracting firms; (3) the execution of development programs was carried out by the same group of foreign monopolies that led to the impoverishment of the economy; and (4) the Development Board was too lax in its followup and accounting procedures and too tolerant of foreign firms' abuse of contracts.

In a nutshell, the development policies led to strengthening the dependency of the economy on oil, wasting of Iraq's most important resource, consolidating and strengthening the feudal base of the economy, total neglect of industrialization, failure to develop a public sector that would exercise leadership in the progress of economic growth, disproportionate boost to trade sector, corruption of the bureaucracy, and finally the retention by the economy of all features of backwardness and underdevelopment.[1]

Although the regime that followed the 1958 revolution prepared no formal statement outlining its economic philosophy and objectives, the reading of various announcements, official documents, and acts indicates that the two overriding goals of the revolution were the attainment of economic independence and the achievement of more equitable distribution of wealth and income. The main economic principles that guided subsequent economic policies may be summarized as follows: (1) economic planning is an important instrument to guide and direct the whole economy; (2) curbing monopolies and strengthening the middle class; (3) liberating the economy from the shackles of imperialism; (4) abolition of land tenure system; (5) establishing trade relations with all countries; (6) closer economic ties with Arab countries; (7) strengthening and expanding the public sector; (8) encouragement of the private sector; and (9) a higher rate of economic growth.[2]

The new regime decided to abolish the Development Board and replace it by a Ministerial Committee. The new committee, however, decided to continue the implementation of the board's program (but at a slower rate) until a new plan can be drawn up and a new structure for its implementation be organized.

The new structure was introduced in 1959 when the Economic Planning Council was established and the Ministry of Development was replaced by the new Ministry of Planning.[3] At the same time a Provisional Economic Plan (PEP) was adopted to provide continuity for work on projects that had already been started while the new ministry of planning prepared a detailed economic plan.[4]

This Provisional Economic Plan (the fifth since 1951) was to cover the period 1959/60–1962/63 with a total expenditure of ID 392 million to be spent as shown in Table 3.1 (see p. 38). Although the PEP did not provide revenue estimates it stated that its projects will be financed by 50 percent of the oil revenues and that any shortfall would be covered through internal borrowing.[5]

Almost two years after the adoption of the provisional plan, the Detailed Economic Plan (the sixth since 1951) was adopted to cover the period 1961/62–1965/66 with total expenditures of ID 556 million and revenues of ID 424 million (see Table 3.1).

The PEP's total planned expenditure of ID 392.2 million was distributed as follows: agriculture got 12.2 percent, with only 4 percent of the total allocated this time to dams; industry received 12.4 percent; transportation and communications were given nearly 26 percent; and the remaining 49 percent went to building and housing.

Table 3.1
Provisional and Detailed Economic Plans (ID Millions and Percentages)

	Provisional Economic Plan 1959/60-1962/63 Millions	(%)	Detailed Economic Plan 1961/62-1965/66 Millions	(%)
Expenditures				
Agriculture	47.9	12.2	112.9	20.0
Industry	48.7	12.4	166.8	29.4
Transportation and Communication	100.8	25.7	136.5	24.1
Buildings and Housing	190.7	48.7	140.1	24.7
Other	4.0	1.0	10.0	1.8
Total	392.2	100.0	566.3	100.0
Revenues				
Oil	---	---	315.8	55.8
Foreign Loans	---	---	77.2	13.6
Deficit Finance (Implied)	---	---	142.6	25.2
Miscellaneous	---	---	30.8	5.4
Total	---	---	566.4	100.0

Source: Government of Iraq, Law No. 181 of 1959 and Law No. 70 of 1961; United Nations, Studies on Selected Development Programs in Various Countries in the Middle East, 1969 (New York, 1969), p. 6.

The importance of housing is reflected in the allocation of ID 76.4 million or 19 percent of the plan's total budget. This is an unprecedented commitment for this type of social welfare.

The Detailed Economic Plan (DEP), which became effective in January 1962, was an improvement over the previous plans in its sophistication. It established a target rate of growth, calculated in an elementary way the capital-output ratio, and concluded that investment should be about 35 percent of the national income. Because the marginal productivity of agricultural investment is lower, according to the plan, than investment in industry, it was decided to allocate more investment funds to the latter sector. The DEP introduced the principle of calculating the cost of each project and the proportion that can be financed during the plan's five-year period. The DEP continued to follow the principle, which was introduced by the Provisional Economic Plan, of separating planning from implementation with the various ministries being in charge of executing the plan's projects.

The DEP had a total expenditure of ID 566.4 million distributed among the four major sectors as follows: agriculture, 20 percent; industry, 29 percent; transport and communications, 24 percent; and building and housing, 25 percent. Revenues were estimated to be ID 413.8 million, plus a deficit of ID 142.6 million. The deficit was to be financed by internal and external loans and by selling equity shares in completed projects to the private sector.[6]

It should be noted that the planners of DEP were determined to accelerate the pace of industrial development when they allocated nearly 30 percent of the total planned expenditure to this sector. Allocation for industry under DEP was nearly 250 percent of what had been allocated to industry under the fourth plan (1955–60).

In assessing the performance of the plans under Qasim's regime, the following observations are offered: (1) There was a noticeable shift in emphasis from irrigation to industry. This can be explained by the fact that some irrigation projects had been completed while other projects were not urgently needed. Yet agriculture seemed to have been pushed to the background as it received the lowest share of the total funds. (2) The DEP gives the impression of emphasizing housing by allocating 25 percent of the funds to this sector. However, an inspection of the details reveals that out of a total of ID 140.1 million, ID 40 million was allocated to the Ministry of Defense, ID 10 million to army officers' housing, ID 8 million for sewage in Baghdad alone, and only ID 14 million for low-income housing. (3) The DEP did not pay much attention to how to integrate the private sector in the plan. (4) The rate of performance in terms of actual spending manifested a high degree of variation.

Since the period 1958–64 was covered by three plans organized differently, an attempt will be made to evaluate the performance on an annual basis.

For the first nine months of the fiscal year 1959–60, actual expenditure was 62 percent of planned expenditure. This was higher than the previous two years' rates of 52 percent and 57 percent. The deliberate policy of slowing down spending on irrigation projects is reflected in the decline in the rate of actual spending from 45 percent in 1957–58 to only 28 percent in 1959–60. Actual spending on roads, on the other hand, rose from 25 percent of planned spending in 1958–59 to 76 percent in 1959. Spending on industrial development declined from a peak of 108 percent in 1958–59 to 57 percent in 1959–60.

For the year 1960–61, the performance was very poor, with actual spending only 33 percent of the planned expenditure.

In 1961, the rate of performance began to improve, rising from 41 percent in 1961 to 54 percent in 1962. This upward movement, however, proved to be only temporary. In 1963, the rate of performance dropped to 45 percent and was followed by an even lower rate, 41 percent, in 1964. This may be explained by the political upheavals that engulfed the country in February and November 1963.

Table 3.2 shows planned and actual expenditures under PEP and DEP for the period 1958/59–1962/63.

The most important change to take place during Qasim's era, however, was the enactment in 1958 of the Agrarian Reform Law. The new law limited agricultural land holdings to 1,000 and 2,000 donums, depending on the method of irrigation. Land in excess of these limits was to be taken over by the government. The landowners were to receive compensation in the form of treasury bonds. Peasants were to receive small holdings, 30 to 60 donums, and to join cooperative societies supervised by civil servants. The law set five years for the completion of the process of land distribution.[7]

This revolutionary change in the land tenure system was not accompanied, however, by corresponding increases in investment in the agricultural sector. On the contrary, and as was stated earlier, agriculture was not made a top priority by the new regime. First, agriculture received the lowest share of the total funds allocated for development under the DEP. Second, the DEP estimated that agricultural development requires ID 389.5 million; of this amount, only ID 112.9 million or 29 percent of the total was allocated. This is much less than the allocation to industry, which received 76 percent of the funds needed for industrial developments as projected by the planners.

While the relatively heavy emphasis on industry can be explained by the fact that this sector was virtually neglected under the monarchy, the same can be said about agriculture, which was also starved of funds.

Table 3.2
Planned and Actual Development Expenditures, 1958/59–1962/63

Expenditures	Planned (Millions)	Actual (Millions)	Actual:Planned (Percentage)
Agriculture	118.6	49.8	42.0
Industry	76.1	39.9	52.4
Transportation and Communication	159.8	58.3	36.5
Building & Housing	179.2	95.7	53.4
Other	43.2	23.8	55.1
Total Expenditure	576.9	267.5	46.4
Total Actual Revenue		289.6	
Actual Expenditure: Actual Revenue			92.4

Source: Table 3.1; Central Bank of Iraq, Quarterly Bulletin (various issues).

The inadequacy of investment funds allocated to agriculture is shown by the gap between capital requirement in this sector as estimated by the Food and Agriculture Organization (FAO) and planned investment. According to FAO, the agricultural sector should have received during the period 1958–65 ID 40 million per annum.[8] The DEP by contrast planned to invest ID 22 million per annum.

Any criticism of Iraq's agricultural development policy under the Qasim regime must take into consideration, however, the disruptive impact of internal political instability on the entire development process. The Qasim regime was threatened by a military uprising in the northern part of the country in 1959. This was followed by the 1961 Kurdish revolt in the northeastern part of the country. While this revolt was going on, a coup d'etat brought a new government to power in February 1963.

These military and political upheavals, needless to say, were damaging to the economy in terms of their human and material costs. The frequent reorganization of the economic and political apparatus to suit the goals of each new government inflicted more damage on development by making it impossible to provide direction and guidance for any length of time.

In addition to the effects of political instability, the engagement of the armed forces in a campaign to put down the Kurdish revolt had its own crippling effect on the economy as mobilization for such fighting takes precedent over all other pressing economic, political, and social needs.[9] Among the casualties of the instability was the decline in agricultural output and the unavoidable delay in the implementation of land reform.

The extent of the failure of Iraq's agricultural development policy is reflected in the significant decline of the contribution of the agricultural sector in both absolute and relative terms. Thus the value of agricultural output—which stood at ID 85.7 million in 1953, in 1956 prices—rose by an average rate of 1.1 percent, to ID 86.7 million, during the five-year period 1959–63.[10] It is important to note that FAO projected that the contribution of the agricultural sector to the national income in 1965 would be ID 280 million, in 1956 prices. But such contribution was ID 80.4 million in 1963 and ID 120 million in 1965.[11]

The failure of agricultural development policy is also reflected in the decline in agricultural productivity. Thus, while the cultivated area of wheat, barley, and rice increased from 2.8 million in 1957 to 3 million hectare in 1963, the total output of these three main field crops declined from 2.5 million tons to 1.4 million tons respectively.[12] While the failure of agricultural development policy had the effect of turning Iraq from a food-exporting to a food-importing country, the land reform failed to achieve any measurable redistribution of income.[13]

While agricultural development failed to receive the attention it deserved under the Qasim regime, the industrial sector fared better. The regime's attention to industry took several forms, such as the raising of the capital of the Industrial Bank and the extension of more protection to domestic industry. The DEP's allocation for industry was nearly 2.5 times what was allocated to this sector in the last six-year plan drawn by the pre-1958 regime. This shift in favor of industry may be explained as a reaction to the dearth of industrial allocation under the Development Board, as well as the need to implement industrial projects which had been drawn up and approved for implementation as far back as 1952. Moreover, the Qasim regime viewed industrialization as the only means for Iraq to liquidate her state of economic dependency on foreign interests. The argument ran as follows: Iraq's main source of wealth, oil, is regulated by a small group of foreign firms whose ultimate interest is the maximization of their profits, which are derived from a number of sources — including Iraq. The revenue from oil, thanks to pre-1958 development policies, had been dissipated on foreign imports. This meant the return of Iraq's wealth to the economies of the home countries of the oil companies. To loosen and lessen this state of economic dependence and ultimately achieve economic independence, industrialization had to take place at all costs. Furthermore, industrialization would ultimately raise individual income, which — together with agrarian reform — would reduce inequalities and achieve social justice. Another explanation for emphasizing the industrial sector was that, given the same amount of investment, the return in this sector is higher than the return in other sectors. This is so because capital-output ratio in industry was lower than in other sectors.[14]

While appropriation for industry received more attention under Qasim, actual spending did not show any substantial change. As was the case in agriculture, one of the primary explanations for the low rate of performance in the industrial sector was the political instability that disorganized the development effort and affected industrial investment in both public and private sectors.[15] From a look back at the 1958-63 Qasim era, it can be said that the achievements of the regime may be found in areas other than the rate of actual to planned spending.

The single most important achievement was the regime's decision, soon after it came to power, to enact agrarian reform. This had the twin effects of destroying the power base, both political and economic, of the landlords and bringing about a more egalitarian distribution of land. It is true, of course, that agrarian reform failed to reach its proclaimed targets in the assigned period; but such failure should be attributed to other factors, such as the lack of trained agricultural cadres and personnel, lack of agricultural credit, lack of mechanization, low utilization of fertilizers, and the general underdevelopment of the agricultural sector (and, for that matter, of the whole economy).

Other accomplishments of the Qasim regime include the expansion of social services to lower-income classes, the attempt to diversify Iraq's foreign trade by inaugurating trade relations with the Soviet Union and other centrally planned economies, the withdrawal from the sterling area (thus ending one of the last vestiges of British colonialism in Iraq), and the serious attempt to plant the seeds of a national oil sector – evident by the enactment in 1961 of Law 80, which expropriated all parts of the oil concession area that were not actually utilized by the foreign owned oil companies – the IPC group.

DEVELOPMENT PLANNING UNDER
THE AREF BROTHERS

In February 1963, a bloody coup d'etat led by the Baath party succeeded in overthrowing the regime of Qasim. The leaders of the regime, both military and civilian, had no program for the country or the government. As Hanna Batatu noted, the new leadership of the country was attended by a glaring ineptness and want of imagination, compounded by conceit, negligence, personal rivalries, improvisation, and a rush upon status and fat emolument. This judgment is supported by the leading civilian personality of the regime, who asserted that the leaders of the new regime were lost in the government and that their coup had the characteristic of a leap into the unknown.[16]

The problem of the new regime was hopeless in that the Baath party itself had no program. Instead it had ideas that were too general and too ill-defined and little that was the result of disciplined thinking upon the living condition. In other words, a Baathi would have looked in vain through the whole literature of his party for a single objective analysis of any of the serious problems besetting Iraq. In the absence of a program for the development of the country and the presence of increased repression, the Baathists found themselves extinguished by the divisions within their own ranks.[17] In November 1963, the military wing of the government, under the leadership of the president, Abdel Salam Aref, succeeded in purging the government from its civilian counterpart. Abdel Salam Aref remained in power until his death in a helicopter crash in 1966, when his brother Abdel Rahman Aref succeeded him as president. In July 1968, he was overthrown by another military–civilian coalition, which brought the Baath party back to power – where it has remained until the present time.

To the extent that normal functions of the government could be carried out, the new regime continued to implement the Qasim government's

Detailed Economic Plan until it could formulate its own plan—the Five-Year Economic Plan for the years 1965–69.

As a document, the Five-Year Plan (FYP) was the most articulate and sophisticated of all the plans that had been drawn up since the inception of development planning in Iraq in 1950. The FYP articulated overall qualitative general objectives and provided an outline of target-specific economic and social goals and an outline of conditions for the success of the plan, stressing also the importance of the role of fiscal policy, monetary policy, trade policy, and wage policy.[18]

As to the overall general objectives, FYP adopted the objectives outlined in the constitution: Iraq is a democratic socialist state that derives its system from Arab heritage and the spirit of Islam; economic planning is a vehicle to provide direction for the economy; and both public and private sectors are essential to the process of development to increase production and raise living standards. Although private capital cannot be used against the interests of the people, private property rights are to be respected. The FYP stressed that the primary purpose of economic development was to provide a better life for all the people and to combat poverty, disease, and illiteracy. In order to achieve these goals, the economy had to be developed on the basis of comprehensive planning. Having outlined these general principles, the FYP goes on to outline specific targets and objectives.

The economic objectives could be articulated as follows:

1. A rise in standard of living at a rate of no less than 8 percent per year was essential.
2. In order to lessen dependence on imports and accelerate economic diversification and to lessen dependence on oil as the primary source of income and foreign exchange, the FYP adopted annual growth rates of 7.5 percent for agriculture and 12 percent for industry.
3. Economic stability in the short term is necessary.
4. The FYP was designed to expedite the process of Arab economic integration and economic unity, especially with Egypt. Toward this end, FYP goods-producing projects were to be designed with capacity that assumed the existence of an Arab common market.

As to the social objectives, FYP acknowledged that a high proportion of the people were living at the margin of existence and that its policies should attain the following:

1. The FYP should aim to achieve full employment and to eliminate both structural and disguised unemployment. The plan, however, recognized that such goals cannot be reached in five years because of the large size of labor force relative to investment.

2. Expansion of social services, such as health and education, as a means to raise productivity and increase output and welfare.

3. A wider geographic distribution of planned expenditure in order to narrow the income gap between urban and rural population.

4. The benefits of the process of economic growth should accrue in large measure to the poorer classes with limited income, and the plan should aim to reduce gradually the concentration of income and wealth.

The document furthermore underlined the importance of coordinating fiscal, monetary, trade, and wage policies with the policies and objectives of the FYP.

As to fiscal policy, the plan outlined three tasks: (1) fiscal policy should see to it that government spending does not grow by more than the 8 percent per year envisaged for the economy during the plan period; (2) fiscal policy should regulate government spending to moderate sharp fluctuations in economic activity; and (3) fiscal policy should lessen inequality in the distribution of income.

The FYP also called upon monetary policy to be flexible and coordinate its actions with the plan by expanding the money supply to accommodate the rising national output to avoid recession.

The linkage between the goals of the FYP and trade policy was also highlighted. The plan maintained that its goals would be frustrated if a serious rise in the general price level is allowed to take place, since such inflation would result in lower investment, lower rate of economic growth, and lower real income for large segments of the population. To avoid such consequences, the planners proposed that the country should have sufficient stocks of goods to be used to stabilize prices when needed.

Finally, the planners felt that it was necessary to have a wage policy that would see to it that wages are kept within certain limits in order to regulate consumption and encourage saving for investment.

THE ECONOMY'S PAST PERFORMANCE AS A GUIDE FOR THE PLAN

In projecting the growth of the economy for the years 1965–69, the FYP provides important and illuminating data regarding the performance and the changing structure of the Iraqi economy during the 1953–63 period.[19] Some of the changes are the following:

1. Gross domestic product grew at an annual rate of 6.4 percent. Such a relatively high rate, it should be remembered, was influenced by the growth of the oil sector, which was determined by decisions taken by foreign oil firms outside the context of the Iraqi economy. The GDP growth rate also encompassed the fast-growing ordinary budget, especially defense, which tended

to expand with the rising oil revenue. By the same token, the relatively high growth rate should be qualified by the growth in the service sectors of trade, banking, and transportation, which also depend on the flow of oil earnings as such earnings increase imports and consequently stimulate the demand for these services.

2. Leaving the oil sector aside, it was found that the nonoil GDP grew at an annual rate of 5.5 percent.

3. The growth rate of agriculture was found to be zero.

4. Nonagricultural sectoral annual growth rates were industry, 11.5 percent; electric power, 16.7 percent; banking and insurance, 11.3 percent; transportation, 6 percent; public administration and defense, 10.5 percent; wholesale and retail trade, 5.7 percent; services, 8.3 percent; and construction and building, 2.4 percent.

5. While nonoil exports declined by 34 percent during this period, imports increased by 67 percent. This imbalance found Iraq's nonoil exports financing only 19 percent of its imports in 1963 compared to 35 percent in 1953.

In order to improve the performance of the economy, raise living standards, lessen dependence on oil, increase employment, and improve balance of trade, the FYP projected the following changes in the economy by 1969–the last year of the FYP:[20]

1. An increase of 47 percent in GNP or an annual rate of growth of 8 percent.

2. An increase of 34 percent in consumption or an annual growth rate of 6 percent.

3. An increase of 44 percent in the value added in agriculture or an annual rate of growth rate of 7.5 percent.

4. An increase in the value added of the industrial sector of 76 percent, or an annual rate of growth of 12 percent.

A glaring built in failure of the plan was its admission that it could not provide employment to all the new entrants in the labor force. Although the plan projected an increase of .664 million workers in the size of the labor force, it also projected that only .322 million workers would find employment. This meant that the unemployment rate, said to be 3.1 percent in 1964, would rise to 13.5 percent in 1970, with the number of unemployed rising from .076 million to .418 million during the same period.[21]

SECTORAL EXPENDITURE UNDER THE FYP

To attain its objectives, the plan allocated ID 668 million.[22] The sectoral breakdown of the appropriation for the plan's five-year period is shown in Table 3.3. To finance its projected investment, the plan budgeted ID 561.2 million.

Table 3.3
Allocated, Budgeted, and Actual Expenditure and Revenue: Five-Year Plan, 1965/66–1969/70 (ID Millions)

	Allocated		Budgeted		Actual	Actual to Allocated
	Millions	(%)	Million	(%)	Million	(%)
Expenditures						
Agriculture	173.6	26.0	142.0	25.3	56.3	32.4
Industry	187.2	28.0	157.0	28.0	99.5	53.1
Transport and Communication	110.1	16.5	91.0	16.2	66.3	60.3
Building and Housing	134.8	20.2	108.7	19.4	71.2	52.9
Others[1]	62.5	9.3	62.5	11.1	72.2	115.5
Total	668.1	100.0	561.2	100.0	365.5	54.7
Revenue						
Oil			390.0	69.5		
Other[2]			171.2	30.5		
Total			561.2	100.0	392.6	70.0

Source: Ministry of Planning, *Detailed Framework of the Five-Year Economic Plan, 1965–1969* (Baghdad, 1969), pp. 45–47; Ministry of Planning, *Evaluation of the Five-Year Economic Plan, 1965–1969* (in Arabic) (Baghdad, 1971), p. 26.
1. Include international obligations and Ministry of Defense projects.
2. Foreign and domestic loans constitute almost three-fourths of this item.

The data in Table 3.3 give rise to several observations. In the first place, the planning authorities acknowledged that the plan would not meet its own appropriated targets. They adopted a two-tier system of spending – allocated and budgeted. The planners' explanation of this allocated–budgeted approach to development spending was that government ministries tended to submit projects that lacked detailed studies, which made it difficult to ascertain the time of their implementation. Thus it was useful to include in the plan more projects than could actually be implemented. Additionally, the planners thought their spending targets should be flexible enough to meet the needs of other ministries. The plan also took into consideration the fact that contractor actual payments for completed projects are made some time after these projects' period of testing and maintenance. In other words, funds must be appropriated in the plan to meet obligations incurred in previous years.[23]

Whatever the arguments for the divergence between allocated and budgeted spending, the latter was brought into balance with the budgeted income of the plan.

Leaving aside the planners' budgetary and nonbudgetary exercises and considerations, it should be stressed that the FYP's growth targets with regard to national income, consumption, employment, agriculture, and industry were predicated on the investment of ID 668.1 million by the government; and it is on meeting this spending goal that the performance of the plan will have to be judged. It is also necessary to indicate that in addition to the spending of ID 668.1 million the plan assumed the investment of another ID 181 million by the private sector during the plan period.

Looking at the income side of the plan, it is worth noting that oil revenue continues to be the most important source of development spending, providing nearly 70 percent of the plan's total income. The plan also shows a serious inclination to rely on borrowed funds to finance its investment since foreign and domestic loans were projected to contribute 22 percent to the plan's budgeted revenue.

The sectoral distribution of allocated expenditure reveals that agriculture and industry account for 54 percent of the total, with agriculture receiving 26 percent while industry was given 28 percent. But the share of industry would decline if we were to remove the share for power generation, ID 46.3 million. Such a change would reduce the appropriation to ID 140.9 million, or 21 percent of the total.

Allocations for the agricultural sector were designed to achieve an overall annual growth rate of 7.5 percent; to increase the output of principal agricultural crops to meet the needs of domestic consumption by the end of the plan period; to concentrate on the production of agricultural raw materials for domestic industry; to diversify agriculture by adopting intensive methods; to continue the work on projects of flood control, irrigation, and drainage; and to continue the process of land distribution initiated in 1958. It is important to note that of this sector's allocation, irrigation, flood control, and drainage projects received ID 88.5 million, or 52 percent of the total.[24]

The broad objectives of industrial development under FYP were aimed to raise national income, increase employment, and help in economic diversification.

Allocations for this sector were projected at ID 187.2 million. This figure would be smaller if we exclude allocation for power-generating plants, which amounted to ID 46.3 million. The remaining ID 140.9 million was allocated in order to achieve an annual growth rate of 12 percent. This growth rate was to be achieved through productivity enhancement, completion of work on projects already initiated under previous plans, and building new plants and industries.

The thrust of industrial development followed the line of import substitution industrialization, with the exception of petrochemicals which had the export market as a target. Industrial projects, already under construction or slated for construction under the FYP, include projects in such industries as petrochemicals, food processing, building materials, textiles, oil refining, natural gas distribution, furniture, electrical equipment, tobacco, durable goods, and the like. It is worth noting that petrochemical projects were slated to absorb the major share of industrial allocation, ID 47.5 million or nearly 34 percent of the total.

In addition to the increase in projected investment in the two leading nonoil goods-producing sectors, the FYP followed in the path of the previous plan in appropriating funds for infrastructural projects; in raising allocations for housing; and in increasing investment in social services such as medical care, public health projects, and education at all levels – a trend that has received attention since the July 1958 revolution.

ACTUAL PERFORMANCE OF THE FYP

The government that drafted the FYP was overthrown by a coup d'etat in July 1968. The new regime allowed the FYP to run its full course – through March 1970. This makes the FYP the first plan in nearly two decades to have completed its full planning period, thus allowing for a more comprehensive assessment than all the plans that preceded it. The performance of the FYP as measured by the ratio of actual spending to allocations may be seen in Table 3.3 (p. 47).

It can be readily seen from the data in this table that the FYP, not unlike the preceding plans, left much to be desired. For the plan as a whole, actual expenditure was less than 55 percent of allocated expenditure (the performance ratio rises to 65.1 percent if actual spending is related to budgeted spending). Aside from the Ministry of Defense projects (the main item under "others"), which exceeded their target, all other sectors failed to reach their expenditure goals.

In agriculture, which had suffered a decade of stagnation prior to the plan's period, actual spending failed to reach one-third of allocated investment. Both the industrial sector and the building and housing sector managed to spend about 53 percent of their appropriation, while the transportation and communications sector was able to spend 60 percent of its allocation.

While the plan failed to reach its spending target, employment by contrast increased by 427 thousand compared to projected increase of 262 thousand.[25] The primary explanation for this discrepancy may be found in the plan's stress on the employment that its investment was to create, without taking into consideration employment generated by projects initiated before 1965 but completed during the 1965–69 period.

Aside from this bright dimension of employment, all other economic indicators failed to reach their projected targets by a considerable margin. This is to be expected since actual investment was only 55 percent of projected investment spending. This failure in actual investment spending resulted in a total rise in GNP in the five-year plan period by 29 percent instead of 45 percent. Similarly, the total increase in output was 31 percent instead of the projected 48 percent. In Table 3.4 projected rates of growth in several sectors of the economy are compared with actual growth rates by the end of the plan period.

The failure of national output to rise according to the plan's projections can be explained by several factors. First, many large and costly projects such as irrigation, land reclamation, and drainage systems do not contribute to production in the short run since there is a considerable lag between the time of investment and the time when their impact on the economy is felt. Second, agriculture continued to be plagued by low productivity due to lack of modern technology, lack of extension and cooperative services, high levels of soil salination, near absence of drainage canals, and lack of use of fertilizers and pesticides. Third,

Table 3.4
Projected and Actual Growth Rates under the Five-Year Economic Plan, 1965-1969

Economic Sector or Indicator	Projected Growth (Percentage)	Actual Growth (Percentage)
A. Five Year Change (1964 prices)		
Gross Domestic Product	45	29
Total Output of Goods and Services	48	31
Agriculture	44	26
Industry	76	39
Electricity and Natural Gas	147	117
Construction	47	71
Transportation and Communication	44	16
Trade and Finance	43	45
Home Ownership	19	6
B. Annual Change		
Gross Domestic Product	8	5
Agriculture	8	5
Industry	12	7
Electricity and Natural Gas	20	17
Construction	8	10
Transportation and Communication	7	3
Trade and Finance	7	8
Home Ownership	4	1
Total Output of Goods and Services	8	5

Source: Ministry of Planning, *Detailed Framework of the Five-Year Economic Plan, 1965-1969* (Baghdad, 1969), pp. 45-47; Ministry of Planning, *Evaluation of the Five-Year Economic Plan, 1965-1969* (in Arabic) (Baghdad, 1971), p. 26.

there was idle capacity in many industrial projects and factories due to lack of inputs, spare parts, or skilled workers.

While these explanations are important, at least three other considerations must be enlisted to explain this failure. First, in 1964 a number of nationalization measures were enacted that transferred to government ownership a relatively large number of private-sector enterprises such as commercial banking, insurance, cement, cigarettes, and food processing. Such sweeping measures undoubtedly had the effect of discouraging investment in the remaining private enterprises, on the one hand, and diverting private capital to commercial activities characterized by high turnover rate.[26] Second, the process of agrarian reform and land distribution started in 1958 continued its slow pace in the 1960s, thus depriving the agricultural sector of the necessary prerequisites of management, certainty, and growth. Third, while the FYP was in its fourth year, another coup d'etat took place in July 1968, giving rise to different sets of planning, reorganizational, bureaucratic, and political uncertainties that slowed down investment and growth.

A general assessment of the FYP by the Ministry of Planning reached these conclusions:

1. The relative importance of the oil sector in the economy declined from 22.8 percent of GDP in 1964 to 20.4 percent in 1969.

2. Taking into consideration the contribution of the private sector, it was found that some sectors of the economy outperformed their target rates of growth. Such results were found in electricity, construction, distribution, and services. On the other hand, industry, transportation and communications, mining, and agriculture fell behind their target growth rates.

3. The FYP was given credit for laying a strong foundation for the Iraqi economy and achieved a "big push," which will lead to higher growth rates in the subsequent plan.

4. The FYP was also credited with the introduction of modern technologies in industry, power generation, and transportation and communications.

5. Average personal income in real terms increased by less than 12 percent in five years. One of the reasons for this poor performance was the higher-than-projected rise in the rate of population growth. Another reason, of course, was that national income failed to rise in accordance with the projections of the plan.

6. The plan failed to provide proper planning for human resources at the sector level and according to the necessary skills structure in the short run, as well as the long run.

7. Although the relative importance of the oil sector declined slightly, oil continued to represent 85 percent of Iraq's exports.

8. Although the FYP projected that final consumption, both private and public, would absorb 74 percent of GNP by the end of the plan period, the actual ratio was close to 87 percent.[27]

The FYP was in its fourth year when the Baath party seized power in 1968. The new regime allowed the FYP to complete its course while a new five-year plan was being prepared, as is seen in the following chapter.

NOTES

1. See Ibrahim Kubba, *This Is the Path of July 14; Defense before the Revolutions' Court* (in Arabic) (Beirut: Dar al-Taliaa, 1969), pp. 33–39; Government of Iraq, *The July 14 Revolution in Its First Year* (in Arabic) (Baghdad, 1959); Ministry of Planning, *Explanatory Memorandum for Provisional Economic Plan* (Baghdad, 1959), pp. 1–6; Mohammad Salman Hasan, *Studies in the Iraqi Economy* (in Arabic) (Beirut: Dar al-Taliaa, 1966) pp. 143–147, 225–232.
   2. Ibid.
   3. Government of Iraq, *Law No. 74 of 1959.*
   4. Government of Iraq, *Law No. 181 of 1959.*
   5. Ibid., Article 18 and p. 86.
   6. See Ministry of Planning, *Explanatory Statement for the Law of the Detailed Economic Plan for the Five-Years from (1961–1962) to (1965–1966) No. 70 of 1961,* pp. 73–74.
   7. Government of Iraq, *Law No. 30 of 1958.*
   8. Food and Agricultural Organization Mediterranean Development Project, *Iraq, Country Report* (Rome, 1959), p. 30. Henceforth cited as *FAO Report.*
   9. As a testimony to the damaging impact of political instability, the following report is illustrative: Beyond the Euphrates River, a rusty barge lies half buried in sand, miles from the nearest water. Just eight years ago this emptiness was rich farmland, and the barge floated on an irrigational canal. The canal has vanished into a desert.
   At the southern port of Basra, a towering silo built to store wheat for export now houses grain Iraq must import to feed herself. Near Baghdad a huge abandoned agricultural project now supports only six families.
   Iraq is potentially the richest Arab country in the Middle East, but years of mismanagement and political unrest have brought stagnation and instability. See *The New York Times,* January 3, 1965.
   10. See Ministry of Planning, *The Detailed Framework of the Five-Year Economic Plan, 1965–1969* (in Arabic) (Baghdad, 1969), pp. 18–19.
   11. *FAO Report,* p. 23; World Bank, *World Tables,* 3rd ed. (Baltimore: The Johns Hopkins University Press, 1983), p. 90.
   12. *FAO Report,* p. 71.
   13. See A. J. Meyer, "Economic Modernization," in *The United States and the Middle East* (New York: American Assembly, Columbia University, 1964), p. 64.
   14. See Ibrahim Kubba, *This Is the Path of July 14; Defense before the Revolution's Court* (in Arabic) (Beirut: Dar al-Taliaa, 1969); Government of Iraq, *The July 14 Revolution;* Ministry of Planning, *Explanatory Memorandum.*
   15. "In general, private industrial activity has varied with the political cli-

mate, activity slowed down after the revolution, recovered late in 1960, quickened somewhat during 1961 and the first half of 1962, but then slowed down again." K. M. Langley, "Iraq: Some Aspects of the Economic Scene," *The Middle East Journal* 18 (Spring 1964): 188.

16. See Hanna Batatu, *The Old Social Classes and the Revolutionary Movements of Iraq: A Study of Iraq's Old Lauded and Commercial Classes and of Its Communists, Ba'thists, and Free Officers* (Princeton: Princeton University Press, 1982), pp. 1012–1014.

17. Ibid.

18. See Ministry of Planning, *Detailed Framework*, pp. 1–5.

19. Ibid., pp. 14–27.

20. Ibid., p. 55.

21. Ibid., p. 35.

22. In addition to the plan's own appropriation, the Ministry of Planning projected ID 181 million of private-sector investment, thus bringing total projected investment for this period to ID 849 million. For private sector projected investment, see ibid., p. 43.

23. Ibid., p. 45.

24. Ibid., pp. 48, 72.

25. Data in this section, unless otherwise indicated, are either taken or derived from Ministry of Planning, *Evaluation of the Five-Year Economic Plan, 1965–1969* (in Arabic) (Baghdad, 1971), pp. 2–40.

26. For a discussion of the nationalization measures see Abdel Munim Said Ali, "Evaluation of the Role of the State in Arab Countries," in *The Role of the State in Economic Activity in the Arab World*, ed. Ali Nassar (in Arabic) (Kuwait: Arab Planning Institute, 1991), pp. 136–141.

27. Ministry of Planning, *Evaluation*, pp. 42–43.

CHAPTER 4

The Baath Party and
Its National Development Plans

When the coup d'etat of July 1968 brought the Arab Baath Socialist party (the Baath), the Five-Year Plan 1965–1969 was in the fourth year of its implementation. The new regime, which had no economic program of its own, allowed the FYP to run its course while it attempted to consolidate its power and develop its plans for the future of Iraq.

The Baath party, whether in Iraq or in Syria where it was founded in the 1940s, has never distinguished itself for a coherent political, social, or economic program. Whenever it succeeded in coming to power, which it did through coups d'etat, it tended to suffer from a dichotomy between its rhetoric, on the one hand, and its policies, on the other. This failure can be attributed in no small measure to the manner in which the structure of thought of Arab nationalism has developed in the modern era. Since the Baath has been one of the main contending political movements of Arab nationalism (the other was Jamal Abdel Nasser of Egypt – 1952-70) and since it has been the sole party in control of the political and economic destiny of Iraq for the last twenty-five years, it is relevant for this study to examine some of the main tenets, concepts, and principles of Arab nationalism and its Baathist variation.[1]

EVOLUTION OF ARAB NATIONALISM

It can be said that modern Arab nationalism evolved in the broad context of the general historical forces that shaped the emergence of nationalism in Europe and elsewhere. The historical growth of nationalism as an ideology for capitalism was necessary for the market-based growth of modern European economies, which entailed the rise of powerful national states and their institutions. The nation state that gained legitimacy in Europe and America was subsequently extended and adapted to local conditions by elites in colonized countries and regions.[2]

The Ottoman empire – which had ruled the Arab region, including Iraq, for centuries – utilized Islam as the ideological force to rationalize its colonial rule. By the eighteenth century, however, there were at least three trends that worked to undermine Ottoman rule and eventually give rise to Arab nationalist sentiments. These were (1) the realization by the non-Turkish communities that they were not equal to the Ottomans in the eyes of the colonial ruler; (2) European economic and political penetration of the empire and its provinces, which demonstrated to the Arabs the failure of the Ottoman system of government to protect its subjects from foreign invaders; and (3) the decline of control by the Ottoman central authorities over the periphery, including the Arab provinces, which in turn helped local elites to assert a measure of autonomous control in the provinces.

The decline of authority of the central government afforded the elite groups in the Arab region a historic opportunity to enjoy a high degree of autonomy. By the nineteenth century, the idea of an Arab nation based on ethnolinguistic association achieved new strength and clarity and tended to erode the idea of a religiously based allegiance.[3] At this stage, however, Arab nationalism was apolitical. Yet the cultural renaissance of the last century led to the struggle against the alien (i.e., the hegemonic control of the Ottomans and the discovery by the Arabs of their own heritage).[4] Although certain writers asserted that the Arabs in the Middle East should be independent of the Turks, such independence was not to be attained until after World War I.[5]

In 1916, the Arab revolt against the Ottoman rule was declared on the strength of a promise by the British that they would guarantee the liberation of the Arabs and help create an Arab kingdom, which was to consist of the Arab parts of Asia.[6]

As subsequent events have demonstrated, Britain had no intention of helping the Arabs form their own state; it had already agreed with France to carve up the Arab East, with France assuming control over Syria and Lebanon and Britain assuming control over Iraq, Jordan, and Palestine. The League of Nations sanctioned this colonial control by calling it a mandate system under which Britain and France were expected to prepare the mandated areas for political independence.

The first generation of Arab nationalists, who led the Arab revolt and fought for independence, ended up in power with the approval and under the patronage of a new colonial regime that was imposed on their countries by France and Britain. For the elites, it was an act of replacing one dominant foreign power by another.

From the elites' perspective, the mandatory system actually provided new advantages lacking under the Ottomans. In the first place, they had become the de facto as well as the de jure rulers of their own people. In other words, they became the government, but with the mandatory power pulling the strings in order to secure European economic and political interest. This was clearly the case in Iraq. Moreover, a new class of landowners was established by the colonial power to provide political backing for the monarchy. Doreen Warriner observed that the foundation of the new kingdom in Iraq strengthened the position of the tribal sheiks by giving them both legal ownership of land and representation in parliament. And as oil money provided an alternative source of investment in agriculture and other sectors of the economy, the function of these large landowners became simply one of preserving their position in the packed parliament and of resisting any change.[7]

The nature and the implications of the mandatory system in Iraq were assessed by Peter Sluglett as follows:

In any balance sheet for the Mandate, the Iraq people outside the small circle of government ... were the losers. The Government was not carried on for their benefit, but for the benefit of the Sunni urban political class within a framework created and supported by the British authorities. ... When it was clear that British interests would no longer be at risk, and when the necessary mechanism to protect them had been perfected it was time to withdraw. ... It is profitless to blame the British Mandatory authorities for failing to ensure that the Iraq Government concerned itself with the wider interests of the nation, or made efforts to reconcile rather than exacerbate the tensions within the state: to do so would be to misunderstand the nature of imperialism.[8]

The failure of the Arab revolt to achieve political and economic independence meant that the next phase in the evolution of Arab nationalism had to entail the elimination of European domination and its agents – the Arab governments that were installed by France and Britain. The efforts of the Arab nationalists did not show results, however, until after the end of World War II. But while the history of the interwar period was shaped by European colonialism and its local elites, other forces, which eventually undermined these positions, were at work.

As government functions expanded, so did its military and civilian bureaucracies and technocracies. This meant that new recruits from outside the ranks of traditional elites had to be drawn into the labor force. The emergence of these classes coincided with the rise of two other classes – the urban and rural proletariat – caused primarily by the changes in the pattern of landownership and import-substitution industrialization. As the structure of the economy changed, another class of petit bourgeoisie – bankers, shippers, exporters and importers, insurance agents, and the like – tied to the international economy also emerged. As World War II came to an end, the configuration of social classes and their interests had undergone a major change, since the establishment of governments in Iraq and other parts of the Arab region in the aftermath of World War I.

While the traditional elites had, by the end of World War II, continued to link their political and economic fortunes with imperialism, the new classes were challenging the status quo and searching for a new social and economic order. The opportunity to replace the old order forced itself upon the Arab region when the state of Israel was created in 1948 in Palestine – a fact that had the effect of destroying the political legitimacy of the first generation of Arab nationalist regimes. Explanations and rationalizations of this failure included collusion between imperial powers, Arab regime bankruptcy, and superior enemy technology.[9]

The old nationalist order was displaced by a new, younger generation of nationalists in a succession of military takeovers in the core Arab countries – Syria (1949), Egypt (1952), and Iraq (1958). These regimes succeeded in destroying the economic and political power base of landed aristocracy, expanding the public sector, and nationalizing both large domestic enterprises and foreign enterprise whenever such nationalization was feasible.

The new nationalist regimes failed in several areas. One of the hallmarks of these regimes was their repressive systems of government. Another aspect of their failure was their unwillingness, leaving their rhetoric aside, to develop their economies in a manner that would reduce dependency on the international economic system. To do otherwise would have meant a recognition of classes, something the new generation of nationalists chose to reject.

THE POLITICAL ECONOMY OF ARAB NATIONALISM

Changing historical contexts that gave rise to movements such as Arab nationalism, the particular epoch that engendered a given type of struggle, the forces that presented challenges to Arab nationalism, be it foreign or local, are some of the elements that gave rise to various interpretations of the ideological contents and goals of Arab nationalism. Indigenous factors – such as the nature of class and power structure, land tenure, cultural heritage, and distribution of income and wealth – are some of the other elements that affected the evolution of Arab nationalism.

Given the foreign-imposed conditions – from Ottoman control to European colonialism and imperialism – that had to be overcome, the rhetoric of Arab nationalism tended to have revolutionary overtones. Yet it is important to note that Arab nationalism from its very inception to the present is a middle class political movement. Although Arab nationalism did not have a unified organization or a unified political leadership, its underlying sentiments and aspirations have been strong enough both to permit at certain junctures mass mobilizations in behalf of its objectives and ideals and to compel conservatives to accept at least temporarily some of its aims.[10]

These aspirations and sentiments were articulated through two main political movements which succeeded in coming to power in a number of Arab countries in the second half of the twentieth century. One movement was led by Jamal Abdel Nasser, while the other was led by the Arab Baath Socialist party. When Nasser and his fellow army officers succeeded in 1952 in overthrowing the monarchy in Egypt, their focus was to rid Egypt of some of the more flagrant economic injustices and waste that the monarchy had imposed on the Egyptian people. The rise of the tide of Arab nationalism under the leadership of Nasser and Egypt was paralleled by the emergence of another and similar political movement whose philosophy was articulated by the Arab Baath Socialist party which made its debut first in Syria in the 1940s. The core of the Baathist ideology, it is claimed, is that its goals consist of Arab unity, freedom, and socialism. For the Baath, one of the objectives of imperialism is to retard and prevent Arab unity. It follows that existing political divisions and fragmentation must be removed if the Arabs are to overcome stagnation and backwardness. In order not to confuse its own socialism with that of the Communists or the Marxists, the Baath not only rejects the concept of class struggle as the driving force in historical development but also asserts that the well-informed Arab cannot be communist without giving up Arabism since the two, according to the Baath, are mutually exclusive.[11]

Having asserted the supremacy of Arab nationalism and Arab unity and having rejected Communism, Marxism, and non-Arab socialism, one would have expected the Baathists to provide an articulation of an alternative outline of an ideology. But such formulation was not forthcoming. Instead, the emphasis continued to be on the importance of Arab nationalism and Arab unity, an emphasis characterized by a high degree of circularity.

As to the meaning of the Baath's brand of socialism, one of the founders and the leading theoretician of the Baath, Michel Aflaq, stated that "When I am asked to give definition of socialism, I can say that it is not to be found in the works of Marx and Lenin. I say: socialism is the religion of life and of its victory over death." Aflaq went on to say that the Arabs should "take care not to lose their nationalism nor to confuse it with the felonious notion of class interests, so as not to endanger national unity."[12]

The intellectual challenge that Marxism presented in the areas of social justice and a more equitable pattern of income distribution forced the Baath, however, to include such goals in its economic and social program.[13] The most serious challenge to the very essence of the Baath ideology came from the party's own left wing, which claimed that the Baath was too conservative to respond to the needs of the people because of the inherently traditional nature of its ideology.[14]

In short, among the new generation of nationalists that advocated what it called Arab socialism, this socialism turned out in practice to be similar to development policies applied in most countries of the Third World where the public sector had to assume responsibilities the private sector was either unwilling or unable to undertake.

A glaring gap in the ideological structure of Arab nationalist thought is the virtual absence of economic analysis articulating the economic dimensions and objectives of the movement.

An important explanation for the lack of economic analysis may be found in the disdain and the indifference with which some of the leading thinkers of Arab nationalism viewed economics. One such writer was Sati Al-Husri who went so far as to deny the importance of economic forces and interests to the evolution of Arab nationalism. According to him, even to consider economic interests as one of the foundations of Arab nationalism is something contrary to intelligence and logic. Another thinker of Arab nationalism, Abdel Rahman Al-Bazzaz, who has served as secretary general of OPEC and became Iraq's prime minister in the 1960s, echoed Husri's views when he said that it is possible for nationalism to arise among people who are aware of their national existence, their national language, and the spiritual values given them by their common history without the need for a materialistic economic unity to hold the group together.[15]

Another explanation may be found in the nature of the economic development of the Arab region during the nineteenth century. Charles Issawi maintains that the Arab region experienced much less industrialization than either East Asia or Latin America.[16] To the extent that the Arab region suffered from economic stagnation under the Ottomans and from deindustrialization due to European penetration, a case can be made for the lack of economic analysis that would be relevant to the region.

Although interest in economics increased in this century, especially in the second half, there is still an obvious lack of a system or systems of economic thought that can be described as Arab economic thought. Arab nationalism continues to lack an economic content. As the well-known Arab economist, Yusif Sayigh, observed, Arab thinkers — whether they are in power or not or whether they were in positions of intellectual or ideological or party leadership — have so far failed to produce a comprehensive system of thought that could constitute the social and economic content of Arab nationalism.[17] Another economist, Mahmud Abdel-Fadil, reached a similar conclusion when he stated that Arab economists had failed to make serious contributions similar to those made by Latin American or Indian economists.[18] The dearth of economic analysis by the Arab nationalists should not be taken to mean that Arab economists in general failed to pay attention to the problems of their region or their respective countries.

The experiment by Jamal Abdel Nasser of Egypt to restructure the Egyptian economy by expanding the public sector considerably is a case in point. For several years, Nasser's was the only Third World experiment in state-building and economic development along socialist lines outside the Marxist-Leninist model.[19]

The main tenets of Arab socialism, as can be gleaned from the writings of Arab economists who dealt with the subject, include the following: (1) Arab socialism allows a high degree of private property and consequently a high degree of income inequality; (2) Arab socialism sanctions private ownership of means of production and therefore allows considerable room in the economy for a national bourgeoisie; (3) the sanctioning of private property and the right to inherit wealth are rooted in the teaching of Islam, which must be respected; (4) Arab socialism aims to have a high level of output and an equitable distribution of such output; and (5) Arab socialism believes in the economic progress of future generations, but such progress cannot be undertaken at the expense of present generation whose needs should not be sacrificed. Arab socialism, in other words, must be able to strike a balance between the needs of the present generation and the aspirations of future ones.[20]

These principles of Arab socialism were influenced by the policies of Nasser, who stressed the importance of the principle of nonexploitive private property and the principle of equitable distribution of national output. Arab economists' views of Arab socialism were determined to a considerable extent by economic policies and measures adopted by governments in Egypt, Iraq, Syria, and Algeria. In all these countries certain economic activities were either reserved for the public sector or transferred to this sector through nationalization. Public-sector activities in these four leading Arab countries are in line with economic practices in most Third World countries where private capital has shown reluctance to commit itself to risky or long-term economic activities such as industrial production.

In his extensive study of writings on Arab socialism in the 1960s, Abdel-Fadil found himself reaching the conclusion that most of these writings were a restatement of official ideological documents and that many of these writings tended to rationalize public policies that were already in place. Such writings had failed to pay minimum attention to the

problems associated with transition to socialism and the contradictions
that manifest themselves in any serious process of such transformation.[21]

THE NATIONAL DEVELOPMENT PLAN, 1970/71–1974/75 (1970–74)

The National Development Plan (NDP) took two years to prepare
and was drafted with the revolutionary rhetoric that permeated the
planning documents.[22] The NDP is discussed in more detail than the
previous plans because it constitutes a sort of watershed in the history
of planning in Iraq.

In the first place, it is the first plan to be drafted and implemented
and allowed to run its full course under the auspices of the same political power structure. In other words, the regime that prepared the plan
was not changed in the midst of the life of the plan. Second, the planners of NDP had the distinct and great advantage over their predecessors of being able to make use of the wealth of studies, planning and
technical experience, and administrative competence Iraq had been
able to attain over the previous two decades. This advantage was recognized in the preamble to the plan's strategy, which described the
NDP as a comprehensive plan for economic and social development
founded on clear strategy, well defined goals, and adequate implementing structures.[23] Another manifestation of this plan's indebtedness to
past experience was its emulation of most of the previous (1965–69)
plan's structure, analysis, and goals – as is seen later in this chapter.

Another factor that distinguished this plan from all others was the
fact that it was ushered into the world in the midst of the era of rising
oil revenue that started with the conclusion of the Tehran price agreement of 1971 and followed with the oil price explosion of 1973–74.

The NDP also had the dubious distinction of being the last formal
and published five-year plan; after this plan's period, the Baath regime
chose to resort to a series of annual investment programs instead of
the traditional, formal multiple-year plans which had characterized
planning effort in Iraq since 1950.

THE STRATEGY OF THE PLAN

The opening paragraph of the NDP strategy elevated the July 1968
coup d'etat to a revolution and stated that our socialist revolution is
alone equipped to accelerate economic and social development and
that this socialist revolution has a specific strategy for the process of
development and that this strategy was designed to (1) increase production, labor productivity, and the use of modern technology, (2) increase investment and human capital formation, (3) stress saving as a
condition of development, (4) ensure that consumption does not conflict

with the requirements and the need for savings, (5) increase mass aware-
ness of and participation in the process of development, (6) adopt the
principle of "balanced growth" in planning, which entails the efficient
utilization of domestic raw materials and the encouragement of industries to efficiently use such resources to help diversify local production
to meet local needs, (7) expand and diversify exports, (8) adopt a ra-
tional import policy to improve living standards, especially of low-
income groups, and (9) support the private sector through investment
incentives.[24]

The NDP articulated two sets of goals: general economic and social
objectives and sector-specific goals. The general economic and social
objectives include the raising of national income by 7.1 percent per
year, or twice the rate of population growth; concentration on the
goods-producing sectors of the economy (i.e., agriculture and industry);
exploitation of the country's mineral resources to lessen dependence on
oil; a more equitable distribution of projects throughout the country;
pursuance of pan-Arab integration; increase in social services; increase
in employment opportunities; and a more equitable distribution of
income.[25]

The objectives the plan envisaged for the various sectors are these:[26]

1. *Agriculture.* The development of this sector was planned to raise its output
   at an annual rate of 7 percent in order to meet local demand, to meet the
   needs of the industrial sector for agricultural raw materials, to increase agricultural export, and to rely on intensive rather than extensive farming.

2. *Industry.* The industrial sector was projected to grow at an annual rate of
   12 percent. Other goals for this sector include the completion of projects
   already started, increased industrial productivity, increased output of manufactured exports, attainment of a degree of self-sufficiency in manufac-
   tures, and encouragement of industrial integration with other Arab countries.

3. *Transportation and Communication.* The plan recognizes the importance
   of an expanded infrastructure for the growth of the economy. Since infrastructure projects had traditionally received considerable attention, the
   task of NDP was to complete projects initiated in the past and extend the
   networks of transportation and communication (i.e., roads, highways, rail-
   roads, air and sea transport, and telecommunications).

4. *Buildings and Services.* As in the previous plan, the NDP pledged to stress
   the importance of buildings geared to expand social services such as health
   and education.

QUANTITATIVE GOALS OF THE PLAN

To attain the broad objectives of the NDP outlined here, the planners established a series of specific growth rates for each sector. Table
4.1 (see p. 64) shows these target rates and the comparable rates in the
previous plan (1965–69) as well as the actual growth rates achieved

Table 4.1
NDP: Annual Average Sectoral Growth Rates, 1970–1974

Sector	1970–1974 Percentage	1965–1969 Percentage	
		Target	Actual
Agriculture	6.9	7.5	4.7
Mining	1.8	6.0	3.5
Manufacturing	12.0	12.0	7.0
Electricity	11.4	20.0	17.3
Construction	15.0	8.0	10.3
Transportation and Communication	7.7	7.4	3.0
Trade	8.5	---	---
Finance	9.6	7.4	7.7
Homeownership	3.4	3.5	1.2
Defense and Government	5.5	---	---
Other Services	7.6	8.7	6.4
All sectors	7.1	8.0	5.2

Source: NDP Law, p. 140; NDP Guide, p. 38.

under that plan. Based on these growth rates, the plan projected certain structural changes in the economy by 1974. Thus it was projected that the relative importance of the mining sector to GDP would decline from 32.6 percent in 1969 to 26.4 percent in 1974, while that of industry would increase from 9.1 percent to 11.4 percent and that of agriculture from 19.1 percent to 19.7 percent during the same period.

The plan also projected increases in a number of economic indicators. These are summarized in Table 4.2. To reach its projected growth targets, the Ministry of Planning estimated that ID 1.144 billion of investment would be required. This projected requirement was divided as follows:

1. ID 537 million, 47 percent of the total, was to be invested by the central government under the direction and supervision of the Ministry of Planning (i.e., NDP).

2. ID 322 million, 28 percent, was assigned to government enterprises, autonomous agencies, and the municipalities.

3. ID 285 million, 25 percent, was to come from the private sector.

Sectoral allocations under the national development plan, as well as the various sources of finance, are shown in Table 4.3. The NDP sectoral allocations reveal that the planners decided to alter the pattern of the sectoral priorities which had characterized the 1965–69 plan. Thus, while allocations to the three primary investment sectors under NDP

Table 4.2
NDP: Projected Total Increases in Certain Economic Indicators, 1970–1974

Indicator	Projected Increase Percentage
National income indicators (1969 prices)	
Gross domestic product	34.6
Gross national product	39.2
Gross domestic investment	89.8
Personal income	37.6
Private Consumption	33.7
Public consumption	27.6
Imports of goods and services	26.2
Exports of goods and services	14.2
Other indicators	
Employment	24.3
Worker Average Annual Income	13.1
Savings	62.9
Per Capita Income	19.6

Source: NDP Law, pp. 140–159.

Table 4.3
NDP: Sectoral Allocations and Revenue, 1970–1974 (ID Millions)

	Original		Revised	
	ID	Percentage	ID	Percentage
Sectoral Allocations				
Agriculture	185.0	34.4	366.2	19.0
Industry	132.0	24.6	391.0	20.2
Transport and Communications	60.0	11.2	219.3	11.4
Buildings and Services	67.0	12.5	283.0	14.6
Other	92.9[1]	17.3	672.5[2]	34.8
Total	536.9	100.0	1932.0	100.0
Revenue				
Oil	425.0	79.2	1554.4	90.0
Other[3]	111.9	20.8	172.6	10.0
Total	536.9	100.0	1727.0	100.0

Source: NDP Law, pp. 9, 145, 150; *Annual Abstracts of Statistics.*
1. Includes loans to government enterprises and international obligations.
2. Includes, in addition to items in note 1, other investment expenses and general reserve.
3. Includes foreign and domestic loans and loan repayments.

agriculture, industry, and infrastructure were 35, 25, and 24 percent of total allocations respectively, the comparable ratios under the 1965–69 plan were 25 percent, 28 percent, and 35 percent. It should be noted that while the relative importance of agriculture increased appreciably between the two plans, the relative importance of the other two primary sectors moved in the opposite direction.

The pattern of the sources of finance changed little in that oil revenues continued to supply most of the plan's estimated income. It should be noted, however, that the relative importance of oil revenue under NDP increased to 79 percent of total plan revenue, compared with 70 percent under the previous plan.[27]

NDP investment, however, was only one component of total projected investment, accounting for 47 percent of total allocation. The other two components were (1) ID 322 million to be invested by government enterprises and municipalities and (2) private-sector projected investment of ID 285 million. Table 4.4 shows the plan's total sectoral projected investment of ID 1.144 billion by each of the three components.

The data in Table 4.4 give rise to several observations. First, the division of investment between private sector and public sector tends to increase the role of the former by raising its share from 22 percent of total investment in the 1965–69 plan (FYP) to 25 percent in NDP. Second, although the share of central government investment declined from ID 561 million or 68 percent of the total under FYP to ID 537 million or 47 percent of the total under NDP, the allocation of government enterprises by contrast increased from ID 79 million (or less than 10 percent of total investment under FYP) to ID 322 million (or 28 percent of the total under NDP) thus bringing up total public-sector investment to 75 percent of the plan's projected investment, compared with 68 percent under the FYP.[28] The data in Table 4.4 reveal an important aspect of NDP in that, within the government enterprises component of the plan, the lion's share (66 percent of the funds) was allocated to industry. Of this sector's appropriation, 86 percent was allocated to the projects of the national oil and mineral companies.[29]

The large allocation for investment in the oil sector is a reflection of a number considerations, some of which go back to 1961. When the Qasim regime nationalized the bulk of the land (more than 99 percent) covered by the three concessions, neither it nor the successor regime were successful in developing Iraq's considerable oil reserves. Although the Iraq National Oil Company (INOC) was created in 1964 with the intent to develop these reserves and build a national oil industry, the company was not given the necessary resources or the political backing to accomplish its mission. The regime that came to power in 1968 decided to put into effect policies that would attain the original goals of INOC by providing it with enabling legislation and funds. The

Table 4.4
NDP: Aggregate Sectoral Distribution of Planned Expenditures, 1970–1974 (ID Millions)

Sector	NDP ID	Govt. Enterprises ID	Total Govt. ID	Sector Share in Total Govt. Expenditures Percentage	Private Sector ID	Grand Total ID	Share of Govt. in Total Expenditures Percentage	Share of Private Sector in Total Expenditures Percentage
Agriculture	185.0	8.0	193.0	22.5	18.0	211.0	91.5	8.5
Industry	132.0	212.0	344.0	40.0	50.0	395.0	87.0	13.0
Transport and Communications	60.0	54.0	114.0	13.3	35.0	149.0	76.6	23.5
Buildings and Services	67.0	48.0	115.0	13.4	182.0	297.0	38.7	61.3
Other	92.9	---	92.9	10.8	---	92.9	100.0	---
Total	536.9	322.0	858.9	100.0	285.0	1144.9	75.0	25.0

Source: Derived from *NDP Law*, pp. 9, 145, 150; *NDP Guide*, p. 92.

long-term implication of these policy decisions was to increase rather than lessen the role of oil in the economy of Iraq, hence increasing the dependence of the economy on this particular sector. In addition, in 1969, a number of agreements with the Soviet Union, East Germany, and Hungary were concluded that provided for loans, technical assistance, training, and equipment to help INOC build a national oil industry. A novel aspect of these agreements was that the repayment of the loans would be made in the form of oil which these agreements were to help produce.[30]

Another feature of the plan's aggregate spending is the role of private-sector investment. While the share of this sector's investment is 25 percent of total investment, most of its investment (64 percent) was geared to housing. It should be noted that while the private sector was projected to provide 8.5 percent, 13 percent, and 23.5 percent of the investment in agriculture, industry, and transport and communications respectively, its role in the buildings and services sector was much higher – 61.3 percent. Indeed it can be said that the housing market was left virtually in its entirety to the private sector since public-sector investment in housing was limited to less than ID 1 million.

A significant feature of the plan was the high share of the industrial sector, which was projected to receive 40 percent of public-sector investment, while the agricultural sector was allocated 22.5 percent, followed by buildings and services with 13.4 percent, and transportation and communications, which was slated to receive 13.3 percent of public-sector projected investment. It is clear from these allocations that the government must have concluded that industrial development, especially the development of the oil sector, should receive priority over all other sectors.

It is also significant to note that of the 234 projects in the agricultural, industrial, transport and communications, and the buildings sectors, only 58 new projects were to be initiated by the NDP. These new projects were slated to absorb ID 101 million, 23 percent of the ID 444 million to be invested in these sectors during the plan's period. Table 4.5 shows the distribution of the new projects in the various investment sectors. In this sense, NDP became a mere extension of previous plans since the bulk of its investment was allocated to complete projects that had already been started.

ASSESSMENT OF THE NATIONAL
DEVELOPMENT PLAN

The planners of NDP had considerable advantage over all past planners. In the first place, they had two decades of past experience to build on and to learn from. Over these twenty years, there had been a

Table 4.5
NDP: Distribution of Development Projects by Sector, 1970–1974 (ID Millions and Percentages)

Sector	Total Number of Projects	Total Invest- ment (Millions)	Number of New Projects	Per- centage of Total	Investment in new Projects (Millions)	Percentage of total Invest- ment
Agriculture	65	185	4	6.1	8.5	4.6
Industry	24	132	7	29.2	63.9	4.8
Transport and Communi- cation	58	60	20	34.5	21.2	3.5
Buildings	92	67	27	29.3	6.9	10.3
Total	239	444	58	24.3	101.0	22.7

Source: Derived from *NDP Law,* pp. 9–40.

steady accumulation of data, statistics, and economic analysis; a rise in the number of technical personnel; an increase in experience; and wider and more complex interaction with foreign firms and enterprises of all stripes and nationalities. These firms were retained to perform a variety of technical tasks such as advisory services, preparation of feasibility studies, drawing up of contracts, project building, and follow-up and maintenance. In all these activities, these firms served as an important source of technical knowledge, which enhanced the country's reservoir of knowhow and technology in many fields. In short, the drafters of the NDP were in the enviable position of approaching their task with experience, knowledge, sophistication, and relatively sizable cadres of specialists and experts.

In addition to the expertise the planners had at their disposal, they also had the time to prepare the plan. The government made a wise decision in allowing the 1965-69 plan to run its course, thus giving itself and its planners nearly two years to prepare the new plan. The relatively voluminous literature that surrounded the plan supports the contention that the planners did not draft the plan in a hurry.[31]

The NDP, however, was issued by a regime that described itself as "revolutionary" and "socialist," which will effect "radical" changes in Iraq's economic and social structures. Such assertions should have led, one would expect, to the formulation of a plan that would result in a clearcut break with those of previous regimes, especially the one it overthrew in 1968.

Yet a casual inspection of the plan, its literature, its allocations, its revenue, and its modus operandi leads to the conclusion that far from constituting a clearcut break with the past or even a major point of departure, the new regime's development policies and its NDP were nothing but a faithful continuation of past development policies and plans, especially the 1965–69 development plan. In other words, there was nothing that can vaguely be described as revolutionary or radical. Suffice it to say, as is shown in Table 4.5 (p. 69), only 58 out of the NDP's 239 projects were new; and these new projects were slated to absorb ID 101 million, 23 percent of the plan's total allocation.

Comparison of total allocation, sectoral distribution, and plan performance between NDP and earlier plans breaks down to the point of irrelevance starting in 1971, the second year of NDP, because of the series of oil price increases in the 1970s.

In February 1971, the Organization of Petroleum Exporting Countries (OPEC) succeeded in its negotiations with the oil companies to raise government per-barrel revenue by raising the tax rate on company profit from 50 percent to 55 percent and by agreeing to a series of price increases over the next five years. These changes were followed by further increases to take into account the decline in the value of the dollar because of its devaluation in the aftermath of the collapse of the Bretton Woods system. The combined effect of these changes increased government per-barrel revenue for the key Arabian Light crude from $0.91 before the conclusion of the Tehran agreement to $1.46 by June 1973.[32]

But the provisions of the Tehran agreement were superseded by market developments and the events of the Arab–Israeli war of October 1973 when the Arab oil-producing states and other members of OPEC decided to raise the price from $3.01 per barrel on October 1 to $11.65 per barrel by January 1, 1974.[33]

These sharp increases, coupled with Iraq's success in nationalizing the Iraq Petroleum Company, led to sharp increases in Iraq's oil revenue from ID 280 million in 1970 to ID 2.4 billion in 1975. In comparing Iraq's oil revenue during the two five-year periods of the two plans 1965–69 and 1970–74, we find that during the first period Iraq's total revenue amounted to ID 1.2 billion or an annual average of ID 249 million. The corresponding figures for 1970–74 were ID 3.5 billion and ID 696 million.

While such a dramatic increase in revenue was most welcome, in that it increased government options, opportunities, and flexibility, at the same time it removed any restraint on spending and eroded the integrity of the plan and the planning process.

It will be recalled that NDP was formulated and adopted in 1970 with a total allocation of ID 537 million. As a result of the rise in oil revenue total allocations were raised to reach the unprecedented level of ID 1.9 billion, 360 percent of the original allocation.

The success of the plan as measured by the ratio of actual spending to planned spending, the NDP performance was not a major advance over the previous plan. The plan succeeded in spending 61.6 percent of its appropriation compared with 67 percent under the previous five-year plan. Sectoral implementation shows that the industrial sector outperformed all other sectors, as the data in Table 4.6 show.

Ironically, the oil price explosion of the 1970s dashed the hope of NDP planners to change the structure of the economy. Thus, instead of lowering the contribution of the oil sector to GDP to 26.4 percent in 1974, its share actually increased to 60.4 percent. By contrast, with agriculture and manufacturing, which were slated to contribute 19.7 and 11.4 percent of 1974 GDP respectively, their actual contributions in 1974 amounted to 6.9 and 5.2 percent. Table 4.7 (see p. 72) provides quantitative comparison between actual and target values of several economic indicators.

THE 1975 INVESTMENT PROGRAM

The 1970–74 NDP, which covered the five-year period and ended by the end of fiscal year 1974–75 in March 1975, was followed by a nine-month investment program to cover the period April-December 1975. This short-term program was intended to accommodate the change in the fiscal year from April through March to January through December. Total allocation under this transitional program amounted to ID

Table 4.6
NDP: Revised Allocations, Actual Expenditures, and Revenue, 1970–1974
(ID Millions)

	Revised Allocation	Actual Expenditure	Actual to Allocation (Percentage)
Expenditures			
Agriculture	366.2	208.5	56.9
Industry	391.0	329.7	84.3
Transport and Communication	219.3	177.5	53.6
Building and Services	283.0	171.3	60.5
Other	672.5	293.8	43.7
Total	1932.0	1180.8	61.6
Revenue			
Oil	1554.4	1389.1	89.4
Non Oil	172.6	150.3	70.8
Total	1727.0	1539.4	89.1

Source: NDP Law, pp. 9, 145, 150; Annual Abstracts of Statistics.

Table 4.7
NDP: Target and Actual Values of Certain Economic Indicators, 1974
(ID Millions)

Economic Indicator	Target	Actual	Percentage of Actual to Target
Gross domestic product	1163	3347	288
Oil extraction	409	2023	495
Total exports	465	1943	418
Total imports	263	906	344
Agriculture	317	232	73
Manufacturing	401	176	44
Construction	174	69	40
Transportation and Communication	186	124	67
Electricity and Water	35	14	40
Private Consumption	684	1047	153
Public Consumption	321	477	149
Employment (Thousands)	3165	2800	88

Source: NDP Law; Arab Monetary Fund, National Accounts of Arab States 1971–82
(Abu Dhabi, 1983); World Bank, World Tables, 3rd ed.; United Nations, Monthly Bulletin of Statistics.

1.1 billion. The distribution of this sum was as follows: agriculture, 19.3 percent; industry, 41.6 percent; transport and communications, 15.4 percent; buildings and services, 17.5 percent; the remaining 6.2 percent being appropriated to all other projects and undertakings.[34]

DEVELOPMENT PLANNING AFTER 1975

In the early 1970s, the planners in the Ministry of Planning were looking beyond the last year of the 1970–74 NDP. They were thinking of a long-term development plan, 1975–95, that would serve as the overall framework for medium-term plans of the five-year variety. And within the latter, they would draw up annual investment programs. Indeed, in 1974 the Ministry of Planning announced that the next NDP would be part of the long-term plan.[35] This approach to planning had much to recommend it in that it provided continuity, stability, and flexibility. It also had the advantage of providing an important element of predictability for the entire economy, thus reducing the severity of shocks associated with unplanned increases in development spending or oil revenue. Furthermore, the contemplated approach was conceived at a time when oil revenue was flowing into government treasury at ever-rising rates. A long-term plan would have provided an automatic stabilizer for public-sector spending over a two-decade period and rationalized import programs and avoided bottlenecks and inflation and unplanned recycling of petrodollars.

Acceptance of new planning approaches and innovations is determined in the final analysis not by the force of their logic, no matter how impeccable and convincing such logic might be, but by the political agenda of the country's leadership, which was lodged in the Revolutionary Command Council (RCC) composed of few men.

The RCC is a unique nonelected authority that concentrated in its hands all political, legislative, and executive power. In short, the small group that comprised the RCC was (and still is) the supreme governing body in the country. It was this body that, in practice, rejected the planners' new approaches and decided instead to resort to what might be called segmented, annually approved investment programs. In other words, the RCC decided to abandon the continuity and stability features of planning in favor of investment programs decreed annually. The 1975 investment program was followed by another investment program for 1976 and another one for 1977.

In 1977, however, the RCC adopted the National Development Plan, 1976–1980. Unlike the plans that preceded it over the previous decades, the law failed to publish the usual sectoral allocations of investment or even the plan's aggregate expenditure. Nor did the law make any mention of the plan's estimated revenue. Instead, the law stated that the national plan shall be ratified and that it consists of the following documents: (1) the national development plan for the years 1976–80, (2) the Minister of Planning's Explanatory Note dated April 19, 1977, (3) the indicators and recommendations of the investment program 1977, and (4) the indicators and recommendations of the import program 1977.[36]

While the government chose not to make the plan's investment allocations public, it chose to announce the following annual growth rates: national income, 16.8 percent; per capita income, 13.3 percent; crude oil, 15.5 percent; manufacturing, 32.9 percent; agriculture, 7.1 percent; distribution, 16.9 percent; and services, 10.4 percent. The law also decreed that the contribution of the oil sector to the GDP should be reduced to 50.6 percent by 1980.[37] Moreover it was projected that the goods-producing sectors would raise their share in the GDP to 76 percent, while the distribution and service sectors would contribute the other 24 percent of the GDP by 1980. In the meantime, employment was projected to increase by .548 million workers, raising the size of the labor force to 3.5 million in 1980.[38]

A compilation of sectoral allocations under the five annual plans that comprise the five-year period of the plan, 1976–80, shows that total allocations amounted to ID 15.7 billion. The data in Table 4.8 (see p. 74) reveal that the share of industry was the highest, followed by buildings and services, transport and communications, and agriculture in that order.

Table 4.8
Sectoral Allocations under Annual Plans, 1976-1980 (ID Millions)

Sector	Allocations ID	Share of Total Percentage
Agriculture	2157	13.7
Industry	4490	28.5
Transport and Communications	2318	14.7
Buildings and Services	2458	15.6
Other Allocations	4312	27.4
Total	15735	100.0

Source: Derived from *Annual Abstracts of Statistics.*

It is significant to note that more than 27 percent of the total projected investment, ID 4.3 billion, was lumped in the category of "other allocations." In the absence of a published detailed plan, one is compelled to speculate as to the nature of such allocations. An explanation for such large allocation may be found in the unexpected rise in oil revenue brought about by the rise in crude oil prices in the context of the Iranian revolution of 1978. Thus, as Iraq's oil revenue increased from ID 3.1 billion in 1976 to ID 8.9 billion in 1980, "other allocations" increased from a mere ID 61 million in 1976 to ID 1.6 billion in 1980.

Although this explanation informs that receipts and allocations were affected by the rise in oil revenue, it fails to inform us where the funds were intended to be invested. Since projected investment in the traditional sectors – agriculture, industry, and the like – was not made public, the unpublished funding may very well have been intended for defense and internal security projects. What lends credence to this inference is the high share of defense spending in the ordinary budget, which in turn must have entailed considerable capital spending. Thus, for the years 1971, 1972, 1973, and 1974, the government reported total ordinary expenditures of ID 341.4 million, ID 345.4 million, ID 454.9 million, and ID 921.4 million respectively. The share of defense and police forces in these years amounted to 44.9 percent, 44.4 percent, 47.2 percent, and 53.3 percent.[39]

Although the government ceased to publish data about the economy, available information indicates that between 1975 and 1980 certain economic indicators have registered these annual growth rates in real terms (1975 prices): GDP, 11 percent; mining, 6.5 percent; agriculture, 2.6 percent; industry, 14.2 percent; construction, 15.8 percent; transportation and communications, 20.3 percent; and government services,

13.5 percent. The reconfiguration of sectoral contribution to GDP by 1980 was as follows: production sectors contributed 67 percent of the GDP instead of the projected 76 percent while the distribution and service sectors contributed the remaining 33 percent instead of the projected 24 percent. As to employment, it increased by .3 million instead of the projected .548 million.[40]

After 1980, Iraq's development experience was first halted under the impact of the Iran–Iraq war then negated in the aftermath of Iraq's invasion of Kuwait in 1990, as discussed in the following two chapters.

Moreover, fragmentary data on development spending for the years 1975, 1976, and 1977 show that such spending amounted to ID 2.6 billion, or 51.6 percent of the ID 4.9 billion planned for the same period.[41] The outbreak of the Iran–Iraq war in 1980 changed development spending dramatically as Iraq had known it for the previous thirty years.

NOTES

1. For a more detailed treatment of these issues see Abbas Alnasrawi, *Arab Nationalism, Oil, and the Political Economy of Dependency* (Westport, Conn.: Greenwood Press, 1991), Chapter 2.

2. For a detailed analysis of these points, see Maxime Rodinson, *The Arabs* (Chicago: University of Chicago Press, 1981), pp. 89–90.

3. Ibid., pp. 24–25.

4. See Bassam Tibi, *Arab Nationalism: A Critical Inquiry* (New York: St. Martin's Press, 1981), pp. 72–77.

5. For a detailed analysis of these issues, see Albert Hourani, *Arabic Thought in the Liberal Age, 1798–1939* (London: Oxford University Press, 1962), Chapter 11; Tibi, *Arab Nationalism*, Chapter 5.

6. Tibi, *Arab Nationalism*, p. 88.

7. Doreen Warriner, *Land Reform and Development in the Middle East: A Study of Egypt, Syria and Iraq* (London: Royal Institute of International Affairs, 1957), pp. 137–138. According to Samir Amin, landed aristocracy was directly established as such by imperialism during the 1920s in Iraq, Morocco, and the Sudanese Gezireh. See Samir Amin, *The Arab Nation: Nationalism and Class Struggle* (London: Zed Books Ltd., 1978), p. 29.

8. Cited in L. S. Stavrianos, *Global Rift: The Third World Comes of Age* (New York: William Morrow & Co., 1981), p. 535.

9. See Muhammad A. Shuraydi, "Pan Arabism: A Theory in Practice," in *Arab Nationalism and the Future of the Arab World*, editor Hani A. Faris (Belmont, Mass.: AAUG Press, 1987), pp. 95–114.

10. See Anouar Abdel-Malek, editor, *Contemporary Arab Political Thought* (London: Zed Books Ltd., 1983), pp. 1–14.

11. For a good outline of the main points of the Baath's program, see J. M. Abdulghani, *Iraq & Iran: The Years of Crisis* (Baltimore: Johns Hopkins University Press, 1984), pp. 30–33.

12. Cited in Tibi, *Arab Nationalism*, p. 175.

13. See Sadoon Hammadi, "Arab Nationalism and Contemporary Challenges," in Centre for Arab Unity Studies, *The Evolution of Arab Nationalist Thought* (in Arabic) (Beirut, 1986), p. 344.

14. See Tibi, *Arab Nationalism*, p. 178.

15. See Mohammad Labeeb Shuqair, "The Economic Dimension in Arab Unity Thought: The First Stage, from the Beginning of Arab National Thought to the Mid Fifties," *Al Mustaqbal Al Arabi* (in Arabic) 3 (September 1978): 76–85.

16. Charles Issawi, *An Economics History of the Middle East and North Africa* (New York: Columbia University Press, 1982), p. 155.

17. Cited by Mahmoud Abdel-Fadil, *Arab Economic Thought and Issues of Liberation, Development and Unity* (in Arabic) (Beirut: Centre for Arab Unity Studies, 1982), p. 87.

18. Ibid., p. 178.

19. Maxime Rodinson, *Marxism and the Muslim World* (New York: Monthly Review Press, 1981), p. 268.

20. See Abdel-Fadil, *Arab Economic Thought*, p. 91; see also Tareq Y. Ismael, *The Arab Left* (Syracuse: Syracuse University Press, 1976).

21. Abdel-Fadil, *Arab Economic Thought*, pp. 90–93.

22. The details of the plan, as well as the rationales for the plan, are contained in Planning Board and Ministry of Planning, *Law of National Development Plan for the Fiscal Years 1970–1974 and the Explanatory Memorandum* (in Arabic) (Baghdad, 1970). Henceforth *NDP Law;* Ministry of Planning, *Guide to the National Development Plan, 1970–1974* (in Arabic) (Baghdad, 1971). Henceforth *NDP Guide.*

23. *NDP Law*, p. 125.

24. Ibid.

25. Ibid., p. 127.

26. Ibid., pp. 131–137.

27. For a breakdown of revenue sources under the 1965–1969 plan, see Ministry of Planning, *Detailed Framework of the Five-Year Plan for 1965–1969* (in Arabic) (Baghdad, 1969), p. 45.

28. See *NDP Guide*, p. 70.

29. Ibid., p. 92.

30. See "Dimensions of Iraq National Oil Policy," *Dirasat Arabiyah* (in Arabic) 6(10):136–157; see also Iraq National Oil Company, *Oil in Iraq: From Concessions to Direct National Investment, 1912–1972* (in Arabic) (Baghdad, 1973), pp. 15–17.

31. In addition to *NDP Law* and *NDP Guide* cited earlier, the Ministry of Planning published other documents and studies related to the plan. Some of these documents (in Arabic) include: *Synopses of Planning in Iraq* (1969); *Preliminary Detailed Framework of the National Development Plan 1970–1974: Analysis of the Iraqi Economy to the Base Year 1969* (1970); *Law of National Development Plan 1970–1974 and the General Objectives of the Plan* (1971); *Detailed Objectives of the Components of the National Development Plan, 1970–1974* (1971); *National Income Accounts and Sectoral Accounts of Capital Formation and Its Financing* (1971); *Transportation, Communication and Storage Sector* (1971); *The Industrial Sector* (1971); *The Agricultural Sector*

(1971); *Sources of Finance in Central Government Sector* (1971); *General Summary of Investment in the Central Government and Self-Financed Investment in the Public Sector and Non-Sectoral Investment Allocations* (1971); *Buildings and Services Sector* (1971); *Collection of Laws and Regulations Relating to the Formation of Planning Systems in Iraq and Laws of Development Programs and Economic Plans 1950–1970* (1971).

32. Ian Seymour, *OPEC: An Instrument of Change* (London: The Macmillan Press, 1980), p. 88.

33. For a more detailed treatment of these points, see Abbas Alnasrawi, *OPEC in a Changing World Economy* (Baltimore: Johns Hopkins University Press, 1985), pp. 20–31.

34. See Abdul Wahab Al-Ameen, "Investment Allocations and Plan Implementation: Iraq's Absorptive Capacity, 1951–1980," *The Journal of Energy and Development* 6(2):263–280.

35. Ministry of Planning, *Progress under Planning* (in Arabic) (Baghdad, 1974), pp. 9–10.

36. See *Law 89 of 1977,* Article 1.

37. Ibid., Article 3.

38. See Al-Ameen, "Investment Allocations," p. 272; Economist Intelligence Unit, *Quarterly Economic Review, Iraq* 4(1977):10.

39. Central Bank of Iraq, *Quarterly Bulletin* (various issues).

40. These ratios were derived from World Bank, *World Tables,* 3rd ed. (Baltimore: Johns Hopkins University Press, 1983); Arab Monetary Fund et al., *Joint Arab Economic Report* (annual); and United Nations, *Monthly Bulletin of Statistics.*

41. See *Annual Abstracts of Statistics* and Isam Al-Khafaji, *The State and Capitalist Development in Iraq 1968–1978* (in Arabic) (Cairo: Dar Al-Mustaqbal Al-Arabi, 1983), p. 30.

CHAPTER 5

The Iran–Iraq War and the Demise of Development

On September 22, 1980, Iraqi jets attacked ten Iranian air bases, and its ground forces invaded Iran at eight different points. Iran retaliated by bombing Iraq's oil-exporting facilities, thus forcing it to suspend oil shipments from its southern fields four days after the outbreak of hostilities. Although some oil exports were resumed, such exports were suspended by the end of November in the aftermath of the destruction of Iraq's offshore oil terminals with 2.5 million barrels per day (MBD) export capacity. This in turn slashed Iraq's oil export by 72 percent, from 3.281 MBD on the eve of the war to a mere .926 MBD, pumped through the pipelines across Turkish and Syrian territories.[1] The war, which the Iraqi government undoubtedly thought would be a short and successful blitzkrieg, lasted eight years, with disastrous human and economic consequences from which the Iraqi society and economy will continue to suffer for many years.

THE WAR AND THE IRAQI ECONOMY

When the government of Iraq initiated hostilities, the economy was in the first year of what was promising to be another decade of economic growth. Following the nationalization of Iraq Petroleum Company (IPC) and its affiliates and the oil price explosion of 1973–74, Iraq found itself in a position to push forward with its development and other spending plans unhindered by lack of capital or foreign exchange. Furthermore, the 1975 Algiers agreement with the Iranian government enabled the Iraqi government to repress the Kurdish rebellion, thus freeing itself from the burden of its military expedition against the Kurds.

One of the historical ironies of the 1970s was the success of the Iranian revolution in overthrowing the militarily powerful Shah's regime in Iran in 1979. The newly established Islamic Republic's policy to lower oil output and export created an opportunity for Iraq to expand its oil export, making it the largest OPEC oil exporter after Saudi Arabia.

The changes in Iraq's oil fortunes in the early 1970s and the rise in oil prices that accompanied the Iranian revolution pushed Iraq's oil revenue from ID 219 million in 1972 to ID 1.7 billion in 1974 to ID 3.7 billion in 1978 and to ID 8.9 billion in 1980 (Table 1.1, p. 11). In other words, Iraq's oil revenue increased by forty times in less than a decade.

A favorable regional context, combined with the sharp increase in oil revenue, allowed the government to increase spending on infrastructure, goods-producing sectors, social services, imports, and the military. These favorable conditions pushed almost all economic indexes to unprecedented high levels. Thus, between 1970 and 1980 average rates of growth were as follows: GDP, 11.7 percent; government consumption, 13.6 percent; private consumption, 13.2 percent; gross fixed capital formation, 27 percent; imports of goods and services, 22.5 percent; industrial activity, 10.2 percent; manufacturing, 13.4 percent; construction, 28.4 percent; and transport and communications, 19.9 percent. Agriculture, by contrast, registered an average rate of growth of 1.4 percent.[2] Such rates could not, of course, be sustained for a long time under normal peace time conditions – not to mention war conditions. Moreover, it is worth stressing again that the boom of the 1970s was fueled by the sharp rise in the export earnings of a single commodity – oil. Therefore, as soon these export earnings start to decline, for whatever reason, the impact of the decline is transmitted with a multiplier effect to the rest of the economy. And this is precisely what happened to the economy of Iraq once the war erupted.

The first casualties of the war, as indicated earlier, were the oil facilities, including loading terminals, pumping stations, refineries, and pipelines. This, in turn, forced oil output to decline from 3.4 MBD in August 1980 to .140 MBD two months later. In terms of actual income, Iraq's oil revenue declined from $26.1 billion in 1980 to $10.4 billion in 1981. This decline in turn reduced the share of the contribution of the oil sector to GNP from two-thirds in 1980 to only one-third in 1981.

In addition to the decline in oil revenue, the closure of Iraq's ports to the Persian Gulf forced it to resort to overland routes through Kuwait, Jordan, and Turkey, which had the effect of raising delivered prices of imports. Another general effect of the war was the gradual exhaustion of foreign reserves and the rise in dependence on foreign supplier credit, and later on long-term foreign debt. In addition to drawing down its foreign reserves, Saudi Arabia and Kuwait provided Iraq with considerable financial support, especially in the early phase of the war.

The availability of accumulated foreign assets and Arab financial assistance enabled the Iraqi government to carry on a policy of what might be termed "guns and butter," which sought to continue civilian levels of spending while expanding its military budget at the same time. This can be seen in the sharp rise in imports from $4.2 billion in 1978 to $21.6 billion in 1982, an increase of more than 400 percent. A close examination of their composition reveals that nonmilitary imports accounted for the bulk of the increase. Thus, between 1978 and 1982, the value of nonmilitary imports increased from $2.6 billion, 61.9 percent of total imports, to $17.3 billion, 80.1 percent of the total.[3] It is relevant to note here that foreign trade was a monopoly of the state. This means that any increase in imports must be the outcome of a deliberate policy decision by the government. Thus the sharp increase in nonmilitary imports must be looked at as a political strategy by the government to lessen the impact of the war on living standards by making consumer goods available in large quantities. This view is supported by this assessment:

The apparent capacity of the Ba'ath regime in Iraq to weather the war against Iran is indicated by the return to normality to Baghdad. The slogan of the Ba'ath that business is as usual is being converted there to providing a flow of foodstuff and consumer goods to the population on a scale rarely observed before the war.[4]

Nor did the government policy of guns and butter confine itself to higher levels of consumer-goods imports. As is shown in the previous chapter, allocations for development spending were sharply increased. Thus, while such allocations amounted to ID 2.8 billion in 1978, they were raised to ID 5.2 billion in 1980, to ID 6.7 billion in 1981, and to ID 7.7 billion in 1982 (Table 5.1 on p. 82). According to one study, the value of contracts with foreign enterprises for nonmilitary projects increased by 64 percent from $14.8 billion in 1980 to $24.3 billion in 1981.[5]

This massive planned increase in development spending was nothing but political rhetoric. In the first place, even prior to the war the economy was suffering from a number of serious problems and bottlenecks — inflation, inability to spend allocated investment funds, skilled manpower shortages, and inadequate infrastructure. An illustration of the last problem was the transport system. As Abdul Wahab Al-Ameen noted, the inadequacy of the transport system became painfully evident when imported goods increased from less than $.9 billion in 1973 to $2.6 billion in 1974 and the system could not handle the influx of

Table 5.1
Investment Programs and Annual Plans, 1976–1983 (ID Millions)

Year	Agriculture	Industry	Transport and Communication	Building and Services	Other	Total
1976	269	709	243	213	61	1494
1977	390	966	352	288	382	2377
1978	500	800	438	381	681	2800
1979	500	842	436	462	1043	3283
1980	505	1173	850	1114	1598	5240
Subtotal	2158	4490	2318	2458	4312	15736
1981	681	1246	1284	1899	1632	6743
1982	768	1316	1387	1653	2576	7700
1983	484	811	809	1105	2142	5350
Subtotal	1434	3373	3480	4657	6349	19793
Total, 1976–1983	2302	7863	5799	7115	10662	35530

Source: Government of Iraq, *Annual Abstract of Statistics.*
Note: Details may not add up to totals because of rounding.

cargo. This inadequacy was compounded by the limitation imposed by storage capacity.[6] Given this problem, it is obvious that the transport and storage systems were far from adequate to handle the volume of goods associated with the $21.6 billion of imports for 1982 without a great deal of delay and waste, not to mention the costs associated with the war-induced rerouting of trade.

Similarly, the pace of development since the 1950s has been hindered not by lack of funds but by lack of skilled manpower, especially in the areas of administration and management. Lack of familiarity with the technical processes of projects and confidence in their administrative, financial, and technical ability to carry out projects from conception to implementation forced many government departments to employ the services of foreign contractors according to the "turnkey" formula.[7] The point at issue here is the question of how the Baath regime could seriously expect to build a much larger number of projects during wartime when it could not do so before the war broke out. Moreover, the diversion of manpower from the civilian economy to the war fronts only added to the economy's manpower problems, especially at a time when foreign contractors were withdrawing their workers from a country engaged in hostilities. In short, the war with Iran made Iraq's chronic labor shortages only worse.

On top of these perennial problems, Iraq simply did not have the financial resources to fund these massive allocations. In spite of the government's brave face and high projected budgets, there was no escape from the destructive realities of the war. The Iraqi regime's pretentious claims and wishful thinking came to an end in 1982 as the war front moved to Iraqi soil, where it continued for the next six years. In the following pages, a more detailed analysis of the impact of the war on the economy of Iraq is undertaken.

THE WAR, IRAQ'S OIL, AND SAUDI ARABIA'S OIL POLICY

In 1979, Iraq was OPEC's largest oil exporting country after Saudi Arabia. Its export in that year amounted to 3.3 MBD, 11.4 percent of OPEC's total export. Iraq's oil revenue amounted to $21.4 billion, 10.5 percent of OPEC's. By 1983, Iraq's oil exports and revenue plummeted to .740 MBD and $7.8 billion, 5.1 percent of OPEC's oil export and 5 percent of its combined oil revenue.[8] The reasons for this sharp decline include the war-caused decline in export, the general decline in demand for oil (particularly OPEC's oil), and the decline in oil prices. Another reason for the decline in Iraq's oil export and income was the 1982 decision by the Syrian government to close Iraq's oil pipeline across Syrian territory. This closure caused Iraq to lose an export outlet of .4 MBD, which in turn limited its export outlets to only one pipeline through Turkey with export capacity of about .750 MBD – about one-fourth of its export capacity on the eve of the war.

The sharp decline in oil revenue forced the Iraqi regime to adopt programs of retrenchment and austerity and to halt development projects, except for those related to the war effort. An indicator of the impact of the war, oil conditions on development may be found in Iraq's declining share in the value of projects contracted by members of the Organization of Arab Petroleum Exporting Countries. In 1979, Iraq's share in such contracts was 17 percent; it rose to 30 percent in 1980 and 31 percent in 1981. This ratio declined to 9 percent in 1982 and again to 2 percent in 1983.[9] The impact of the war on Iraq's oil must be considered in its long-term ramifications rather than in its unavoidable effect for the duration of the war.

In a market where there are few producers selling a homogeneous product such as crude oil, it is almost certain that as one producer's share of the market shrinks other producers will expand their sales, acquiring their competitor's lost market share. This is especially true when producers have excess capacity or can expand capacity in a short time. This is actually what happened when Iran, in the context of its revolution, decided to cut its oil export by 2.3 MBD between 1977 and 1979. This decline was more than offset by the rise in oil exports from Iraq, Saudi Arabia, and Kuwait. By the same token, the decline in Iraq's (and Iran's) oil export because of the war was offset by other producers, mainly Saudi Arabia. Taking Middle East OPEC countries as a group, oil export and revenue data show that Saudi Arabia received 40 percent of the group's oil revenue and was responsible for 40 percent of total oil export in 1978. By 1981 Saudi Arabia's share of export rose to 60 percent while its share of revenue increased to 62 percent. Another way of looking at Iraq's changed position relative to that of Saudi Arabia is to measure the change in the relationship between the two countries' levels of revenue. In 1979, Iraq's oil revenue was 34 percent of that of Saudi Arabia. By 1981 the ratio had plummeted to 9 percent.

It is important to note in this context that Saudi Arabia persisted in keeping its output at an unusually high level, in spite of the generally recognized glut in the world market. Indeed, OPEC's total oil export peaked at 28.9 MBD in 1979 and declined to 16.5 MBD in 1982, while Saudi Arabia's share of the total grew from 32 percent in 1979 to 37 percent in 1982.

This Saudi policy of overproduction was perceived by Iraq's President Saddam Hussein to be harmful, a perception he expressed as follows:

We direct our friendly but also serious criticism toward some Arab brothers whose production and marketing policies have led to the creation of a glut in the oil market. We cannot possibly find convincing arguments in favor of this policy and its goals. Its harmful effects upon the Arab oil producing states and others is very clear. If some oil producing states have financial surpluses, we do not all possess such an accumulation of wealth. We also do not see any wisdom in production that leads to glut in the oil market.[10]

The Saudi oil policy came under a more pointed attack by Iraq's oil minister who maintained that the objective of the oil glut policy was to prolong the Iran–Iraq war.[11]

The Saudi policy of overproduction did not inflict revenue losses on Iraq alone, of course. Other OPEC members joined Iraq in condemning the policy of harming their economic interests as well.[12] The fact that Saudi Arabia was responsible for the oil glut was not an unfounded allegation. The Saudi oil minister himself acknowledged in no uncertain terms that the glut was engineered by his government's policy:

Well, as a matter of fact, this glut was anticipated by Saudi Arabia and almost done by Saudi Arabia. If we were to reduce our production to the level it was at before we started raising it, there would be no glut at all. We engineered the glut and want to see it to stabilize the price of oil.[13]

But this policy of overproduction exerted downward pressure on market prices over which the Saudis had no control. Although the Saudi government believed that it could stabilize the official price of oil through the manipulation of its output and that the glut was a temporary phenomenon that would disappear in mid-1982, the behavior of other oil producers proved the Saudis to be wrong.

A key explanation of the change can be found in Iran's success in expanding its oil output and export by offering sizable discounts off the official OPEC price in order to regain some of the market share it had lost to Saudi Arabia. Thus between 1981 and 1982 Iran was able to increase its exports from .855 MBD to 1.804 MBD. Nor was Iran alone in lowering prices. In their attempt to protect their market shares, other OPEC countries such as Libya, Algeria, and Nigeria followed Iran's example by reducing their selling prices. This in turn caused Saudi oil exports to decline from 9.5 MBD in 1981 to 6.2 MBD in 1982 and to 4.3 MBD in 1983. In order to stem the decline in its oil exports, revenue, and power, the government of Saudi Arabia joined forces with other members of the Gulf Cooperation Council in attacking the price cutters for their "irresponsible behavior" and "misguided actions" and ironically calling upon them to raise their prices.[14]

In retrospect, neither the Saudi government nor OPEC as a whole could have done much to stem the decline in oil exports. The decline in demand for oil in general and for OPEC's oil in particular was a result

of the success of industrial countries' energy conservation and substitution measures, on the one hand, and the rise in non-OPEC oil exports, on the other. These changes drove OPEC's total oil exports by
1985 to 13.3 MBD from their 1979 peak of 28.9 MBD. By the same
token, in 1986 the price collapsed to as low as $7 per barrel, from $34
per barrel in 1982, yielding total revenue for OPEC of $76.8 billion in
1986, down from $284.5 billion in 1980.[15]

Throughout these turbulent changes in the oil market, Iraq was no
more than a bystander, since its exports remained well below capacity
as a result of the closure of its export outlets through the Persian Gulf
and Syria. By 1986, Iraqi oil revenue had declined to $6.9 billion from
$26.3 billion in 1980. Ironically, as the war continued to be fought on
Iraqi soil and oil revenue continued to decline, Iraq's dependence on
this source of income intensified since this dwindling income had to
pay for essential military and nonmilitary imports, to service foreign
debt, and to serve as the basis for fresh borrowing.

An important consequence of this changing picture of Iraqi oil was the
increasing dependence of the Iraqi regime on the financial support its
neighbors, especially Saudi Arabia and Kuwait, were willing to provide.

These two countries perceived the danger of the policies of the Irani
regime to the stability of their own family-based governments and ac-
cordingly supported the government of Iraq in its war with Iran. The
financial support to Iraq took several forms. First, there was the extension of outright economic assistance. Second, the two countries agreed
to produce and sell some .3 MBD of oil from their own oilfields on
behalf of Iraq. Third, Saudi Arabia expressed willingness to bolster
Iraq's creditworthiness in the international financial markets.

These changes meant that Iraq's economic and military survival revolved around oil revenue, Arab economic aid, and foreign supplier
credit. As one observer put it: "One of the main props of Iraqi military
turnaround since the parlous days of 1982 has been the supply of foreign credit. Total economic collapse was staved off through the gener-
osity of the Arab states of the Gulf and then the pumping in of OECD
and Soviet credit."[16]

In addition to oil and economic and financial assistance, the Saudi
government allowed the government of Iraq to build pipelines across
Saudi territories to increase and to handle its exports from the southern oilfields. Turkey also allowed Iraq both to expand the capacity of
existing pipeline and to build another to handle more oil from Iraq's
northern fields. These new pipelines increased Iraq's oil-export capacity
from less than 1 MBD in the early 1980s to 3.3 MBD by 1989, thus
making the reopening of the pipeline through Syria, which the latter
had closed in 1982, unnecessary.

It is to be noted, however, that by building its pipelines through Saudi Arabia and Turkey, the Iraqi government exchanged Syrian control over its oil export for Saudi and Turkish control – as the 1990 Iraqi invasion of Kuwait amply demonstrated. It should be noted also that although oil exports increased from .740 MBD in 1983 to 2.2 MBD in 1988 (or by 198 percent), its revenue increased by 40 percent only – from $7.8 billion to $11 billion during the same period because of the persistent stagnation of oil prices.

THE WAR AND THE DETERIORATION
OF THE IRAQI ECONOMY

The decade of the 1970s, especially the second half, witnessed an unprecedented high rate of growth in oil output, oil revenue, national income, per capita income, industrial growth, construction, and public and private consumption. Iraq also had a balance of payments surplus that resulted in the accumulation of nearly $40 billion of foreign exchange on the eve of the decision of the Iraqi government to invade Iran.

Yet beneath this encouraging picture there were structural problems the government either chose to neglect or could not tackle. These problems included labor shortages, stagnant agriculture, rising urban population, persistent inflation, rising dependence on foreign consumer goods (especially foodstuffs), and rising dependence on oil.

Policy makers could deal with these problems so long as oil revenue continued to generate foreign exchange sufficient to import agricultural products and other consumer durables and nondurables, raw materials and capital goods, military equipment, and foreign labor and expertise. Moreover, being the recipient of the largest share of gross national product (i.e., oil revenue), the government was in a position to be the largest spender in the economy, the largest employer, employer of last resort, and the arbiter of the distribution of income among groups, classes, and regions of the country. In addition to these economic tools, oil revenue enabled the government to employ a variety of coercive and repressive measures to ensure acceptance of its rule.

Leaving the economic and strategic importance of oil to the major consumers aside, the Baath regime (like other governments of oil-producing countries) failed to recognize that in the last analysis, the demand for oil is not inelastic in the long term. The failure to comprehend this simple fact, that the demand for oil actually declines if prices remain high, proved to be disastrous for the economy.

In the case of Iraq, the rise in oil revenue in the 1970s was so blinding that the regime seems to have assumed that the upward trend was irreversible. And the realization that Iraq's oil reserves were much higher than had been thought only added to the false belief that there was no limit to the fiscal resources the regime enjoyed. Even if Iraq's oil export capacity had not been drastically reduced in the aftermath of the decision to invade Iran, its export and revenue would have been sharply reduced because of the general decline in demand for oil, as is noted earlier. The point here is that, in the last analysis, Iraq's revenue from the export of this particular commodity is externally determined and beyond any exporting country's oil policies.

Thus, when the war broke out and lasted far longer than the Iraqi regime had expected, the regime had no choice but to transform the economy to a war economy. Although the government attempted in the first two years of the war to insulate the people from its effects by increasing consumer-goods imports and continued with its annual investment programs and increased their allocations, the realities of the war forced the hands of policy makers in 1982 to reverse gears and adopt wartime policy measures. As is stated earlier, 1982 marked a turning point in the eight-year war, in that Iran was able to expel the invading forces from its territories and carry the war to Iraqi soil. In turn, the war became a destructive stalemate for the following six years.

No sooner had the war started than Iraq's oil exports from the southern fields were stopped by Iranian bombing of oil export facilities and of Iraq's harbors on the northern edge of the Persian Gulf. This phase of the bombing cut off Iraq's access to the only harbors that handle its imports. This in turn forced Iraq to resort to overland routes through Kuwait, Jordan, and Turkey — with longer delivery periods and higher delivered prices. The early phase of the bombing, before 1982, resulted also in the destruction of Iraq's core industrialization program, including petrochemicals and iron and steel, which happened to be located in the southern part of the country within easy reach of Iran's air force. The projects that were not damaged or destroyed in the course of the war were halted by the withdrawal of foreign personnel.

In short, the destructive and disruptive effects of the war in the first two years led to general deterioration of the economy, exhaustion of Iraq's owned foreign reserves, general decline in output, high inflation rates, expansion of the armed forces, decline in agricultural and industrial output, rerouting of foreign trade, labor shortages, curtailment of investment spending, rise in food dependency, curtailment of imports, rise in foreign indebtedness, rise in military spending, and the confinement of development spending to the war effort.

The failure of Iraq's military machine to stem the advance of the Iranian troops into Iraq forced the Iraqi government to finally acknowledge that it had no choice but to deal openly with the war and its consequences instead of relegating it to a special enclave.

THE WAR AND THE END OF DEVELOPMENT

Although the government failed to publish a five-year plan for the period 1976–80, it nevertheless published annual plans or investment programs. Table 5.1 (p. 82) provides sectoral allocations under these plans or programs for the years 1976–83.

The single most striking feature of the programs for the years 1976–83 is the absence of any serious link to the reality of Iraq's oil revenue. Historically, oil revenue supplied the bulk of development finance in Iraq. In the early 1950s, all revenue from oil was earmarked for development. This was later changed to 70 percent; and in 1959 it was reduced to 50 percent, a ratio that remained in effect at least officially through 1974 — the last year of the last formally adopted and published five-year plan. Thus, for the 1976–83 period, although total allocations for development amounted to ID 35.5 billion, 50 percent of the cumulative oil revenue during the same period was ID 17.8 billion. The disparity between oil revenue and announced allocations for the three-year period 1981–83 is even more pronounced. In those three years, total allocations were ID 19.8 billion, yet one-half the oil revenue during the same period was only ID 4.7 billion — less than one-fourth of total allocations. Given these disparities, it can safely be said that the government could not have been serious about development planning, let alone implementation, during the war. One estimate placed Iraq's development spending in 1983 at $670 million (ID 215 million), down from $3.9 billion (ID 1.3 billion) in 1982.[17] In the context of its professed investment programs, the government could not finance more than 16.8 percent and 1.2 percent of the allocations for 1982 and 1983 respectively. This should not be surprising, given the drastic decline in oil revenue and the claims of war conditions on Iraq's meager financial resources.

It is obvious from the data that development spending as practiced in Iraq for more than three decades came to an end by 1982. In order to ensure its own political survival, the Baath regime had to sacrifice the country's development program.

While the war and the collapse of the oil market provided the immediate and obvious justification for the termination of development spending, there is a fundamental structural condition that goes beyond these temporary phenomena. This condition relates to the very nature of the political regime that seized power in a coup in 1968. Lacking an economic program of its own, the Baath tended to constantly change economic policies to suit the needs of the day so long as these policies ensured its retention of political control of the country. The phenomenal increase in oil revenue allowed the regime a high degree of freedom to

increase development and military spending, change the configuration
of spending between sectors, accelerate or decelerate imports at will,
emphasize or deemphasize industrial and agricultural investment, concentrate investment on hydrocarbon-based industries, import foreign
labor, provide foreign economic assistance, expend considerable human
and fiscal resources to put down armed and unarmed political opposition, expel large segments of the population, and engage in costly forced
relocation of significant segments of the population to different areas
of the country.

Although it is beyond the scope of this study to analyze the nature
of the rule of the Baath in Iraq, it is useful to say few words about the
power structure and decision making. The locus of political and legislative power in government in Iraq since 1968 has been the Revolutionary
Command Council (RCC) which was described by Iraq's interim constitution, enacted by the RCC itself, as the supreme institution of the
state and thus accountable to no other institution or authority. At various times, the composition and the size of RCC changed to reflect the
factious power struggle within the leadership of the Baath. Throughout
the years, one constant force in the leadership was embodied in the person of Saddam Hussein, acknowledged as the regime's strong man
long before he assumed formal power as president in 1979. Prior to
1979, he had the title of deputy chairman of RCC. Following the departure from the political scene of President Ahmad Hassan Al-Bakr in
1979, Saddam Hussein became the chairman of the twenty-two-member
RCC (reduced to nine members in 1982), president of the republic, leader
of the party, commander in chief, prime minister, and head of the all-
pervasive and powerful intelligence services. In short, he became the
fulcrum of power and the supreme political (and therefore economic)
authority in a single-party state.

Given this degree of concentration of political and economic power,
it follows that the government, in the sense of cabinet ministries, ceased
to have any power of its own and became the agency to implement decisions made by the RCC or by the president. Moreover, with this highly
personal political system, it would be surprising if the leadership wished
to be burdened by lengthy processes of decision making or by the long-
term commitments embodied in five-year economic plans.

An early example of economic decision making outside the ordinary
institutions may be found in the creation, in 1971, of the Follow Up
Committee under the chairmanship of Saddam Hussein himself. Ostensibly the committee was to negotiate and ensure the implementation
of international economic agreements. Yet in the decade of the 1970s,
the committee ended up planning policies for the oil sector, with the
ministry of oil and the Iraq National Oil Company providing technical
advice to it. The committee furthermore succeeded in appropriating to

itself power over all facets of the Iraqi economy, including the central bank, oil-sector projects, and the marketing of oil. Given the importance of the oil sector, this in turn gave the committee absolute control over the economy's resources and the patterns of their spending without the benefit of debate or accountability.[18]

The nature of the Iraqi regime may also explain why the political authority chose to ignore recommendations made by its own economic planners to have a series of five-year economic plans within a twenty-year economic framework. Instead, the political authority resorted to issuing annual investment programs, a practice that gave it considerable latitude to change total and sectoral appropriations. Such a practice obviously reveals the Baath regime's lack of serious commitment to economic growth and diversification. Ironically, it was the war with Iran that finally forced Saddam Hussein to pay attention to economic growth. He realized then that such growth had become a political imperative for his survival.[19]

Yet in the midst of a destructive and scarce-resource-using war, the regime's nonmilitary resources were being squandered on prestige projects. One such project was building a metro system in Baghdad. The project, which has been shelved in 1977, was updated in 1981 at a cost of $3 to $4 billion. Construction was initiated in the midst of the war, but it had to be stopped for lack of resources. Indeed, this type of spending was considered by Iraq's financial supporters, Saudi Arabia and Kuwait, to be one of the reasons for the cutback in their assistance. As Thomas Stauffer noted:

One reason for the cutback in their aid was precisely the fact that Iraq, enjoying almost unabated net cash flow, had continued major development projects, such as the Baghdad subway, which its allies deemed to be low priority; they were unwilling to finance guns, butter, and also the dolce vita.[20]

The new rapid underground system in Baghdad was only one of a number of projects, such as a new international airport, new hotels, and new conference facilities, that the regime was trying to complete prior to the 1982 summit meeting of the Non-Aligned Movement.[21]

Ultimately, the exhaustion of foreign reserves, the decline in foreign aid and export earnings, and the rising demands of the war forced the regime to abandon its unrealistic and business-as-usual posture and shelve its development projects.

WAR LABOR MOBILIZATION AND THE ECONOMY

In 1970, Iraq had 2.9 percent of its labor force, or 62,000 persons, in its armed forces. Five years later, the corresponding figures were 2.9

percent and 82,000. But by 1980, the share of Iraq's labor force drafted into the armed forces had increased to 13.4 percent, or 430,000. As the data in Table 5.2 show, by the time the war ended in 1988 the government was using more than 21 percent of the labor force, or one million, in the armed forces.

The rise in the size and the relative importance of the armed forces to the labor force had several implications for the functioning of the economy both during the war and in the postwar period. First, the data show that in the five-year period 1975–80 the labor force increased by 400,000 persons. By contrast, the increment in the size of the armed forces in the same period amounted to 348,000 persons, or 87 percent of the entire increase in the labor force. Second, as the size of the armed forces increases, so does the number of support workers in the civilian economy who are called upon to provide the nonmilitary requirements of the armed forces such as management, maintenance, and supply services. In other words, the negative impact of the rising size of a standing army on the civilian economy goes beyond the mere increase in the size of the armed forces. A corollary of this change in the structure of employment was the inevitable drain on the level of employment in agriculture and industry. This is so because, as the armed forces and support employment increased, the government had to draw on already-employed unskilled, semiskilled, and skilled workers in other sectors of the economy. In addition, the government had either to extend the draft of those who were already in the armed forces or divert new en-

Table 5.2
Labor Force and Armed Forces, 1970–1988 ($ Millions)

Year	Labor Force	Armed Forces	Ratio of Armed Forces to Labor Force
1970	2.4	.062	2.9
1975	2.8	.082	2.9
1980	3.2	.430	13.4
1981	3.3	.392	11.9
1982	3.8	.404	10.6
1983	4.0	.434	10.9
1984	4.1	.788	19.2
1985	4.2	.788	18.0
1986	4.4	.800	18.2
1987	4.5	.900	20.0
1988	4.7	1.000	21.3

Sources: World Bank, World Tables; League of Arab States et al., Joint Arab Economic Report (Annual); U.S. Arms Control and Disarmament Agency, World Military Expenditures and Arms Transfers (Annual).

trants into the labor market to the armed forces. As the war continued, so did the increase in the size of the armed forces, which reached one million, 21.3 percent of the labor force, by 1988—the last year of the war.

The consequences of the rise in the size of the armed forces for the sectoral distribution of the labor force may be seen in the decline of the share of agricultural employment from 42 percent in 1975 to 12.5 percent in 1985–88. Because of the war, as well as other factors, the depopulation of rural Iraq had a stagnating effect on agriculture and resulted in the decline of wheat output from an annual average of .8 million tons in the period 1974–76 to only 300,000 tons in 1984.[22] This in turn increased Iraq's food imports at a time when it could ill afford larger allocations of declining oil export earnings to pay for them.

Similarly, industrial employment declined from 25 percent to 7.8 percent during the same period.[23] As the data in Table 5.3 show, between 1975 and 1988 employment in the armed forces increased by 918,000 while the size of the labor force rose by 1.9 million. In other words 48.3 percent of the net increase in the labor force was conscripted into the armed forces.

This pattern of mobilization for the war had other implications for the economy. In the first place, it intensified Iraq's perennial problem of labor shortages. The economy—thanks to the government policy of heavy investment in capital-intensive industries, especially oil—found

Table 5.3
Military Expenditures, Oil Revenue, and GDP, 1970-1989 ($ Billions)

	Military of Expenditures (Milex)	Oil Revenue	Ratio of Milex to Oil Revenue	GDP	Ratio of Milex to GDP
1970	.7	.8	87.5	3.6	19.4
1975	3.1	8.2	37.9	13.8	22.5
1980	19.8	26.4	75.0	53.6	38.8
1981	24.6	10.4	236.5	37.3	66.0
1982	25.1	10.1	248.5	43.7	57.4
1983	25.3	7.8	324.4	42.5	59.5
1984	25.9	9.4	275.5	47.6	54.4
1985	19.0	10.7	177.5	49.5	38.4
1986	11.6	6.9	168.1	47.9	24.2
1987	14.0	11.4	122.8	57.9	24.2
1988	12.9	11.0	117.3	55.9	23.1
1989	12.9	14.5	89.0	64.4	20.0

Source: U.S. Arms Control and Disarmament Agency, *World Military Expenditures and Arms Transfers* (Annual); Stockholm International Peace Research Institute, *SIPRI Yearbook 1992* (Annual); United Nations, *National Accounts Statistics: Analysis of Main Aggregates, 1988-1989* (New York, 1991).

itself in the paradoxical position of having to suffer simultaneously from high rates of unemployment and labor shortages in many skills. The war, in other words, accentuated already existing distortions in the labor market. Labor shortages were so severe that when new projects were contemplated the government stipulated that they could not be labor intensive.[24] Second, the government – in order to soften the negative impact of mobilization on the economy – encouraged the entry of women into the labor force. Third, policy makers encouraged the inflow of Arab workers from Egypt, and to a lesser extent, from Morocco and the Sudan. The other side of this influx of labor was its drain on the balance of payments because of remittance transfer to country of origin.

MILITARY EXPENDITURES AND IRAQ'S GNP AND OIL REVENUE

Another important impact of the war was its financial claims on Iraq's resources. Not only did the war result in lower oil output and income, as well as added labor force difficulties and shortages but, as was to be expected, it forced the diversion of the country's resources to underwrite the cost of the conflict with Iran.

In 1970, the Iraqi government spent less than $1 billion on its military, or 19.4 percent of the GDP – a high ratio by world standards. By 1975, it increased military spending more than fourfold to $3.1 billion, or 22.8 percent of GDP. By 1980, it raised military spending more than sixfold over the 1975 level to $19.8 billion, 38.8 percent of GDP. The share of military spending of GDP, as the data in Table 5.3 (p. 93) show, continued to rise to absorb between one-half and two-thirds of GDP during the 1980s.

Another way of measuring the burden of military spending is to relate it to the country's oil revenue. Although military expenditure increased sharply between 1970 and 1975, its relative importance to oil revenue actually declined because of the much sharper rise in oil revenue in the early 1970s. But by 1980 military spending absorbed 75 percent of Iraq's oil income. In subsequent years, the government spent several times the country's oil revenue on its war with Iran. Thus during the five-year period 1981–85, military spending amounted to $119.9 billion or 245 percent of the same period's oil revenue, which amounted to $48.4 billion. In other words, while oil revenue averaged $9.7 billion per year, military spending averaged $23.9 billion. This five-year deficit of $71.5 billion between oil income and military spending was financed by grants from Saudi Arabia and Kuwait, suppliers' credit, draw down of international reserves, foreign debt, abandonment of development plans, and curtailment of imports and social services.

The data on GDP provide another insight on the impact of the war on living standards. Thanks to the oil price revolution, per capita GDP increased tenfold between 1970 and 1980, when it peaked at $3864 to decline to $3176 in 1988. Moreover, per capita GDP purchasing power suffered from another serious erosion – inflation.

A study of the severity of inflation in Iraq by Ali and Ganabi shows that the inflation rate, as measured by the consumer price index, rose from an average annual rate of 5 percent in the decade of the 1960s to more than 6 percent in the early 1970s. It took off in 1975, however, when it reached 18 percent, going all the way up to 68 percent in 1979, with 1973 as the base year. Because of the sharp rise in government spending and the war conditions, the inflation rate jumped to 95 percent in 1980, 139 percent in 1981, and 369 percent in 1988.[25] Under these conditions, it can be concluded that a major part of per capita GDP was wiped out by inflation.

THE WAR AND MILITARY AND NONMILITARY IMPORTS

In an open economy such as that of Iraq, foreign trade plays a vital role in shaping economic and social outcomes, including but not limited to economic growth, levels of public and private consumption, economic diversification, technology, research and development, patterns of international economic relations, and the degree of dependence on foreign markets. Foreign trade is especially crucial in a country that derives its foreign exchange earnings from the export of a single commodity.

Given the narrow base of its economy and its rising dependence on foreign markets for a wide range of foodstuffs, consumer goods, intermediate and capital goods, and military goods, any unplanned decline in exports or imports would affect the level of economic activity, employment, income distribution, and prices, among other economic magnitudes. The impact will, of course, be magnified depending on the size of the multiplier in the economy. An earlier section in this chapter examines the impact of the war on the oil sector. In this section, an examination of the impact of the war on imports is undertaken.

In a country that depends on foreign suppliers for its military hardware, it is only natural that military imports should increase under war conditions. Import data in Table 5.4 (p. 96) show that Iraq's imports of military goods increased from $.5 billion in 1975 to $2.4 billion in 1980, only to jump to $7.1 billion in 1982 and to $9.2 billion in 1984. Although military imports declined after 1984, they continued to remain at a high level up to 1989. Thus, while the ratio of such imports to total imports was 17 percent in 1980 and peaked at 83 percent in 1984, it declined to 45 percent in 1988 and 36 percent in 1989. According to

Table 5.4
Nonmilitary and Military Imports, 1970–1989 ($ Billions)

Year	Total Imports	Arms Imports ($)	Arms Imports Ratio to Total	Nonarms Imports ($)	Nonarms Imports Ratio to Total	GDP	Ratio of Total Imports to GDP
1970	.5	.1	20.0	.4	80.0	3.6	13.9
1975	4.2	.5	11.9	3.7	88.1	13.6	30.8
1980	13.8	2.4	17.4	11.4	82.6	51.0	27.1
1981	20.5	4.2	20.5	16.3	79.5	37.3	55.0
1982	21.5	7.1	33.0	14.4	67.0	43.7	49.2
1983	12.2	7.0	57.3	5.2	42.7	42.5	28.7
1984	11.1	9.2	82.9	1.9	17.1	47.6	23.3
1985	10.5	4.7	44.8	6.1	55.2	49.5	20.2
1986	8.7	5.7	65.5	3.0	34.5	47.9	18.2
1987	7.4	5.5	74.3	1.9	25.7	57.6	12.8
1988	10.6	4.6	45.0	6.0	55.0	55.9	19.0
1989	13.8	4.9	35.5	11.1	80.4	64.4	21.4

Source: U.S. Arms Control and Disarmament Agency, *World Military Expenditures and Arms Transfers* (Annual); Stockholm International Peace Research Institute, *SIPRI Yearbook 1992* (Annual); United Nations, *National Accounts Statistics: Analysis of Main Aggregates, 1988–1989* (New York, 1991).

the data in Table 5.4, total imports of military goods during the period 1980–88 amounted to $50.4 billion, an average annual expenditure of $5.6 billion. Another estimate placed Iraq's average annual imports of military goods and services during the period 1979–89 at $6.8 billion.[26] The Iraqi government acknowledged that the value of military hardware purchased and used in the war amounted to $102 billion.[27]

As to nonmilitary imports, their value increased sharply at the early phase of the war, rising to around 80 percent of total imports in 1981. Starting in 1983, however, their value exhibited a sharp decline. In 1984 and 1987, the government could not import more than $1.9 billion of nonmilitary goods, or 17 percent and 26 percent of total imports respectively.

PRIVATIZATION UNDER WAR CONDITIONS

One of the major decisions of the regime in the context of the war was the adoption of a series of measures to encourage the private sector. These measures culminated in the formal adoption of a policy of privatization in 1987 as the regime's way out of its economic problems.

In the aftermath of the disintegration of Iraq's war machine, the Syrian closure of oil pipelines, the general decline in oil exports and prices, and the economic retrenchment and austerity measures the regime had to put in place, the war forced the regime to reorient its policy toward the private sector and its role in the economy. In a state-run economy where the government was the recipient of nearly two-thirds of GDP and its management of the economy permeated every segment of it – agriculture, land distribution, foreign and domestic trade, industry, construction, banking – the scope of private-sector activity was influenced by the pattern of state spending, as well as by its policies toward the private sector.

Thus, while the private sector was responsible in 1981 for 20 percent of gross fixed capital formation, one-third of the GDP, and 15 percent of imports, its sectoral contribution to GDP varied considerably. In 1981, for example, the private sector contributed nearly 49 percent of the GDP generated in the agricultural sector, 45 percent of manufacturing, 44 percent of internal trade, and 72 percent of transport and communications. Not surprisingly, its share of mining was negligible, 1.3 percent, since this sector was dominated by oil. In the construction sector, by contrast, the share of the government was only 4.7 percent.[28] It is worth noting that construction constituted 42 percent of private sector contribution to GDP, which in turn amounted to close to 14 percent of GDP.

While war conditions supplied the context for policy shift in favor of the private sector, this shift did not occur suddenly. The Baath regime has been moving in that direction even before the war started. As John Townsend reported: "But it can be pointed out that there were signs immediately before the war of what was being described in government circle as 'an opening to the private sector' and that President Saddam himself had said in various speeches that 'the government was withdrawing from direct involvement in the agricultural sector.'"[29]

Like all such policy shifts, the opening or *infitah* to private sector agriculture can be explained by a number of economic and noneconomic factors. It was postulated that in order to establish his unchallenged authority when he became president in 1979, Saddam Hussein decided to fracture the Baath party elite through the historic 1979 purge of the party leadership and to encourage the private sector. These actions on the part of the new president helped him to preempt any potential challenge to his authority, on the one hand, and to create a group or class that would provide a degree of political base and legitimacy for his rule, on the other. As Robert Springborg observed, the decision as early as 1979 to increase the role of private enterprise in agriculture was driven by political and economic embarrassment at the failure of the government to achieve food self-sufficiency (a major goal of the Baath economic plan), the rising food import bill, decline in agricultural labor, rise in the number of foreign agricultural workers and technicians, and the acknowledgment that the massive infusion of capital into agriculture had failed to result in the hoped-for rapid gains in productivity.[30]

A similar assessment was arrived at in 1978 by another study that concluded that after ten years of promises to the effect that agricultural development is a priority in the Baath program of modernization and after billions of dollars of investment, the sector remains languishing in a depressed state with a generally declining level of cultivation affecting most areas of the country. And while this failure is attributable to the failure of the plan and administrative inefficiency, the situation was aggravated by constant legal changes associated with land reform and by the rapid flow of immigrants from rural areas to towns.[31] Underlying this neglect of agriculture was the regime's drift towards a largely oil-based economy.[32]

And so, when the oil economy collapsed under the impact of the war, the regime and the Baath party decided to reach out to the private sector to shift to it some of the public sector's economic functions in order to help the government cope with the economic crisis. In July 1982, the Baath party took a political decision to expand the scope of private-sector activity in the economy. This decision, which was not translated immediately into economic policies, was endorsed publicly by Saddam Hussein in 1984 and 1986 when he declared that "all activities of the private sector form part of the national wealth, and are as important as the activities of the socialist sector."[33] The Iraqi president underlined his commitment to the new policy in 1987 when he stated that "our brand of socialism cannot live without the private sector whether now, or after the war."[34]

In February 1987, the regime announced an ambitious program of economic liberalization and privatization. The main features of the program include the sale by the government of state lands, farms, and factories to the private sector. In time, other measures were announced, with the intention to provide for competition in the banking industry, deregulation of labor market, incentives to private enterprise, creation of a stock exchange, and opening up of the economy to foreign investment. Along the same policy lines and in order to curtail fiscal claims on its oil revenue, the government reduced its subsidies to state enterprises and relaxed policies that sought to set price ceilings on a large number of commodities.

But the economy's structural problems of stagnant agriculture and industry, compounded by the destructive consequences of the war, could not be ameliorated by a program of privatization that was driven by political expediency. Instead of solving Iraq's economic crisis, the new policy measures had the effect of exacerbating them, as evidenced by the rapid increase in prices of a wide range of consumer goods. The manner in which importers took advantage of the new rules provides a good illustration of this failure.

In 1984, the government decreed that importers who had access to foreign exchange were exempt from obtaining import license.[35] The assumption behind this measure was that importers would be enticed to repatriate their foreign-held financial assets and consequently in-

crease the supply of goods, thus exerting a downward pressure on inflation. But as Isam Al-Khafaji noted, instead of using their foreign-held
balances to finance their imports, what these importers did was to export Iraqi dinars to neighboring countries and sell the currency at lower
rates, then import foreign goods for sale in Iraq at inflated prices. This
practice in turn encouraged other sellers in the economy to charge
higher prices and caused higher rates of inflation. In addition to its inflationary bias, this process tended to divert funds from goods-producing
sectors to foreign trade and other speculative transactions that prom-
ised high rates of profit in a very short period of time.[36]

Nor did the government take the necessary time to develop appropriate financial, economic, and legal frameworks for the transfer of state-
owned enterprises to the private sector. The expediency of the new
policy is manifested by the government's willingness to sell these enterprises at prices that were below book value or replacement value.
Indeed: "In most cases, the prices paid barely covered the market cost
of the land the factories were built on."[37]

It can be argued, however, that the government's decision to sell
these assets at low prices was part of broader scheme to bolster the private sector rather than a reflection of administrative ineptitude. In its
desire to confine itself to strategic and other large projects such as oil,
defense, petrochemicals, and other heavy industries, the state was
anxious to withdraw from other enterprises by shifting them to the
private sector. But since the private sector was obtaining high rates of
return outside the goods-producing sectors, the state found it necessary
to offer the private sector such strong incentives as to enable it to
achieve rates of profit high enough to induce it to shift its resources to
these enterprises.[38]

Yet these policies failed to attain their goals. They had to, given the
deeply embedded economic crisis (a crisis that was made worse by the
transfer of state enterprises to the private sector), the discontinuation
of the policy of setting price ceilings, declining government subsidies,
and the failure to control inflation. The resultant decline in purchasing
power forced further decline in the living standards of the overwhelming majority of the people. In the face of such failure, the government
was forced to retreat from these policies when it decided to lower
prices, decree price freezes on many consumer goods, renationalize
some enterprises, increase agricultural subsidies, raise civil servant
salaries, and set lower profit margins for state and mixed enterprises.[39]

AN ESTIMATE OF THE COST OF THE DESTRUCTION

In the longest war of the twentieth century, hundreds of thousands
of people, both civilian and military, lost their lives. The two govern-

ments have not published the extent of the human toll. At the end of the its fourth year, it was estimated that the war had claimed a million casualties.[40] More recent conservative estimates put the total of war dead at 367,000 – Iran accounting for 262,000 and Iraq for 105,000. Another 700,000 were estimated to have been injured.[41] Iraq's loss of 105,000 persons translates into 16 percent of the average size of its armed forces during the period 1980–88.

In addition to the human loss, there is the explicit or quantifiable economic cost of the war and the implicit or nonquantifiable cost. Under the implicit cost, one can include morbidity and early mortality; disability; cost of welfare and veterans; inflation; missed opportunities for growth; opportunity cost of the armed forces and arms imports; loss of income from destroyed, damaged, or uncompleted projects; and disorganization of planning.

The explicit cost elements include military expenditure and arms imports, replacement cost of destroyed assets, lost oil revenue, cost of trade rerouting, and decline in GDP.

In a comprehensive study of the economic losses both Iraq and Iran incurred during the war, Kamran Mofid concludes that the combined loss of the two countries was $1.097 trillion – $644.3 billion for Iran and $452.6 billion for Iraq. Iraq's losses included these elements:

1. $91.4 billion in potential GNP losses: losses incurred in the oil sector, industry, agriculture, energy, telecommunications, housing, and health.
2. $197.7 billion oil-revenue losses.
3. $78.8 billion losses in foreign exchange reserves due to the loss of $35 billion in original reserves plus accumulated interest earnings for the duration of the war.
4. $80 billion potential losses in foreign exchange reserves resulting from high military spending.[42]

A measure of the magnitude of the cost of the war to the Iraqi economy is to relate it to oil revenue. Between 1931, when the government received its first payment for oil export from the oil companies operating in Iraq, and 1988, the cumulative oil revenue amounted to $179.3 billion. Relative to the $452.6 billion of war losses, this means that in its eight years of war with Iran the Baath regime succeeded in spending 254 percent of all the oil revenue Iraq received in fifty-seven years.

Another measure of the extent of the loss is to relate the economic cost of the war to Iraq's GDP during the period 1980–88. Thus, during this period, Iraq's GDP amounted to $433.3 billion, or $48.1 billion per year. Since the economic cost of the war is estimated to be $452.6 billion, or $50.2 billion per year, this means that the annual cost of the war amounted to 104 percent of Iraq's GDP during the nine-year 1980–89 period.

The impact of the war on the evolution of the industrial origins and utilization of GDP and its sectors may be seen in Table 5.5. It can be seen from the data that once it declined under the impact of war conditions in the early 1980s, Iraq's GDP never returned to its 1980 level. The data show that although both public and private consumption increased, the increase was a relative one since such consumption was both related to lower levels of GDP and constrained by inflation. Gross fixed investment also declined drastically during the war years from 46 percent in 1981 to 17 percent in 1986, reflecting the sharp decline in development spending. The cutbacks in investment were dictated by

Table 5.5
Changing Composition of GDP, 1975–1988

	1975	1980	1981	1982	1984	1986	1988
GDP by Type of Expenditure							
GDP in Current prices (ID bn)	4.1	15.8	11.0	13.0	14.8	14.9	17.4
GDP in 1975 prices (ID bn)	4.0	7.1	5.8	5.7	5.3	5.7	6.3
Distribution of GDP(Percentage)							
Government Consumption	21	15	30	36	32	30	30
Private Consumption	35	23	38	46	53	53	53
Change in inventories	9	8	18	13	-8	-1	5
Gross fixed investment	26	22	46	44	27	23	17
Exports of goods & services	51	63	33	26	25	19	22
Imports of goods and services	41	31	64	65	29	31	28
GDP by Origin (Percentage)							
Agriculture	8	5	9	10	13	15	16
Industry-total	57	66	37	32	34	27	33
manufacturing	7	4	7	7	8	11	12
Construction	9	7	16	17	10	9	6
Trade	5	5	10	12	13	13	11
Transport and Communication	5	4	7	7	5	7	7
Other Activities	17	13	24	24	28	32	29

Average Growth Rates of Selected Economic Indicators, 1970-1989

	1970-80	1980-85	1985-89
GDP	11.7	-8.1	-1.7
Government Consumption	13.6	-1.3	-4.4
Private Consumption	13.2	-7.6	-4.6
Gross Fixed Investment	27.6	-0.3	-1.5
Export of Goods and Services	4.4	-8.8	-1.1
Imports of Goods and Services	22.5	-8.2	-2.9
Agriculture	1.4	6.3	-6.7
Industry	10.2	-7.3	11.4
Manufacturing	13.4	0.3	-3.1
Construction	28.4	-7.8	-16.2
Domestic Trade	16.8	1.3	-10.8
Transport and Communication	19.9	-12.4	1.8

Sources: United Nations, *National Accounts Statistics: Main Aggregates and Detailed Tables, 1989, Part I* (New York, 1991); United Nations, *National Accounts Statistics: Analysis of Main Aggregates, 1988-1989* (New York, 1991).

the sharp decline in oil revenue that provided 63 percent of GDP in 1980 but only 22 percent in 1988. Imports, as the data indicate, absorbed nearly two-thirds of GDP in 1981 and 1982 but had to decline to 28 percent of GDP in 1988. The rise in imports in the early phase of the war reflects the regime's decision to flood the market with consumer goods in the hope of containing the impact of the war on consumption levels. By the same token, the decline in imports after 1982 reflects the failure of the regime's "guns and butter" policy and its recognition that austerity measures were unavoidable.

As to the evolution of the relative importance of sectoral contribution to GDP, it can be seen that the sharp decline in the contribution of the industrial sector reflects the sharp decline in oil output, export, and prices. It is this decline that should explain the rise in the relative importance of the agricultural and manufacturing sectors. Other sectors remain more or less stagnant since they are driven primarily by government development spending, which was forced to decline, as mentioned earlier.

The deterioration of the Iraqi economy under the impact of the war can also be looked at through changes in average growth rates. These changes inform of the toll both the economy and ordinary citizens had to pay because of the regime's policies.

Note from the data in Table 5.5 (p. 101) that the double-digit growth rate the economy registered in the 1970s turned into a negative growth rate that averaged 8.1 percent in 1980–85 and 1.7 percent in 1985–89.

Private consumption was hard hit by war conditions. Consumption, which had grown at an average rate of 13.6 percent in 1970–80, plummeted to a negative growth rate of 7.6 percent in 1980–85 and a negative growth rate of 4.6 percent in 1985–89.

Another key sector for future growth was gross fixed capital formation. In the period 1970–80, gross fixed investment registered an impressive average growth rate of 27 percent, only to turn negative in the 1980s. Similarly, average growth rates were very high in the 1970–80 period in trade, construction, and transport and communications; but such rates could not be sustained in the 1980s, when they turned into negative ones either in the first or the second half of the decade, or both. In both agriculture and manufacturing, negative growth rates were exhibited in the second half of the 1980s.

The picture that emerges from the figures of Table 5.5 (p. 101) is one of a high degree of buoyancy in the 1970s followed by grim devastation in the 1980s. In the 1970s, Iraq had an economy where every indicator was showing high rates of growth by historical and contemporary standards – in relation to other countries. Consumption, investment, exports, imports, infrastructure, and industry were all advancing at a fast pace. The invasion of Iran put an end to that growth and, indeed, turned it into negative growth.

This vast turnaround in the fortunes of the people and their economy proved to be but a curtain raiser for the disaster that engulfed Iraq following the decision by its government to invade Kuwait in August 1990, a subject to which the next chapter is devoted.

NOTES

1. For a good history of the war see Dilip Hiro, *The Longest War: The Iran-Iraq Military Conflict* (New York: Routledge, 1991).

2. See United Nations, *National Accounts Statistics: Analysis of Main Aggregates, 1988–1989* (New York, 1991), pp. 126–197.

3. See Abbas Alnasrawi, "Economic Consequences of the Iraq-Iran War," *Third World Quarterly* 8 (3): 869–895, especially Table 3.

4. See Economist Intelligence Unit (EIU), *Economic Review of Iraq* 3 (1981): 10.

5. See John Townsend, "Economic and Political Implications of the War: The Economic Consequences for the Participants," in *Iran–Iraq War: An Historical Analysis*, ed. M. S. El Azhary (New York: St. Martin's Press, 1984), p. 62.

6. See Abdul Wahab Al-Ameen, "Investment Allocations and Plan Implementations: Iraq's Absorptive Capacity, 1951–1980," *The Journal of Energy and Development* 6 (2): 263–280, especially p. 276.

7. United Nations, *Studies on Selected Development Problems in Various Countries in the Middle East, 1969* (New York, 1969), p. 12.

8. Data on oil output, export, and revenue are derived from OPEC, *Annual Statistical Bulletin 1991* (Vienna, 1992).

9. Derived from OAPEC, *Secretary-General's Annual Report* (Kuwait, annual, 1980 through 1984).

10. *Middle East Economic Survey (MEES),* July 27, 1981, pp. 1–2.

11. *MEES,* September 7, 1981, p. 2.

12. Ibid.

13. *MEES,* April 27, 1981 (Supplement), pp. 1–2.

14. See *MEES,* October 18, 1982, p. 3.

15. See OPEC, *Annual Statistical Bulletin, 1991;* Abbas Alnasrawi, *Arab Nationalism, Oil, and the Political Economy of Dependency* (Westport, Conn.: Greenwood Press, 1991), Chapter 7.

16. Economist Intelligence Unit (EIU), *Economic Review of Iraq* 4 (1984): 11.

17. Ibid.

18. See Iraqi Consulting Group, *Proceedings of Egyptian–Iraqi Dialogue* (in Arabic) (Vienna, 1991), pp. 133–134.

19. See EIU, *Economic Review of Iraq* 2 (1981): 9.

20. See Thomas R. Stauffer, "Economic Warfare in the Gulf," *American-Arab Affairs* 14 (Fall 1985): 108.

21. See EIU, *Economic Review of Iraq* 4 (1982): 10.

22. Food and Agriculture Organization, *1984 FAO Production Yearbook* (Rome, 1985), pp. 108–114.

23. Derived from the World Bank, *World Development Report 1979,* p. 163 and United Nations Development Program, *Human Development Report 1991,* p. 150.

24. See EIU, *Economic Review of Iraq* 2 (1982): 17.

25. See Abdel Moneim, S. Ali, and Hail A. J. Ganabi, "Political Economy of Inflation in Iraq, 1988–1992," *Arab Economic Journal* (in Arabic) 1 (Autumn 1992): 91–113.

26. See Congressional Budget Office, *Limiting Conventional Arms Exports to the Middle East* (Washington, 1992), p. 10. It should be mentioned that the calculations in the CBO's study are in 1992 U.S. dollars.

27. See "Documentation on Iraq–Kuwait Crisis," *MEES,* July 23, 1990, pp. D1–D9.

28. Computed from Government of Iraq, *Annual Abstract of Statistics 1983.*

29. Townsend, "Economic and Political Implications," p. 64.

30. For a good treatment of these issues, see Robert Springborg, "Infitah, Agrarian Transformation, and the Elite Consolidation in Contemporary Iraq," *The Middle East Journal* 40 (1): 33–52.

31. See EIU, *Economic Review of Iraq* 2 (1978): 12.

32. Ibid., p. 5.

33. *Middle East Economic Digest (MEED),* February 15, 1986, p. 17.

34. *MEED,* March 28, 1987, p. 18.

35. See Isam Al-Khafaji, "The War and the Iraqi Economy," *Al-Thaqafa Al-Jadida* (in Arabic) June 1989, pp. 4–34.

36. Ibid., pp. 11–12.

37. See Kiren Aziz Chaudhry, "On the Way to Market: Economic Liberalization and Iraq's Invasion of Kuwait," *Middle East Report* (May-June 1991), p. 18.

38. See Al-Khafaji, "The War and the Iraqi Economy," p. 19.

39. *MEES,* January 23, 1989, pp. B3–B4; *MEES,* September 18, 1989, pp. B1–B2; EIU, *Country Report, Iraq* 4 (1989): 8.

40. See *The New York Times,* September 23, 1985.

41. Dilip Hiro, *The Longest War: The Iran–Iraq Military Conflict* (New York: Routledge, 1991), p. 250.

42. Kamran Mofid, *The Economic Consequences of the Gulf War* (London: Routledge, 1990), Chapter 10, especially p. 133.

CHAPTER 6

The Invasion of Kuwait and the Destruction of Development

It has been said that historical analysis of nations at war throughout the centuries suggests that the true economic consequences of a war appear only after the last shot is fired, and, irrespective of victor and vanquished, each country would start the postwar period impoverished.[1]

When the war was finally ended in 1988, Iraq had incurred some $452 billion, nearly ten times its average GDP during the war period, in explicit economic cost. Even if the actual economic cost is lower than the figure cited here, it would still be several times its GDP. Therefore, it would be no exaggeration to say that Iraq started the postwar period with its economy in ruin and its people impoverished.

ABUNDANCE OF PROBLEMS VERSUS SCARCITY OF RESOURCES

Iraq's prewar list of economic difficulties had to be expanded now to include new war-induced problems. Thus, when the ceasefire came into effect on August 20, 1988, Iraq was starting its postwar period with most of its major oil exporting capacity destroyed, blocked, or closed; basic and heavy industries were destroyed or in need of repair; the infrastructure was extensively damaged; a major segment of its labor force was under arms; industrial growth left much to be desired; agriculture was stagnant; and rural workers had either been drafted into the army or moved to urban centers; the large number of workers imported during the war had become a burden on the economy; dependence on food imports had increased; development planning had virtually ceased; hyperinflation was beyond control; dependence on the oil sector had increased; privatization was not succeeding according to expectations; Arab and foreign capital could not be enticed to flow in the economy; levels of imports had fallen; and the servicing of Iraq's rising foreign debt was consuming a significant portion of its foreign exchange earnings.

Facing such a daunting list of difficulties was an oil sector on which the entire economy had come to depend but whose performance left much to be desired. In 1986, the year of the collapse of the oil market, Iraq's oil revenue reached a low level of $6.9 billion. Following OPEC's decision to stabilize member-country output, Iraq's revenue reached $11.4 billion in 1987 but declined to $11 billion in 1988, to rise again to $14.5 billion in 1989 – 55 percent of what it had been in 1980. Against this declining but highly vital source of revenue, the government had to balance a multitude of urgent claims. These included the need for more imports, foreign debt service, expenditure on reconstruction and development, financing ordinary government functions, and funding an ambitious program of military industrialization. In the meantime, the government was called upon to fight abnormally high rates of inflation. In the following paragraphs, an examination of how the government balanced its priorities versus the contribution of the oil sector is undertaken.

GOVERNMENT BORROWING, MONEY SUPPLY, AND INFLATION

One of the structural features of an oil-based economy like Iraq's is the lack of symmetry between national income and the composition of national output. The root of the problem is that in generating between one-half and two-thirds of the GDP, the oil sector is absorbing no more than 2 or 3 percent of the labor force. Since the goods-producing sectors, agriculture and industry, contributed less than one-fifth of the national output, it follows that any domestically spent portion of the income generated by the oil sector is bound to exert an upward pressure on domestic prices. But because government development spending to increase national output takes a long time to show results, the only avenue left to policy makers is to increase imports while the national output of goods and services is being raised. In the absence of such a policy of development, or if the policy fails to increase output, the country will tend to be increasingly dependent on imports; and the economy will become merely a mechanism that exports oil in exchange for imports. Increases in living standards may be attained, but such increases become hostages to the forces that shape the demand for and the price of oil – forces beyond the reach of the governments of oil-producing countries.

In the case of Iraq, the problem was made even worse by a series of decisions by the ruling Baath party in the 1970s to invest in the oil sector, thus perpetuating the phenomenon of an oil-based economy. The regime could have its way so long as government receipts from the oil sector were not overwhelmed by abnormal claims such as war and foreign debt service that might drain the pool of revenue available for domestic spending. The problem is made worse when such abnormal claims are superimposed on an economy when its sole foreign-exchange earner is faltering. This is more or less what happened in Iraq and caused inflation rates to jump beyond control.

It can be said that the period 1960–73 was one of relative price stability – consumer prices increased at an average rate of 5 or 6 percent per year. The picture, however, changed drastically after 1973. Starting in 1973 as the base year, prices increased between 19 percent and 68 percent between 1975 and 1979. Inflationary conditions worsened during the eight-year war with Iran when the inflation rates jumped sharply from 95 percent in 1980 to 369 percent in 1988.[2]

This rise in inflation was clearly caused by the increase in government spending, which could not be accompanied by proportionate increase in output or imports. Following the oil price explosion of the 1970s, the government accelerated its spending, thus raising disposable income at a time when the economy was not in a position to expand output. The problem of skilled labor shortages, which has plagued Iraq, was exacerbated by the influx of foreign firms implementing government project contracts. The competition with existing employers, especially the government, prompted the latter to hold onto its technicians and civil servants by issuing a decree that foreign firms might not pay Iraqi employees more than the government was paying its own employees.[3]

Even when the government attempted to blunt the rise in prices in the 1970s by increasing imports, it found that these attempts were undermined by the lack of the necessary infrastructural facilities to handle large volumes of goods. This should not be surprising, given the sudden increase in revenue and expenditure. Moreover, a major portion of government spending was devoted to expanding the civil service and modernizing and expanding the armed forces – which increased personal incomes without any corresponding increase in the level of national output.

Behind these policies were the regime's own priorities which did not include concentrating its attention on the difficult issue of promoting agriculture and industry. While the regime's planners and bureaucrats recognized the importance of these two sectors for the future of the economy, advocated a gradualist approach to development, and recommended that resources be devoted both to them and to the creation of managerial and technical cadres, the politicians had other ideas. The main concern of the latter was to press for rapid industrialization, prestige, and spectacular projects. Even when funds were allocated to agriculture, the largest segment of such funds was sunk into irrigation and water-control structures with minimum linkage to the local problems of agricultural production.[4] This in turn forced the government to recycle an increasing amount of its petrodollars to import food for an expanding population with more income to spend.

Given time, the imbalance between aggregate supply and aggregate demand of the type that prevailed in the 1970s would have been corrected through an increase in national output or imports or both. Such prospect was not given time to be tested. Instead, the eruption of the Iran–Iraq war in September 1980 changed most everything in the economy.

The destruction of physical assets, such as infrastructure, farms, factories, export facilities, harbors, roads, and the like, led to a decline in domestic product. This was made worse by expanding the size of the armed forces, an expansion that accentuated the problem of labor shortages – a problem further complicated by the withdrawal of foreign workers from industrial and construction sites. The diversion of economic resources to the war effort only added to the problem of supplies for the civilian economy. The rise in the price of imports due to the rerouting of trade and the induced delay in delivery added to the cost of such imports. The eventual decline in imports after 1982 not only deprived the economy of consumer goods but also reduced the flow of inputs, spare parts, and capital goods – making it even more difficult to stem the decline in output.

Moreover, as the government exhausted its previously accumulated foreign reserves and as its oil revenue declined, it found itself forced to seek domestic sources of finance. In a country like Iraq, where the contribution of tax revenue to total government revenue has traditionally been insignificant, war time was not the right time to raise taxes. Nor could the government borrow in the open market, since there was no financial system outside the government-owned banking system.

Given these constraints, in order to finance its war effort in the face of declining revenue, the government found itself increasingly borrowing from the banking system. This practice, which resulted in raising the supply of money in the system, had the effect of intensifying inflationary pressure in the economy, causing the budget deficit to increase and thus forcing the government into another round of borrowing and setting the stage for inflationary spiral.[5] Since the central bank is government owned and the commercial banking system was a government monopoly, such borrowing from the banking system was tantamount to printing money, one step removed.

The high rates of inflation, combined with the war-induced shortages and the general deterioration of the economy, caused impoverishment to spread as living standards continued to fall, thus reinforcing the country's economic crisis.

THE EMERGING PROBLEM OF EXTERNAL DEBT

Iraq has always been one of the few developing countries that managed to stay away from contracting foreign loans. The only significant exception was a number of loans extended by the Soviet Union and other centrally planned economies, most of which were to be paid in oil.

As the war with Iran continued, the government found itself forced to borrow to finance the war. Three sources of loans were identified. First, loans extended by the Arab Gulf states, mainly Saudi Arabia and Kuwait, soon after the outbreak of the war. The government of Iraq has always maintained that such funds, which amounted to $40 billion, were supplied as assistance rather than loans to help it in its war with Iran. Another $35 billion was owed to Western governments and banks. Third, another $11 billion was owed to the Soviet Union and other East European governments.[6] It should be pointed out that Iraq's debt-service obligations in 1990 were projected to be $8 billion, 55 percent of its oil revenue in 1989.[7]

For its part, the government admitted that its foreign debt amounted to $42.1 billion. To service this debt, the government projected total payment of $75.1 billion to its creditors over a five-year period, 1991–95.[8] An average debt service of $15 billion, it should be pointed out, exceeds Iraq's oil revenue of 1989 by $.5 billion. Such was the depth of Iraq's economic crisis before its decision to invade and occupy Kuwait in 1990.

MILITARY INDUSTRIES AND THE
USE OF SCARCE RESOURCES

Inflation, partial demobilization, unemployment, heavy debt payments, low oil revenue, currency depreciation, nonresponsive private sector, stagnant output, falling living standards and general impoverishment, and lack of funds for reconstruction are some of the burdens under which the Iraqi economy was laboring in the postwar period.

While some debt rescheduling agreements were reached with some governments and supplier credits were obtained from other sources, such arrangements could not begin to scratch the surface of Iraq's economic crisis. Nor did the government seem to be focusing its attention on the immediate problems of the economy. A few examples of government spending will illustrate the point.

During the war with Iran, the regime succeeded in building a significant military industry. By the time the war came to an end, Iraq had the largest military industry in the Arab world after Egypt. Iraq's capabilities in this field were demonstrated in 1984 when its forces used domestically produced chemical weapons against Iran. In the spring of 1988, it succeeded in using some 300 surface-to-surface missiles against Iranian cities and forces. During the second half of the 1980s, Iraq's military industry was producing a wide range of arms, weapon systems, munitions, and electronics. The speed with which the government was able to build such an industry under war conditions reflects the decision of the government to commit human and financial resources on a large scale to this undertaking. It has been estimated, for example, that some 100,000 workers were employed in this industry. Although the government succeeded in building a national military industry, it nevertheless imported considerable amounts of inputs, intermediate and capital goods, designs, parts and components, and technology from many sources in the West.[9]

In its attempt to build a domestic military industry, the government sought to overcome the control or interference practiced by arms exporters, to avoid the consequences of potential arms embargo, to free itself from political pressures that might be exerted by arms exporters, and to ensure the secrecy of its military needs.[10]

The conclusion of the war with Iran in 1988 did not bring a weakening in the resolve of the regime to continue to invest in the military industry. Nor did the lack of funds seem to persuade the government to slow down such investment. The merging of the Military Industrialization Organization and the Ministry of Industry into one body called Ministry of Military Industrialization and Industry underlined the importance the government attached in the postwar period to integrating all industrial projects under one management.

Guided by its desire to lessen its dependence on foreign suppliers and capitalizing on the large war-generated pool of new skills in technology, industry, logistics, and management, the government singled out military industrialization as the favored sector to receive huge amounts of funds and large numbers of skilled workers soon after the war ended.[11] The decision to invest heavily in this sector was one of four objectives of postwar economic policy announced in 1988 "to better exploit the technological experience gained in the military-industrial sector."[12]

To appropriate scarce resources to the military industry immediately after a devastating war in a crisis-ridden economy is indicative of the regime's priorities toward the civilian economy and the immediate needs of the people. The regime's economic priorities may be gleaned from another form of spending. Before the war ended, the president decided to go ahead with the construction of a new presidential palace which would require eight years to build. Given the length of time necessary to complete the work and given the president's personal involvement with the project's architects, artists, and historians, it is not difficult to surmise that the project was likely to be very costly.[13]

In addition to official neglect of the civilian economy and development and economic mismanagement, there were also widespread corruption and illegal dealings practiced at higher levels of the government, as was publicly acknowledged by the president himself.[14]

The 9 percent decline in 1989 real GDP over the 1988 level appears to have shocked the government into adopting austerity measures in the public sector. Thus it was decreed to lower government spending in 1990 by 7 percent from the 1989 level. Government departments were ordered to cut the size of their staffs by 50 percent.[15] The decline in the 1989 GDP must have been a severe blow to the government, since oil revenue that year increased to $14.5 billion, 31.8 percent greater than the 1988 revenue of $11 billion.

But such measures could not be effective since the crisis of the economy has become a condition rather than a temporary phenomenon. Nothing short of some draconian measures would have sufficed. But draconian measures required that oil income rise to meet the urgent needs of the economy. This need to raise oil revenue led the regime to its oil confrontation with Kuwait and set the stage for the invasion of August 2, 1990.

OPEC FAILURE AND THE IRAQ-KUWAIT OIL CONFRONTATION

Iraq, like the other twelve OPEC member countries, declares periodically that it will set its oil output and prices according to OPEC oil ministers' collective decisions. Such decisions are much easier to adhere to when, generally speaking, there is a seller's market or when member countries are producing at capacity. Obversely, when there is excess capacity, member countries attempt to expand their sales through hidden discounts, countertrade arrangements, or outright price cuts. Since there is an intense degree of interdependence among the sellers, any increase in the sales of one oil-producing country is bound to affect other countries' sales and revenues. This high degree of interdependence among the few sellers is similar to the oligopolistic price behavior of the oil companies discussed in Chapter 1.

The similarity in price behavior between oil-producing countries and their predecessors, the major oil companies, should not be carried too far. Although the oil companies, like all business firms, are guided by the principle of profit maximization, governments of oil-producing countries are guided by political considerations as well. Like any other government, the government of an oil-producing country owes its political survival to the manner in which its income is distributed throughout the economy. Furthermore, as oil became the single most important source of revenue, to the exclusion of almost all other sources such as taxes, it conferred upon the state unprecedented power over the economy, over regional and personal distribution of income, over urban-rural income differentials, over the level of employment and its sectoral distribution, over the structure of the economy, and ultimately over the very nature of the state and the future of the country itself.

The availability and level of oil revenue also give the state certain leverages in the regional context and, indeed, on the international stage to influence events and developments beyond its borders. It can be said, therefore, that the interest of the state in changes in oil output, price, and revenue goes beyond the mere commercial interest as these changes impinge not only on the domestic economic agenda but also on the state's regional and international agenda, linkages, and obligations. With this in mind, the Iraq-Kuwait oil dispute must be considered.

Over its life since 1960 when OPEC was created, its decisions over prices and output were guided by the perceptions of its member countries of their own national interests. The principle of the sovereignty of the state was, in the final analysis, the guiding principle of each state. In this context, national interest took precedent over the collective interest of the group.

Since member countries varied considerably in their resource endowment of oil reserves, in the size of their populations, in the stage of their economic development, and in the network of their commitments outside OPEC, it was natural that they would have different assessments of the value of their oil reserves and consequently the amount of oil to be produced and the price at which it would be sold.

One group of countries, led by Saudi Arabia and supported by other Arab Gulf states – Kuwait, United Arab Emirates, and Qatar – viewed stable or even relatively low price to be important for all member countries' long-term interests. In order to keep prices from rising, these states were prepared to increase oil output. Their ability to pump more oil to sell at lower prices and still maintain their revenue was bolstered by the fact that they had small populations, considerable accumulated financial investments, and large oil reserves.

The Gulf states argued that it was in the interest of oil-producing countries to maintain prices at levels acceptable to the main consuming countries – the industrialized countries of the West – in order to avoid driving the West to finding alternative sources of oil or of energy or to adopting excessive conservation measures. Another factor that influenced the oil policies of these states was their considerable investment in Western economies. They believed that low oil prices would contribute to general price stability and therefore protect the value of their assets.

If Saudi Arabia and its allies within OPEC can be described as "output maximizers," another group of countries may be described as "price maximizers." Countries with smaller oil reserves but larger populations tend to have lower per capita incomes than members of the other group. Moreover, these countries tend to run balance-of-payments deficits and therefore incur foreign debt obligations. Their position on the price of oil is dictated by their smaller oil reserves. They want to get as much income as possible. Their position is also influenced by their ambitious development plans which call for a large component of foreign exchange. Since all oil-exporting countries are paid in U.S. dollars for their oil, these countries want to see upward price adjustments to offset any erosion in the value of the dollar caused by inflation or foreign exchange fluctuations. Countries in this group include Algeria, Iran, Iraq, Libya, Nigeria, and Venezuela.

One of the notable features of Saudi oil policy and OPEC since the 1973 oil price explosion was the ability of the Saudi government to impose its policy of relative price freeze on other members of OPEC. The tactic was simple but effective. Whenever member countries advocated a price increase that was not in line with Saudi thinking, the Saudi government threatened an increase in output that would lower prices and yield a smaller market share to the country raising prices. This Saudi oil policy in turn helped serve the U.S. government's longstanding objective of access to adequate supplies of Middle East oil at reasonable prices. The policy coordination between the governments of Saudi Arabia and the United States was described by the General Accounting Office in these terms:

To achieve the U.S. objective of access to adequate supplies at "reasonable prices," the United States uses its bilateral relationships with friendly producers in attempts to influence their pricing and production decision. This is especially apparent with Saudi Arabia with which . . . the United States has a "very active" bilateral policy. Frequent visits by cabinet-level officials including the Secretaries of State, Treasury, Defense, and Energy, during the past several years illustrate this bilateralism.[16]

This policy of raising output in order to influence the price of oil was maintained in the course of the Iranian revolution and the early phases of the Iran–Iraq war. As is stated earlier, the decision of the Saudi government to persist in its policy of overproduction in the face of glut conditions in the oil market drew sharp criticism from Saddam Hussein and his oil minister.

The continued erosion of OPEC's market share and revenue after

1982, once the panic demand conditions were satisfied, was transformed into a disastrous price collapse in 1986 as OPEC abandoned all restraints on output in order to regain its market share. But this unrestrained behavior forced the price down from $29 per barrel in 1983 to less than $10 per barrel (at one point $7 per barrel) in 1986 and caused the combined oil revenues of OPEC to plummet from $131 billion in 1985 to $77 billion in 1986 while its combined oil exports increased by 17 percent during the same period.

The 1986 price collapse forced OPEC, in October of that year, to return to its system of quotas and to an agreed-upon official or reference price of $18 per barrel, a price that was deemed by all member countries to be necessary for their social and economic development.[17] The significance of this accord was the linkage member countries established between their economic and social development, on the one hand, and certain level of output to be sold on the world market at a given price, on the other. Therefore, any attempt by a member country to produce above its quota means that it would have to sell its oil at a lower price than the $18-per-barrel reference price agreed upon by OPEC. This in turn means that the noncomplying country will expand its share of the market at the expense of fellow producers, causing a decline in their oil revenue and unwanted implications for their economic and social development.

A number of countries nevertheless failed to abide by their own agreement and allowed their output to rise and exert downward pressure on the price, which fell well below the $18 per barrel benchmark – averaging $16.92 per barrel in 1987, $13.22 in 1988, and $15.69 in 1989. While Kuwait and the United Arab Emirates (UAE) were among the countries that increased their exports, Iraq was not in a position to do so, since its export outlets were severely limited. The government felt doubly frustrated as the country's economic crisis continued to deepen. The oil price movements prior to the invasion of Kuwait illustrate the chaos in the oil market shown by the following brief review.

In October 1988, the selling price of oil had sunk to $12 per barrel. But by the end of 1988, it had recovered to reach $14 per barrel. This was a welcome improvement over $12 per barrel but still significantly below the reference price. The upward movement continued throughout 1989, and it reached $18.84 by December. This trend continued in January 1990, when the price reached $19.98 per barrel. But this price was not allowed to continue; Kuwait and other producers increased their output, causing the price to fall sharply to $14.02 by June – a decline of 30 percent that wiped out a major portion of the oil income of many countries.

The position of a leading output maximizer within OPEC was articulated in February 1990 by the oil minister of Kuwait, Ali Khalifa Al-Sabah, when he stated the following:

First of all, I will tell you that we are producing above quota at the moment. Let us not beat about the bush on that. And I think that our obligation to stay within the quota applies when the price of the OPEC basket is below $18/B and if the price is above $18/B, I think everyone should be, and even encouraged to be, producing above quota.[18]

The oil minister went on to say that the current OPEC price of $18 per barrel would remain at that level and would not be adjusted for inflation or dollar depreciation for at least three or four years. As to the OPEC quotas, he said he would like to see them scrapped as soon as possible. From a practical standpoint they were already irrelevant, so all that was needed was a recognition of that fact.[19]

These statements provide a coherent oil policy for Kuwait the elements of which are (1) the nominal price of oil should remain stable at $18 per barrel, (2) the OPEC quota system should be scrapped, and (3) whenever market forces push the price above $18 per barrel, member countries should expand their output to force it down.

It should be noted that if Kuwait were not a member of OPEC, such a policy would have made considerable sense since its production capacity was about 2.5 MBD, 1 MBD above its quota. In addition, its oil reserves are vast and its population is very small. Moreover, Kuwait had invested considerable capital to buy downstream outlets and facilities for its own oil in Europe; and it had a large investment portfolio producing income that exceeded its revenue from oil in some years. By contrast, Iraq could not increase its exports; it wanted to adhere to the OPEC quota system; it had no investment in retail outlets; and it had no portfolio to produce income. Instead, Iraq had become more dependent than ever before on oil revenue.[20]

Aside from the particular situation of Iraq, the problem with Kuwait's policy position was the central fact that Kuwait was not acting in a vacuum. There was a high degree of interdependence among oil-producing countries, and one country's gain could be attained only at the expense of other countries. Moreover, Kuwait could not announce the demise of the quota system and still remain a member of OPEC. In short, neither Kuwait nor any other member of OPEC could have it both ways.

The consequences of the downward slide in the price of oil, which declined by one-third in the first six months of 1990 from nearly $20 per barrel to $13.67 per barrel, triggered a series of reactions by Iraq. In early May, the Baath party organ, *Al-Thawra*, carried a statement by Iraq's foreign minister attacking the production policy of Kuwait and the UAE.

On May 30, Saddam Hussein made a statement at the Arab Emergency Summit Conference in Baghdad in which he spoke of the economic damage inflicted upon Iraq as a result of the oil price decline. Given Iraq's export capacity at the time, he asserted that a drop in price of $1 per barrel meant a loss of $1 billion in oil revenue per year. Moreover, he expressed the Iraqi government's belief that the price could be raised to $25 per barrel within two years without harming export levels. This in turn meant that the longer the price remained low the larger the economic loss that Iraq would have to endure.

From Saddam Hussein's perspective, the punishing effects on the Iraqi economy of Kuwait's oil policy were similar to the economic damage inflicted by conventional wars. He expressed this view as follows:

I wish to tell those of our brothers who do not seek war, and those who do not intend to wage war on Iraq, that we cannot tolerate this type of economic warfare which is being waged against Iraq. I believe that all our brothers know our situation and are informed about it and that, God willing, the situation will turn out well. But I say that we have reached a state of affairs where we cannot take the pressure. I believe we will all benefit and the Arab nation will benefit from the principle of adherence to OPEC resolutions on production and prices.[21]

The desperate state of the Iraqi economy was made clear by Saddam Hussein when he said that a few billion dollars could solve much that had been at a standstill or postponed in the life of the Iraqis.[22]

Saddam Hussein's statements on the plight of the economy were followed by an assertion a few weeks later by Iraq's deputy prime minister, Saadoon Hamadi, that the price of oil would rise to $18 per barrel if Kuwait and the United Arab Emirates brought their production back to their OPEC-assigned quotas. In its effort to persuade these two states to adhere to the quota system, Iraq was not alone. Indeed, there was a broader effort to pressure these two countries to lower their output.[23]

In the middle of July, Iraq stepped up its campaign against Kuwait and the United Arab Emirates and widened the scope of its accusations against Kuwait. In a memorandum to the League of Arab States, Iraq accused the government of the UAE of participating with the Kuwaiti government in what was described as "a planned operation to flood the oil market with excess production." The Iraqi memorandum characterized Kuwait's actions as tantamount to military aggression and accused its government of being determined to cause a collapse of Iraq's economy:

As far as the Kuwaiti Government is concerned, its attack on Iraq is a double one. On the one hand Kuwait is attacking Iraq and encroaching on our territory, oil fields and stealing our national wealth. Such action is tantamount to military aggression. On the other hand the Government of Kuwait is determined to cause a collapse of the Iraqi economy during this period when it is confronting the vicious imperialist Zionist threat, which is an aggression no less than military aggression.[24]

In addition to the issues of oil production and borders, the Iraqi government added two other issues to the list of its grievances against Kuwait. The first relates to the dispute over the Rumaila oil field where Iraq accused Kuwait of using diagonal drilling to pump oil from that part of the field located in Iraq's territory. The second relates to the financial assistance Kuwait had extended during the war with Iran. While Kuwait maintained that those funds were loans, Iraq insisted that they were grants. From Iraq's perspective, such assistance or loans or debts should have been written off for several reasons. First, the war with Iran had been waged not only to defend Iraq's own sovereignty but also to defend the eastern flank of the Arab homeland, especially the Gulf region, a view that has been confirmed, according to the Iraqi government, by the leaders of the Gulf themselves. Second, Kuwait benefited financially from the war by selling more oil at higher prices. Third, the length of the war, and therefore its cost, was not foreseen. The military hardware alone that Iraq purchased and used in the war amounted to $102 billion.[25]

On July 17, Saddam Hussein accused rulers of the Gulf states of being tools in an international campaign waged by imperialists and Zionists to halt Iraq's scientific and technological progress and to impoverish its people.[26]

On July 27, in the shadow of Iraqi troops movement along the Iraqi–Kuwaiti border, OPEC agreed to set a higher reference price of $21 per barrel and adopt new quotas without allowing any member country to exceed its allocated share for any reason whatsoever.[27]

But on August 2, Saddam Hussein decided to invade and occupy Kuwait; and on August 8, the Iraqi government announced the annexation of Kuwait. The ensuing imposition of a blockade against any exports from Iraq and Kuwait gave rise to demands that OPEC member countries be allowed to increase output beyond their quotas. On August 29, OPEC decided to suspend quota allocations so that member countries might expand their output without restrictions.[28] This last decision was described as having been adopted by OPEC under considerable pressure from the United States, a pressure that amounted to a direct order.[29]

THE INVASION AND THE ECONOMIC SANCTIONS

Iraq's economic crisis resulted from the Baath regime's military, economic, and political policies, which led the economy to a dead end with no prospect for recovery. The immediate explanation of the crisis was the regime's decision to go to war with Iran. The war-induced economic crisis was deepened by the government's erratic economic policies, its neglect of agriculture and industry, its high levels of spending for rearmament and military industry, and widespread mismanagement and corruption. And the austerity program of 1990 was simply the last in a series of manifestations of the crisis.

Needless to say, other considerations besides the economic crisis entered into the regime's decision to invade Kuwait. The analysis of such considerations, however, goes beyond the scope of the study.[30]

Given Iraq's economic crisis and the regime's failure to keep its promises that living standards would improve after the war, Kuwait – with its vast economic resources, its small size, and its defenselessness – must have looked like an easy target and an expedient solution to its problem.

Indeed, the importance of Kuwait's resources for Iraq's economy – the real reason for the invasion – was underscored by the deputy prime minister for the economy when he said that Iraq would now be able to pay its debt in less than five years; that the new Iraq's oil reserves had doubled; that the "new Iraq" would have an oil production quota of 4.6 MBD instead of 3.1 MBD; that its oil income would reach $38 billion per year and rise to $60 billion in the near future; that there would be considerable expansion in the private sector once the two economies were integrated; and that Iraq would be able to vastly increase spending on development projects and imports.[31] These economic dreams turned into ashes when a number of countries, under the leadership of the United States, took it upon themselves to undo what the Iraqi regime had done on August 2.

On the day of the invasion, United Nations Security Council Resolution (UNSCR) 660 was passed, condemning the invasion and urging the withdrawal of Iraqi troops from Kuwait. The United States, Britain, and France decided on the same day to freeze Iraqi and Kuwaiti assets and to ban trade with Iraq. For its part, the Soviet Union decided to halt arms deliveries to Iraq.

On August 6 UNSCR 661 was passed, imposing mandatory sanctions and embargo on Iraq and occupied Kuwait. This resolution banned all transactions with Iraq and sealed Iraq's economic fate for years to come. As has been stated several times in this study, Iraq's economy is totally dependent on the world market for its oil exports; its foreign exchange earnings; its imports of foodstuffs; consumer goods; raw materials; and other inputs, technology, spare parts, and capital goods.

A measure of the effectiveness of the embargo may be seen in the 86 percent decline in Iraq's oil output from 3.3 MBD before the invasion to less than .5 MBD in subsequent months – enough to meet the needs of local consumption. And since the price of oil had been raised to $21 per barrel, Iraq's oil revenue in 1990 would have been much higher than that of 1989. Even before the new price rise took effect, Iraq's oil revenue of $9.5 billion for the first six months of 1990 was 34 percent higher, on annual basis, than the 1989 level.

The effectiveness of the embargo was so immediate that on December 5, 1990, in testimony before the U.S. Senate Foreign Relations Committee, it was reported that the embargo had effectively shut off 90 percent of Iraq's imports and 97 percent of its exports and produced serious disruptions to the economy and hardships to the people.[32]

The embargo-induced loss to the economy in the six-month period prior to the January 1991 bombing of Iraq was estimated by the Iraqi government to amount to $17 billion – $10 billion in lost oil exports, $5.1 billion in production cuts, $1 billion in increased production costs, $.7 billion in losses resulting from delays in development projects, and $1.3 billion for other losses.[33] In retrospect, such economic losses and hardships were minor in comparison to the destruction inflicted upon Iraq by the 1991 Gulf war.

The six-week bombing campaign, which started on January 16, 1991, was aimed not only at military targets but also at such assets as civilian infrastructure, power stations, transport and telecommunications networks, fertilizer plants, oil facilities, iron and steel plants, bridges, hospitals, storage facilities, industrial plants, and civilian buildings. And the assets that were not bombed were made useless by the destruction of power-generating facilities. The impact of the intensity and the scale of the bombing was assessed by a special United Nations mission to Iraq as follows:

It should, however, be said at once that nothing that we had seen or read had quite prepared us for the particular form of devastation which has now befallen the country. The recent conflict had wrought near-apocalyptic results upon what had been, until January 1991, a rather highly urbanized and mechanized society. Now, most means of modern life support have been destroyed or rendered tenuous. Iraq has, for some time to come, been relegated to a pre-industrial age, but with all the disabilities of post-industrial dependency on an intensive use of energy and technology.[34]

This vast scale of destruction should not be surprising in light of the fact that Iraq, a small country of 173,000 square miles with a population of 18 million, was subjected to 106,000 bombing sorties in 42 days.

AN ESTIMATE OF IRAQ'S HUMAN LOSSES

Neither the U.S. government nor the Iraqi government nor the United Nations has seen fit to release data on the extent of the war-caused human and material losses. Any estimate of the extent of the destruction must be considered provisional for the time being.

The human losses caused by or related to the war fall into three categories: (1) military and civilian losses during the war itself, January 16 to February 28, 1991; (2) civilian and military human losses during the unsuccessful popular uprising of March 1991 against the Baath regime and its institutions; (3) civilian losses that can be attributed to the effects of the destruction of infrastructure and other facilities and the continued embargo.

Estimates of military losses indicate that anywhere between 50,000 and 120,000 Iraqi soldiers were killed in the six-week war.[35] Using different sources, Dilip Hiro concluded that 82,000 Iraqi soldiers lost their lives and that this figure amounted to one-third to one-half of the Iraqi dead during the entire Iran–Iraq war, which went on for 464 weeks.[36]

Civilian losses during the war were estimated to range between 5,000 and 15,000 Iraqis. But in the month-long uprising against the government that followed the war it was estimated that between 20,000 and 100,000 civilians lost their lives. In addition, it was estimated that 15,000 to 30,000 Kurds and other displaced people died in refugee camps and on the road and that another 4,000 to 16,000 Iraqis died of starvation and disease.[37] These staggering figures show that between 94,000 and 281,000 Iraqis lost their lives during the war and the subsequent uprising.

In addition to the loss of human lives, the war and its aftermath inflicted other losses on the civilian population, some of which are difficult to quantify. No data, for instance, have been released regarding the injured, the maimed, and the traumatized, whose numbers and the extent of whose plight are not known. Similarly, it is difficult to estimate the losses endured by the large numbers of refugees and displaced persons whose plight was caused by the manner in which the government crushed the March 1991 uprising.

Suffice it to say that in late March 1991 more than two million people either "got up and left their homes in less than six days" fleeing to Iran and Turkey or sought refuge in the marshes near the Iraq–Iran border.[38] Moreover, more than three years since the conclusion of the

Gulf war, the Iraqi regime is still engaged in an ongoing war against its own people.[39]

There are other lasting effects of the war. The breakdown in health care delivery systems symbolized by the bombing of hospitals; the lack of medicines, food, and purified water; and the destruction of power-generating plants contributed to more deaths among civilians, especially children.

In May 1991, the Harvard Study Team Report projected that some 170,000 children under the age of five would die over the next year from the effects of the war, a doubling of prewar figures.[40]

Another effect of the war is its impact on life expectancy. The Iran–Iraq war had the effect of lowering male life expectancy by ten years. Given this precedent and coupled with the vastly deteriorated living and health conditions in Iraq, there is every reason to conclude that life expectancy will be lowered still further.[41] Another report asserts that 170,000 people have died as a direct or indirect result of the embargo.[42] Furthermore, lack of food and medicine increased the child mortality rate for those under five years old from 29.5 per 1,000 births in 1988 to 92.7 per 1,000 births in 1992.[43]

In short, the huge human losses that Iraq had to endure in the 1991 war, combined with the large losses during the war with Iran and the large number of disabled, will leave their impact on the size of the labor force and its skills, and consequently on the growth of the economy, in the future.

AN ESTIMATE OF IRAQ'S ECONOMIC LOSSES

It will be recalled that the Iraqi decision to invade Kuwait was driven primarily by the desire of the regime to find a solution to the economy's deepening crisis. The economic crisis was a direct result of the bankrupting effects of the Iran–Iraq war. The economic destruction of the Gulf war was superimposed on an economy already reeling from the multiple shocks of a war ended less than two years earlier.

The economic destruction of 1991 took many forms. First was the destruction of nonmilitary and military assets. The extent of the massive destruction of or damage to the infrastructure and other sectors of the economy, as assessed by the United Nations, is referred to earlier.

The scope of the damage widened as the list of targets was constantly expanded in the course of the war. When Iraq invaded Kuwait, U.S. military planners were said to have designated 57 sites in Iraq as strategic targets. In the course of the war, the list was expanded to 700 targets in order amplify the economic and psychological impact of the U.N. sanctions.[44] It was also suggested that a number of targets were destroyed to increase Iraq's dependency on the West, especially the United States, after the war:

Some targets, especially late in the war, were bombed primarily to create post-war leverage over Iraq, not to influence the course of the conflict itself. Planners now say their intent was to destroy or damage valuable facilities that Baghdad could not repair without foreign assistance.[45]

The kind of bombing certain to increase Iraqi dependency was the obliteration of its power-generating plants, which cannot be restored without imported equipment.[46] A study by the United Nations placed replacement of Iraq's power-generating systems at $20 billion.[47]

As to the value of all the assets destroyed during the war, it was estimated to be $232 billion.[48] This replacement cost is several times the level of Iraq's GDP in 1989. In addition, one must calculate the value of lost output, the replacement cost of military equipment and related supplies, inflation-related losses, depreciation of the Iraqi dinar, and lost imports. Furthermore, one must also add the loss of export earnings (i.e., lost oil revenue).

Lost Output and the Multiplier Effect

The most obvious and readily measurable loss is that of lost oil revenue which, according to government estimate, amounted to $22 billion per year.[49] In 1989, Iraq's GDP was $55.3 billion. This means that Iraq lost nearly 40 percent of its GDP from this sector alone because of the sanctions. A reduction in oil revenue of this magnitude is bound to have a devastating impact on private consumption, public consumption, development spending, and private-sector investment.

The effects upon the economy of the embargo on imports are also severe. In an open economy like Iraq's, such an embargo affects not only the availability of consumer goods from foodstuff to luxury commodities but also the availability of inputs and capital goods essential for the functioning of all sectors of the economy. These shortages induce decline in output, on the one hand, and inflation, on the other.

Since the Iraqi economy is totally dependent on its foreign sector and since it is in no position to pull itself up by its own bootstraps, it is only logical to conclude that it will continue to suffer from stagnation and decline so long as the sanctions continue. In other words, the longer the sanctions are imposed the greater their potential impact as a result of the multiplier process. Thus, according to Al-Roubaie and ElAli, the impact of the sanctions will reduce Iraq's GDP by two-thirds in 1994 from its 1990 level.[50]

IMPACT ON PERSONAL INCOME, CONSUMPTION, AND COST OF LIVING

"When people get to the point where they start selling their property and their jewelry, we know, statistically, that they are approaching the famine stage," observed one U.N. expert in describing the conditions of the people in Iraq in August 1991. This should not be surprising in a country where the embargo had been in effect for a year, where inflation had reached a record figure of 2,000 percent, where wages had not risen for more than three years, and where the poorest – about 85 percent of the population – are hardest hit – their situation getting worse every day. The government rationing system provides only 55 percent of calorie requirements. Yet the embargo has barely affected the regime's top cadres, who – far from feeling the pinch – benefit hugely in one way or another from hefty profits in the private sector.[51]

A measure of the collapse of the Iraqi economy is the change in Iraq's per capita GDP, measured in 1980 prices, which rose from $1,745 in 1970 to $4,083 in 1980. By 1988, however, it had declined to $1,756, and by 1991, to $627 (see Table 8.1, p. 152). Indeed, one has to go back to the 1940s to find a comparable per capita GDP.

But per capita GDP data do not tell the full story of the decline in living standards since a major portion of GDP is devoted to military and similar forms of spending. The deteriorating living conditions of most Iraqis were captured by the findings of the International Study Team.[52] After having analyzed the behavior of prices, incomes, and employment for the year ending August 1991, the study team made these observations:

1. While there has been a shift in the distribution of employment from the formal to the informal sectors of the economy, monthly earnings remained stagnant.
2. Consumer prices during the same period increased considerably, especially the food price index which increased by 1,500 to 2,000 percent in that year.
3. Real monthly earnings, or the food purchasing power of private income, have declined by a factor of 15 or 20 or to 5 to 7 percent of their August 1990 level.
4. Real monthly earnings are lower than the benchmark used by the government before 1990 to identify "destitute households" eligible for government support.
5. These earnings are lower than the monthly earnings of unskilled agricultural workers in India – one of the poorest countries in the world.

The data in Table 6.1 (see p. 124) how the extent of poverty that can

Table 6.1
Estimates of Labor Earnings in Iraq, August 1991,
Compared with Various Benchmarks

	Estimate[1] (ID/month)	Index
Nominal monthly earnings, unskilled labor (public sector)	260	100
"Effective" monthly earnings, unskilled labor (public sector)	468	180
Monthly earnings of unskilled labor in India (in calorie-purchasing-power equivalent)	482	185
Value of the Indian poverty line in terms of "calorie-purchasing-power equivalence"	667	257
Value of the "destitution line", which the government of Iraq used before August 1990 to identify households eligible for social security payments[2]	835	321
Value of the average 1990 food basket	1,010	388
Value of pre-crisis real earnings of unskilled labor (public sector)[2]	4,022	1,547

Source: Jean Dreze and Haris Gazdar, "Income and Economic Survey," in International
   Study Team, *Health and Welfare in Iraq after the Gulf Crisis: An In-Depth Assessment*
   (October 1991).
1. All figures are in monthly terms for a household of six with two earning adults.
2. The lower estimate of the food price index has been used as deflator.

be attributed to the invasion of Kuwait, the Gulf war, and the economic
sanctions against Iraq.

More recent data given in Chapter 8 show that living conditions in
Iran have worsened since the sanctions remain in effect. Chapter 7,
however, is devoted to a general assessment of Iraq's development experience during the period 1950–90.

NOTES

1. John Townsend, "Economic and Political Implications of the War," in
Iran–Iraq War: An Historical Analysis, ed. M. S. El Azhary (New York: St.
Martin's Press, 1984), pp. 62–63.
2. See A. M. S. Ali and H. A. J. Ganabi, "Political Economy of Inflation in
Iraq 1988–1992," *Arab Economic Journal* (in Arabic) 1 (Autumn 1992): 99.
3. See Economist Intelligence Unit (EIU), *Economic Review of Iraq* 2
(1977): 8.
4. See EIU, *Economic Review of Iraq* 1 (1978): 9.
5. See Ali and Ganabi, "Political Economy of Inflation," p. 106.
6. See Keith Bradsher, "War Damages and Old Debts Could Exhaust
Iraq's Assets," *The New York Times,* March 1, 1991.
7. See EIU, *Economic Review of Iraq* 2 (1990): 13. It should be pointed out

that 1989 oil revenue was used since Iraq's flow of oil was stopped soon after its invasion of Kuwait in August 1990.

8. See "Iraq Outlines Dire Economic Prospects in Plea to the UN for Five-Year Moratorium on War Reparations," *Middle East Economic Survey (MEES)*, May 13, 1991, pp. D6–D9. Henceforth "Economic Prospects."

9. For a detailed discussion of Iraq's military industry, see Yezid Sayigh, *Arab Military Industry* (in Arabic) (Beirut: Centre for Arab Unity Studies, 1992), Chapter 8.

10. Ibid., p. 234.

11. Ibid., p. 266.

12. See Yousif M. Abdul-Rahman, "Trade with Iraq, An Emerging Market," *American-Arab Affairs* 28 (Spring 1989): 40.

13. See EIU, *Economic Review of Iraq* 1 (1988): 11. Another, but much smaller, project was the construction of an opera house in Baghdad at a cost of $161 million in public funds. See idem 4 (1989): 10.

14. Ibid. 1 (1990): 10–11.

15. Ibid. 2 (1990): 11–12.

16. General Accounting Office, *The Changing Structure of the International Oil Market* (Washington, 1982), pp. 49–50.

17. See OPEC, *OPEC Official Resolutions and Press Releases, 1960–1990* (Vienna, 1990), p. 250–254.

18. *MEES*, February 12, 1990, pp. 1–5.

19. Ibid.

20. For an articulation of Iraq's oil policy, see Ramzi Salman, "Iraq's Oil Policy," *MEES*, March 12, 1990, pp. D1–D6.

21. See "Documentation," pp. D1–D9.

22. Ibid.

23. See "OPEC lobbies overproducers," *Middle East Economic Digest (MEED)*, July 6, 1990, p. 9.

24. See "Documentation," p. D5. It is worth noting that Iraq's accusation that Kuwait was exploiting its economic difficulties to exact border concessions was supported by an official letter sent by Kuwait's director general of the state security department to Kuwait's minister of interior on the former's visit to the CIA: "We agreed with the American side that it was important to take advantage of the deteriorating economic situation in Iraq to put pressure on that country's government to delineate our common border. The Central Intelligence Agency gave its view of the appropriate means of pressure, saying that broad cooperation should be initiated between us, on condition that such activities are coordinated at high level." See Pierre Salinger and Eric Laurent, *Secret Dossier: The Hidden Agenda behind the Gulf War* (London: Penguin Books, 1991), pp. 239–241.

25. See "Documentation," p. D6.

26. See "Documentation."

27. See *OPEC Bulletin*, September 1990, p. 7.

28. Ibid., p. 8.

29. See Youssef M. Ibrahim, "OPEC Members Close to Raising Ouput Ceiling," *The New York Times*, August 28, 1990.

30. For a good study of the historical background of relations between the two countries, as well as a good survey of the factors that led to the invasion,

see Dilip Hiro, *Desert Shield to Desert Storm: The Second Gulf War* (New York: Routledge, 1992), Part I.

31. See "Iraq: Dreams and Figures," *Tariq al-Shaab,* October 1990, p. 5.

32. See *The New York Times,* December 6, 1990, p. A16.

33. See *MEED,* August 30, 1991, p. 22.

34. See *Report to the Secretary-General on Humanitarian Needs in Kuwait and Iraq in the Immediate Post-Crisis Environment by a Mission to the Area Led by Mr. Matti Ahtisaari, Under Secretary-General for Administration and Management,* dated 20 March 1991, p. 5.

35. An explanation for this wide range in military losses may be the overestimate by the United States of the size of Iraq's army in Kuwait on the eve of the ground war. For such estimates, see U.S. House Armed Services Committee, *A Defense for a New Era: Lessons of the Persian Gulf War* (Washington, 1992), pp. 29–33.

36. See Hiro, *Desert Shield to Desert Storm,* p. 396.

37. See Caryle Murphy, "Iraqi Death Toll Remains Clouded," *The Washington Post,* June 23, 1991; and Ruth Sinai, "Greenpeace says 200,000 dies in war," *The Burlington Free Press,* May 30, 1990. A source in the U.S. Census Bureau calculated that as of the end of 1991, 86,194 men, 39,612 women, and 32,195 children died either at the hands of the American-led coalition forces, during the domestic rebellions that followed, or from postwar deprivation. See *Inquiry,* March/April 1992, p. 15.

38. Judith Miller, "Displaced in the Gulf War: 5 Million Refugees," *The New York Times,* June 16, 1991.

39. See Joost R. Hilterman, "Diverting Water, Displacing Iraq's Marsh People," *Middle East Report* 181 (March/April 1993): 36.

40. Harvard Study Team Report, "Public Health in Iraq after the Gulf War," May 1991, p. 1.

41. Carl Haub, "A Demographic Disaster," *Manchester Guardian Weekly,* March 10, 1991.

42. See Francoise Chipaux, "Embargo on Iraq Hits the Wrong Targets," *Manchester Guardian Weekly,* February 21, 1993, p. 22.

43. *MEES,* April 12, 1993, p. A7.

44. Barton Gellman, "Allied Air War Struck Broadly in Iraq: Officials Acknowledge Strategy Went Beyond Purely Military Targets," *The Washington Post,* June 23, 1991.

45. Ibid.

46. See Harvard Study Team Report, Table 6.

47. *MEES,* July 29, 1991, p. D6.

48. See Arab Monetary Fund et al., *Joint Arab Economic Report,* 1992, p. 18.

49. See *Tariq al-Shaab* (in Arabic), January 1993, p. 4.

50. See Amer Al-Roubaie and Wajih ElAli, "The Impact of Economic Sanctions against Iraq," paper presented at the annual meeting of the Middle East Economic Association, Anaheim, Calif., January 1993, p. 15.

51. See Françoise Chipaux, "Saddam Sits Pretty as Iraqi People Suffer," *Manchester Guardian Weekly,* August 11, 1991, p. 13.

52. See Jean Dreze and Haris Gazdar, "Income and Economic Survey," in International Study Team, "Health and Welfare in Iraq after the Gulf Crisis: An In-Depth Assessment," October 1991, pp. 10–32.

CHAPTER 7

Iraq's Economic Development, 1950–1990: An Assessment

Iraq's development experience, its nature, successes, and failures, cannot be separated, of course, from the contextual dimensions – historical, international, regional, ideological, political, social, economic, and above all oil – in which the experience occurred. Iraq's development experience in the narrow sense of the term (i.e., allocation of funds by the state for investment purposes) was and still is the dependent variable determined by the interplay of the contextual forces. Some of these contextual forces are briefly reviewed in the following paragraphs before the assessment of Iraq's development is undertaken.

EVOLUTION OF THE NEW STATE

Iraq, a colony of the Ottoman empire since 1638, was invaded in 1914 by British forces soon after the Turks entered World War I on the side of the Axis. After securing the southern province of Basra, the British drove north toward Baghdad, which they entered in March 1918. In the meantime, in 1916 the Arabs rose in revolt against the Ottomans on the strength of a British government pledge that they would have national independence if they revolted against the Turks. But the British had no intention of honoring their promise, since they had already entered into another agreement with the French to divide up the Arab world once the war was concluded.

The unfulfilled British pledge, combined with outright foreign occupation following the collapse of the old Ottoman order, led to the Iraqi rebellion in June 1920 against the British, who were forced to bring enforcements from England, Iran, and India. The uprising, which was finally put down in February 1921, was soon followed by a new British political project for the country. The new plan, put into effect in August, entailed the coronation of Faisal as king and the formation of an Iraqi cabinet. The new regime was a mere facade for the British who became the mandatory power. The mandatory power was charged by the League of Nations with the responsibility of bringing the new state to the stage of political independence and admittance to the league. While the symbols of power were transferred to the new state, the exercise of power remained in British hands. As William Stivers observed:

Increasingly, the Iraqis were forced to pay the costs of protecting Britain's strategic and economic interests. Given that the king and his ministers were obliged to take the advice of British officials, whose agents colonized the Iraqi administration, Britain effectively controlled an entire civil service financed by the Iraqi taxpayer. Iraq supported an army that could not act unless the British high commissioner concurred.[1]

When Iraq was admitted to the League of Nations in 1932, Britain's position of control was forged in the provisions of a twenty-five-year treaty that obliged Iraq to grant Britain the right to maintain air bases and garrisons to protect them. Moreover, the Iraqi government committed itself to asking for a British military mission to strengthen Iraqi armed forces. It also declared that when in need of foreign administrators it would employ British subjects selected after consulting Britain. These treaty-bound controls prompted Stiver to conclude that

In this fashion was erected a structure of informal controls, grounded in significant measure on a class of local *compradores* who had been raised to their positions of authority under British tutelage, who had remained there behind the shield of British arms, and who were tied to Britain by reason of training and connections, not to speak of common interests and mutual dependency. Having receded into the background, the British were less of a target for nationalist malcontents.[2]

Following his death in 1933, Faisal was succeeded by his son Ghazi who reigned until his death in 1939. During Ghazi's reign, the country suffered from several coups, tribal rebellions and military expeditions to suppress them, frequent cabinet changes, and disruptive and exhausting alliances between politicians and tribal leaders.

Between 1939 and 1953, Prince Abdel-Ilah ruled as regent during the minority of Faisal II. The two men were killed in the course of the July 14, 1958, revolution which ended the era of the British-installed monarchy. The 1939–58 period had its share of coups, uprisings, and rebellions.

One of the most serious eruptions took place in 1941 when certain pan-Arab army officers mounted a coup and installed a veteran politician, Rasheed Ali el-Gailani, as prime minister. The independent course the new government wanted to pursue in its relations with Germany and England forced the regent, who had identified himself with the British in World War II, to escape to a British military base. This was followed by the Thirty-Day war of 1941 in which British force was used to defeat the Iraqi army and reimpose the rule of the regent. In order to preempt another coup, the crown decided to link its fortunes more and more to those of the English and the tribal sheikhs. In other words, the crown developed a vested interest in the continuance of the tribal order and the English connection.[3]

This identification of interests had the effect of alienating most of the political class, as well as the rising and now more educated, more politically aware, and more skilled urban population. This alienation contributed in no small measure to the series of fierce urban mass uprisings of 1948, 1952, and 1956.[4] Within two years of the last uprising the monarchy was toppled in July 1958 and replaced by a republican form of government.

In the less than five years it survived, the republican regime was faced with a number of severe problems and challenges. These included an open split among the military leaders, an open rebellion by a segment of the armed forces, an assassination attempt on the regime's strong man, Abdel Karim Qasim, an open political feud with Nasser of Egypt and his followers in Iraq, a rebellion by the Kurds in the northern part of the country, a falling out with the regime's political supporters, the drift toward erratic and authoritarian rule, unsettled dispute with the oil companies, and a general drift toward stagnation. By 1963, the political power base of the regime was so weakened that its overthrow was accomplished in February 1963, when Qasim was immediately executed by the new rulers.

The military-Baath alliance that succeeded the Qasim regime of 1958–63 and ruthlessly suppressed Qasim's political supporters fell into a quagmire of chaos, arbitrariness, and disintegration that prompted the military wing of the alliance to oust its civilian counterpart in November 1963. The head of the regime, Abdel Salam Aref, who perished in a helicopter accident in 1966, was succeeded as president by his brother, whose regime was toppled in July 1968 by yet another coup organized by another military-Baath alliance. This time it was the civilians who eventually succeeded in bringing the military under their firm control.

Between 1968, when the Baath seized power, and 1979, when Saddam Hussein became president, the Baath succeeded in consolidating its power through a mixture of rewards, coercion, and unprecedented use of internal security methods. The ruling group managed to stave off all attempts to unseat it and stamp out any political opposition from within or without the party. Rebellions were ruthlessly suppressed, and whole communities were deported or relocated in different parts of the country. Another factor that enabled the Baath to remain in power was its success in ending the festering dispute with the oil companies by nationalizing them and the phenomenal rise in oil revenue in the 1970s.

Beginning in 1979, the ruling group under Saddam became preoccupied with its own survival. First, Saddam ruthlessly purged a major segment of the political leadership only weeks after he assumed the presidency. A year later, he took the country into the destructive eight years of war with Iran which ended in 1988. Two years after the end of the war, he gambled with the fortunes of the country when he invaded Kuwait in August 1990. This invasion provoked the imposition economic sanctions against Iraq and was followed by the Gulf war of 1991 which inflicted enormous destruction on the people and the economy and provoked sanctions that are still in effect.

From this brief review of Iraq's political history, several observations can be made. One of the most important features of this history since Iraq emerged as a modern state in 1921 is the predominant position of Britain in the affairs of Iraq during the first thirty-seven years of its history. Such position of control had the effect of shaping the country's political, social, and economic development.

Second, the country's political history can be rewritten as an endless series of coups and countercoups; conspiracies; purges and counterpurges; violent seizures of power; ruthless suppression of dissent; and wars, adventures, and sanctions. In all this history, the people had no voice – there has been a virtual absence of democratic institutions and political parties.

Third, changes in political leadership and personalities entailed changes in priorities, direction, and policies. While well-thought-out or planned changes are necessary and beneficial for development, the changes in Iraq were so frequent and sudden as to negate the benefits of planning. This is particularly true in a country where civil institutions have neither matured nor been insulated from political upheavals. In a country where one man or very few men hold the power to make monumental decisions, men of lesser stature think twice before taking any initiative on their own. Frequent changes in leaders and cabinets led inevitably to prolonged delays in plan formulation, adoption, and execution. Moreover, these changes tended to weaken follow-up and accountability systems – to the extent that such systems actually existed.

REGIONAL AND INTERNATIONAL CONTEXT

Iraq became a battlefield between World War I combatants even before it became a state in 1921, albeit under Britain's control. The state remained under such control under one guise or another for the next thirty-seven years, when the era of the monarchy was ended in 1958. Aside from the demands and the costs of being an appendage of British imperialism, the state had to cope with regional and international issues that threatened stability, siphoned off resources, and delayed economic development.

The most important issue in the Middle East was the partition of Palestine and the creation of the state of Israel in 1948. The Palestine question, which still has not been resolved, meant that the investment of military, political, and economic resources by Iraq and other Arab states in the region was inevitable. At another level, the Palestine question was transformed into the Arab–Israeli conflict, which manifested itself in the war of 1948, the French–British–Israeli invasion of Egypt in 1956, the 1967 June war, the 1973 October war, and the 1982 Israeli invasion of Lebanon. In all these wars, Iraq played a role, either directly or indirectly.

Another regional issue that has affected Iraq since its inception in 1921 was the demarcation of the Iraq–Iran border, especially in the area of Shat al-Arab. This particular dispute plagued the two countries for two centuries – long before Iraq became a state. It was finally settled in 1975 when the two governments signed the Algiers accords, which were abrogated by the government of Iraq when it invaded Iran in 1980.

There are other regional disputes, one with Kuwait over border demarcation; and others with Syria and Turkey involving the division of the waters of the Tigris and Euphrates rivers.

An important regional dimension that impinged directly on Iraq's political system and therefore on economic development was the question of Arab nationalism and pan-Arabism. It can be said that between 1921, when the state was created, and 1945, when the League of Arab States was established, economic policies of Iraq and other Arab countries lacked a pan-Arab dimension. Arab states were either still under outright colonial rule and foreign domination or in the early stages of political and economic formation. Between 1945 and 1993, Iraq's pan-Arab economic policies found their expression in the activities of the Arab League and its specialized agencies. Although several ambitious projects were approved, none was implemented with any lasting degree of success.[5]

The weakness of the Arab League system was structural, and it revolved around the prerogatives of the single state. The central premise of a multilateral organization is the willingness of member states to give up some of their national prerogatives for the perceived benefit of the group. Yet the charter of the league failed to provide for punitive actions against noncomplying states. Moreover, the charter made implementation of ratified agreements subject to a member state's goodwill or its perception of its interests.

While Iraq's political regimes in the period prior to 1963 paid lip serv-ice to the lofty goals of pan-Arabism, economic and political unity was not among their immediate policy objectives. This was in contrast to the post-1963 regimes, which professed adherence to the goal of Arab unity. The economic dimension of pan-Arabism was expressed as one of the goals of the 1965–69 five-year plan. Similarly, the 1970–74 na-tional development plan spoke of the importance of Arab economic integration. Yet neither the five-year plan nor the national development plan nor, for that matter, any other plan made any serious attempt toward Arab economic unity.[6]

While the broad regional context exemplified by Iraq's membership in the Arab League or the rhetoric of Arab nationalism and pan-Arabism exerted little impact, if any, on the country's economic development, the same cannot be said about other regional issues. Longstanding dis-putes with Iran gave rise to the buildup of the military and the diver-sion of resources from the civilian economy. The dispute with Iran took a violent turn in 1980 with the eight-year war. The impact of this regional conflict on the economy of Iraq and its development effort was immense. Not only was the war fought at a very high human and economic cost, but Iraq's booming economic development came to a standstill during most of the 1980s.

The other regional dispute that had the most severe impact on the economy, living conditions, and prospects for recovery was Iraq's inva-sion of Kuwait. The ensuing economic sanctions, which are still in effect, together with the effects of the Gulf war had a devastating im-pact on the economy, as is shown in the previous chapter.

Beyond the regional context, Iraq's development policies were un-doubtedly affected by the evolving international context in the Middle East. From the time when the state was created in 1921 to the 1958 revolution, Iraq's economic policies were influenced by England. The mandatory position that Britain had over Iraq, the treaty obligations that tied Iraq to England, the identification of the political class with British interest, Iraq's membership in the sterling area, Iraq's pattern of foreign trade, and the role of oil in its economy were among the forces that cast Iraq into a dependency relationship with Britain. Eco-nomic development policies and emphases during this period were focused primarily on infrastructural projects, leaving the performance of commodity and service producing sectors to market forces.

Following the 1958 revolution, there occurred a series of major changes in Iraq's foreign and economic policies. It is important to stress that the 1958 revolution was a middle-class-led nationalist movement that had the support of all political parties. Thus, soon after the new repub-lican regime was installed, it decided as an assertion of its independence to withdraw from the sterling area, to leave the Western dominated military alliance Baghdad Pact, to open up diplomatic and economic relations with the Soviet Union and the East European countries, to enact agrarian reform, to expand social services, to nationalize over 99 percent of all the oil concession areas, to prepare the groundwork for a national oil industry, and to expand the role of the public sector in the economy. These changes initiated by the Qasim regime continued to provide the policy framework for all the regimes for most of the next three decades.

IDEOLOGICAL DIMENSIONS

It should be clear by now that the 1958 revolution constituted a break in the ideological underpinning of Iraq's economic policies. Prior to 1958, there was some form of tripartite alliance between the land-owning classes as represented by the tribal chiefs, the crown, and the political class. Behind this domestic alliance was the imperial presence of England in the form of military bases, treaty alliance, oil interests, and civil and military advisers. The role of Britain was demonstrated forcefully in the Thirty-Day war of 1941 when the regent fled but Britain succeeded in reimposing his rule on the country.

The economic orientation of the era of monarchy (i.e., the successive governments that came to power between 1921 and 1958) was, broadly speaking, laissez faire. In the early part of the period, most of the national output was generated in the agricultural sector. By the same token, most of the population worked and lived in rural Iraq. Most manufacturing was of the cottage-industry variety. As time went on, especially in the Depression and the war years of the 1930s and the 1940s, local industrial output found a receptive domestic market. The growth of import substitution industries was rather modest; by the end of the 1940s, only 2,000 people were employed in modern industrial plants.[7]

Although the 1950s witnessed the activities of the newly established Development Board, as well as a substantial growth in Iraq's oil export and revenue, there is no evidence to indicate that the political system was interested in changing the characteristics or structure of the economy. Development policy tended to strengthen the economic status quo because its benefits tended to flow to landowners instead of peasants and urban workers.

The political and economic orientation of 1921–58 was rejected by the 1958 republican regime. This rejection was based on the assertion that the Iraqi economy prior to 1958 was distorted in favor of imperial and feudal interests because the economy had been allowed to grow with the most important sector, oil, at the mercy of foreign oil firms. Moreover, the sheltered status of the foreign-dominated oil sector had permitted it to become a mere financier of feudalism and of the reactionary classes which, in turn, served and perpetuated foreign interests in Iraq at the expense of the majority of the people. The dualism of the economy – reflected in a modern oil sector coupled with a backward agricultural sector and weak industry – was responsible both for the low level of national income and for its maldistribution, as well as the impoverishment of the masses. Although conditions of poverty could have been ameliorated, the policies of the Development Board had served the interests of the large landowners. Moreover, development spending should have encouraged the emergence of market conditions conducive to the rise of a national bourgeoisie; but such evolution failed to occur because a pliant Iraqi government preferred to increase imports rather than domestic output, thus recycling oil revenue to the benefit of foreign exporters and contractors.[8]

In short, the new regime concluded that in order to ease the tension between the ruling elite and the people, it had been decided to increase Iraq's oil revenue, on the one hand, and waste such increase in revenue, on the other. In order to accomplish this task, the Development Board had been created to spend the oil revenue on nonproductive projects for the benefit of the few. The presence of foreign nationals as voting members of the Development Board – supported by a large number of foreign consultants, engineers, and technicians – ensured that the Iraqi economy would remain in state of stagnation and backwardness.[9]

To reorient the economy and change the number and the composition of development beneficiaries, the new regime took it upon itself to change the objectives and policies of development. These changes tended to favor public-sector industrial investment, provide more protection to local industry, enact agrarian reform, and increase welfare programs and social services. It is worth noting that in spite of the revolutionary rhetoric of the new regime its policies tended to encourage the private sector, either through land distribution – in the case of the agricultural sector – or by extending incentives and protection to industry.

While Qasim's regime represented a major break with past economic and development policies and had clear and definite views about steering the country and the economy in a different direction, the leaders of the February 1963 coup that overthrew Qasim had no program or policy. As the political leader of the coup and his associates put it: We got lost in the government, and they admitted that their February coup had the characteristic of a leap into the unknown. The problem, however, was much deeper than just being overwhelmed by the affairs of the state. The problem was one of intellectual vacuum and aridity of thought. In his analysis of the period, Batatu observed that one of the reasons for this problem was that the writings of the Baath's leading intellectual, Michel Aflaq, not only were too general and too ill defined but also contained much that was reminiscent of the products of the old romantic mills of Europe and little that was the result of disciplined thinking upon the living Arab situation. And a Baathi would have looked in vain through the whole literature of his party for a single objective analysis of any of the serious problems besetting Iraq. Poorly nourished on the intellectual side, they put too much trust in naked repression.[10]

Naked repression, the struggle for power, and personal rivalries led to the in November 1963 coup when the military wing of the government decided to oust their civilian partners. The new leaders, who remained in power until July 1968 and who were in sympathy with the policies of Nasser's Egypt, decided to implement in Iraq some of the economic policies of the Nasser regime. The most significant change in the economy which the 1963-68 regime introduced in Iraq in 1964 was the sudden nationalization of a major segment of the private sector.

In July 1964, the government issued a number of decrees transferring to public-sector ownership thirty industrial and trading firms and all commercial banks and insurance companies. In addition to transferring ownership to the public sector, these decrees – which the government called "socialist laws" – established the principle of employee representation on the boards of directors of the nationalized companies, as well as the principle of profit sharing, by earmarking 25 percent of each company's profits for its employees. To oversee and manage the newly acquired public-sector enterprises, an economic organization attached to the office of the prime minister was established. The administration of this body was entrusted to a board of directors composed of a chief executive officer, several cabinet ministers, the governor of the central bank, and representatives from each of the nationalized economic sectors: trade, industry, and insurance. A separate organization was created to manage the nationalized commercial banks.[11]

According to the government, the justifications for the enactment of the nationalization measures included social justice; the drawing of clear lines of demarcation between the private and public sectors; exorbitant private-sector profits at the expense of consumers; and the emergence of a social class with controlling power over banking, insurance, trade, and industry – accompanied by rising economic, social, and political influence. The primary force behind these measures, however, was political – the government wanted to create a degree of economic, social, and political symmetry with Egypt to lay the grounds for political unity between the two countries.[12]

Although the 1964 measures increased the scope of the public sector in the economy, the share of the private sector continued to be predominant. This division in favor of the private sector changed when the Baath party seized power in July 1968.

When the Baath came to power, it proclaimed that its ultimate goal was to establish a socialist economy. In the meantime, the Baath party announced that in the transition it would implement the following measures: expansion of public-sector role in agriculture at the expense of the private sector, total control over foreign trade, central government control over domestic trade, strengthening of the role of public sector in industry, and managing of social services according to the requirements of transition to socialism.[13]

During the 1970s, the government was successful in translating its ideological pronouncements into economic policies, especially after the nationalization of the oil industry. By the middle of the 1980s, the government had almost total control over both manufacturing industry and foreign and domestic trade. The public sector, in other words, displaced the private sector as the predominant sector in the economy.[14] There were exceptions to these conclusions, however. First, the construction sector in general, but especially home building, remained in the hands of the private sector. Second, the government, as early as the middle of the 1970s, began to scale down its involvement in agriculture by allowing much wider scope to the private sector. Third, in the second half of the 1980s, the government formally reversed its position on the private sector and decided to expand its role through its enactment of the privatization measures discussed in Chapter 5.

AN ASSESSMENT OF IRAQ'S DEVELOPMENT,
1950-1990

In a lecture sponsored by the Iraqi Economists'Association in 1960, the noted Iraqi economist Mohammad Salman Hasan observed that the July 1958 revolution had two major interconnected tasks: guarding the country's political independence and achieving economic liberation. His theme was that the two goals are mutually reinforcing in that political independence will be compromised so long as conditions remain that give rise to economic dependence. An important dimension of dependence was the controlling force of foreign investment over the national economy. Given this condition, any national economic policy must, above all else, free the economy from the control wielded by foreign capital. This was a necessary step to rid the economy of its dependency status in order to build it on strong national foundations and thus achieve rapid and balanced growth and development, raise the living standard of the people, and become the true guardian of national independence.

Hasan went on to list five aspects of dependence including the dominant position of the foreign-controlled oil sector in the Iraqi economy; the scant industrial output and concomitant need for industrialization; the semifeudal nature of the land tenure and need for accelerated implementation of agrarian reform; the perennial foreign trade deficit and need to protect domestic industry; and the dependence of the monetary, banking, and financial system and need to achieve its independence. The apparent economic chaos and the visible contrast between Iraq's rich resource endowment and the poor performance of the economy or the contradiction between the wealth of the country and the poverty of its people, Hasan concluded, are the direct outcome of dependency. It is imperative, therefore, that in order to solve these problems economic development must be pursued according to a national development plan that would rid the economy and the people of these contradictions.[15] With certain important exceptions, this analysis, as well as the policy recommendations, provided the framework for Iraq's development policy for most of the period under consideration.

One important exception was the development policy of the pre-1958 regime, which was carried out under the guidance of the Development Board. Another exception was the change in policy direction under the Baath after the middle of the 1980s.

It will be recalled that the development policies in the period 1950–58 tended to neglect industry and agriculture but concentrate on infrastructure and water-control and irrigation projects. With the land-tenure system as it was prior to the 1958 agrarian reform, the benefits of development spending were captured by the upper stratum of the landowning class. The degree of land concentration is revealed in data on land holdings compiled in 1957. Thus out of total land area of 8 million hectares (ha) some .356 million ha, 4.43 percent of the total area, was held by eight owners. And the top 33 owners controlled .758 million ha, 9.8 percent of the total area. At the bottom of the landownership scale we find 162,000 individuals with total ownership of .293 million ha, 3.67 percent of the total area. Further scrutiny of the data shows that 1.7 percent of all owners had 63.1 percent of the area while nearly 84 percent of owners had 15.3 of the land.[16]

This grim picture of land concentration at one end of the scale and minute holdings at the other was made even worse by the plight of the share tenant's situation, which was one of grinding poverty, exploitation, helplessness, and oppression. The tenants or fellahin or laborers not only received a very small portion of the product, ranging beteeen one-fifth and one-fourth, for their labor but were also required to perform other tasks without compensation. This pattern of relationship had the backing of a 1933 law which provided that no laborer could leave the land if he was in debt to the landowner. Since these fellahin were in perpetual indebtedness, they were in effect serfs. These conditions led Warriner to conclude that the main cause of rural misery was that the landowner took most of what the land produces.[17]

With this system of landownership fostered and supported by the state, it was only logical that the benefits of development would flow disproportionately to a small minority of landowners. There was really no escaping this outcome, given the nature of the political system, which was basically a tripod with the crown, the landowners, and the political class as its legs. It is not surprising, therefore, that as one of its first measures the 1958 revolution introduced a change in the land tenure system that put an end to the pattern of relationships responsible for much of the backwardness and poverty in rural Iraq. But the destruction of the pre-1958 landownership system was not a sufficient condition for the process of development to succeed. Land reform was, as indicated earlier, one of several necessary conditions for an independent and growing national economy.

Having disposed of the monarchy, completed the process of political independence, and severed many of the links that had been imposed by Britain, Iraq's new nationalist managers set on the course of development that now must be assessed. Because of the war conditions and their aftermath that have engulfed the country since 1980, the period 1958–93 is divided into two subperiods, 1958–80 and 1981–93.

One of the most outstanding features of the period from 1958, when the republican regime was established, to 1980, when Saddam Hussein took the country to war with Iran, is that the general outline of development — its rhetoric, its framework, its objectives, its sectoral allocations, its total and sectoral performance, its problems, and its utter dependence on oil — remained more or less the same. Although several plans and several regimes and many cabinets and changes characterized the period, the variations did not amount to what successive governments claimed to be revolutionary changes. To be sure, there were different emphases at different times reflecting each regime's political and economic priorities; but by and large the Qasim regime set the tone and the objectives of development for the period under analysis. Even in those instances when this or that regime seemed to have deviated from Qasim's centrist position with respect to the relative importance of the public and the private sector vis-à-vis one another (such as the nationalization measures of 1964 or the attempt to force collective farming or allowing the public sector to overwhelm the private sector), there were always forces at work that ultimately led to or forced a change toward the center. By the same token, when the deviation from the centrist position was found to have gone too far in favor of the private sector, the political authorities found it advisable to steer toward the center again.

It can even be argued that the nationalization of IPC in 1972 had actually started under Qasim back in 1961 when his regime enacted the celebrated Law No. 80 which nationalized nearly 99.5 percent of the areas covered by concession agreements with the oil companies. Another fact that helped the government in its drive to nationalization was the decision by OPEC that oil companies should accept the principle of equity participation by governments in oil concession in their countries, a principle that was accepted by the oil companies in 1971.[18] But there was one major exception, however. That exception relates to the level of oil revenue in the 1970s.

The regime of the Baath had the distinct advantage over all previous regimes that its rule reaped the benefits of regional and international changing conditions – OPEC and the 1971 Tehran oil price agreement, the October 1973 Arab-Israeli war, the transformation of the world oil market from a buyer's to a seller's market – which led to sharp increase in oil revenue and in turn removed constraints on government spending.

DEVELOPMENT PROBLEMS, 1958–1980

In this section two separate but interrelated problems are discussed: implications of political instability for the administration of development and the gap between development goals and achievements.

The Changing Machinery of Development

One of the problems that plagued development in Iraq was the frequent changes of regimes, cabinets, and development machineries.

The original Development Board was empowered with the twin task of drawing its own plans for development and implementing them. To discharge its tasks, oil revenue was earmarked to its budget, which exceeded that of the state. The law that provided for the board's independent status made it an enclave within the economy and the government structure. To curb some of the board's power, a ministry of development was created as a link with the council of ministers. Its technical departments in the areas of irrigation, industry, agriculture, transport, and housing were supposed to work with corresponding government ministries. The board, however, continued to have its independent status, budget, and control over the execution of all major projects.[19]

The 1958 revolutionary regime abolished the board and the ministry of development and replaced them with a planning board composed of cabinet ministers and a Ministry of Planning. A major change in the functions of the new machinery was the separation of planning from implementation. While the planning board and the Ministry of Planning continued to draw up plans, the execution of these plans was distributed among the various ministries. As a consequence of this major functional change, the technical divisions of the Ministry of Planning were transferred to the sectoral ministries. Another major change was the reduction of the share of development budget to 50 percent of oil revenue.

The pendulum swung again in 1964 when the post-Qasim regime decided to give the planning board new and expanded roles in the management of the economy by entrusting to it the formulation of economic, fiscal, monetary, and commercial policies needed for the implementation of the plan. It was empowered also to supervise the preparation of the annual ordinary budget in conformity with the requirements of the plan. The 1964 changes also included the creation of a steering committee to which the board delegated some of its responsibilities.[20] The new powers of the board were so sweeping and so broad that they had no parallel in Iraq's economic and political history. Had the board exercised or been allowed to exercise its newly acquired powers, the entire course of Iraq's economic development could have been entirely different. Although more changes in the planning machinery were introduced during the balance of the 1960s, they were minor.

In 1970, the Baath regime introduced a significant change that expanded the range of the steering committee's functions to the extent that the responsibilities for planning and execution were distributed at three levels: the higher level, or the planning board; the middle level, or the steering committee; and the lower level, or the executing ministries.

One of the more significant changes the Baath introduced was the creation in 1971, under the chairmanship of Saddam Hussein, of the Follow Up Committee. Ostensibly the committee was to negotiate economic agreements with foreign countries and follow up their implementation. Yet it was given considerable power over the development of the oil sector, which had become the cornerstone of Iraq's development strategy. Yet the decisions of the committee, given its political makeup, superseded decisions by the planning board or cabinet ministries.

Another change in the planning machinery introduced by the Baath in 1976 was intended to politicize the planning board by expanding its membership to include high-ranking Baath figures. This process of politization was boosted when Suddam Hussein, then deputy chairman of the Revolutionary Command Council, was appointed chairman of the planning board.[21]

These changes tended to affect the pace of planning and implementation. The decision of the post-1958 regime to combine the legislative and the executive powers in one institution, the council of ministers, meant that whatever stability, continuity, and independence the planning process may have had was destroyed.

Moreover, in a country like Iraq, where development has consistently suffered from shortages of professionals, skilled personnel, and semi-skilled workers, especially in the technical and industrial fields, frequent changes in regimes and administrative machineries deprived the development process of the continuity and stability of trained cadres. This is so because political changes, especially when the changes were violent, placed the continuity of employment of personnel, as well as implementation of projects, in jeopardy. Political purges, forced early retirement, and layoffs were not confined to the bureaucracy's upper rungs but affected project managers, engineers, economists, and many others.

An indicator of the instability that tended to affect planning and implementation adversely was the fact that between 1964 and 1968 Iraq had six ministers of planning. There were also frequent changes in the ministries entrusted with the implementation of the plan. Thus there were eight ministers of industry, eight ministers of transport, seven ministers of public works, and six ministers of agrarian reform.[22]

Ironically, these political changes, while resulting in plan coverage and emphasis to suit the declared policies of the regime in power, in many cases made it necessary to retrieve projects that had been dropped or resume work (at a later period and a much higher cost) on projects that had been stopped. Such projects included irrigation projects, highway construction projects, and industrial plants. A case in point was the sulphur recovery plant at Kirkuk, which was approved in 1956. The documents for its implementation, at a cost of ID 6.8 million, were to be signed in July 1958. The new regime decided to cancel the project. But the 1965 regime decided to go ahead with the project at a cost of ID 8.6 million. The plant started production in 1968, ten years from the time when the contract was about to be signed.[23]

The Gap between Development Allocations and Spending

One of the common and striking features of Iraq's economic development over the thirty-year period 1950–80 is the failure of planners and implementers to spend the funds allocated in development plans and programs. This is true whether one speaks of the market-oriented regime under the monarchy, the centrist regime of the Qasim period, or the Baath regime, which strongly advocated a public-sector-dominated economy. This observation applies also to all sectors of the plan. It is true, of course, that there were variations in performance or in expenditure efficiency or the ratio of actual spending to allocation from year to year or from sector to sector; but at no time did one plan or one program complete its term without a surplus, as can be seen from the data in Table 7.1.

Before we address the question of the relatively low level of expenditure efficiency, a word of caution about the data is in order. While planned expenditures for the entire period and actual expenditures up to 1975 are government-published data, expenditures for the period 1976–80 are author's estimates. It was assumed that the ratio of actual to planned expenditures in this period was the same as the long-term ratio of 1951–75. With this qualification in mind, the data show that in

Table 7.1
Planned and Actual Development Expenditures, 1951–1980 (ID Millions)

	Planned Expenditure	Actual Expenditure	Actual to Planned Expenditure (Percentage)
Agriculture			
1951–1975	1019	488	48
1976–1980	2158	1036	48
Subtotal	3177	1524	48
Industry			
1951–1975	1232	805	66
1976–1980	4490	2963	66
Subtotal	5727	3768	66
Transportation and Communication			
1951–1975	777	526	68
1976–1980	2318	1576	68
Subtotal	3095	2102	68
Buildings and Service			
1951–1975	910	566	62
1976–1980	2458	1524	62
Subtotal	3368	2090	62
Other			
1951–1975	802	667	83
1976–1980	4312	3579	83
Subtotal	5114	4246	83
Total			
1951–1975	4740	3052	64
1976–1980	15737	10072	64
Grand Total			
1951–1980	20476	13128	64

Source: Annual Abstracts of Statistics, various issues, Tables 2-2, 3-1, 3-2, and 3-3.

the first twenty-five years of its development history Iraq planned to spend ID 4.7 billion but actually spent ID 3.1 billion, 64 percent of what was appropriated. Since Iraq's GNP during the same period amounted to ID 22.6 billion, development spending was 13.7 percent of GNP. In the 1976–80 period, the government planned to spend ID 15.7 billion but actually spent 10.1 billion, 23.7 percent of the period's GNP. Taking the entire period 1951–80, we find that Iraq appropriated ID 20.5 billion but actually spent ID 13.1 billion, 20 percent of GNP.

There are several reasons for the failure of the various planning mechanisms and administration to spend their allocations and their consequent failure to achieve the professed goals of economic independence and sustained economic growth.

One of the most serious flaws of Iraq's development strategy since the inception of the Development Board was that it was driven by the level of oil revenue. Regardless of the nature of the political regime – its orientation, its proclaimed philosophy or rhetoric – development was in reality a function of oil revenue. In other words, there was an absence of articulation of what development ought to be in a country like Iraq, which sectors should be promoted, who should benefit from development, what role oil should play in the development process, what linkages should be forged between development plans, on the one hand, and the rest of the economy, on the other.

The picture that emerges is one that called for accelerated growth in the oil sector and the utilization of the oil income to develop the nonoil sectors of the economy. While the first goal was to a considerable extent accomplished, thanks to a combination of a number of factors (including a series of economic and political policy decisions, foreign assistance – especially from the Soviet Union, the influence of OPEC, and the changing nature of the international oil market), the second goal was far from being attained.

What successive governments should have done was establish firm goals, no matter how modest they might have been, for the economy then appropriate funds to attain them. The frequency of changing plans or changing allocations within plans in response to changes in oil revenue indicates a serious lack of understanding of what economic development and planning are all about. While early planners may be forgiven because they were sailing in unknown waters, the same cannot be said about those who followed them and who had the distinct advantage of being able to learn from the trials and errors of their predecessors, of being in a position to benefit from Iraq's cumulative experience and from the experiences of other countries.

The ability to articulate and adhere to a set of economic objectives would have meant also that planning agencies would be able to accumulate the accrued surpluses for use in future years. Instead, successive governments found it easy to divert an increasing share of oil revenue to the ordinary budget. Thus the initial formula of allocating 100 percent of oil revenue to development was changed to 70 percent in the early 1950s; reduced to 50 percent in the late 1950s; and repealed altogether in 1974. Moreover, development plans were called upon to "lend" the state funds or asked to undertake the funding of some ministries' projects that were outside the plan. But this practice had the effect of encouraging the government to avoid the difficult task of raising taxes to finance, at least in part, its current expenditures. How else would one explain the decline in the share of nonoil revenue in ordinary budget from 63 percent in 1966 to 17 percent in 1971 and to 13 percent in 1980. The obverse side of this picture is the continued increase in the relative importance of oil as the prime source of ordinary budget revenue. In 1966, oil revenue provided 39 percent of government revenue, while by 1980 its share has increased to 87 percent of ordinary budget revenue.

The absurdity of the personal income tax system is reflected in the anemic rise in tax collection in comparison to the rise in GDP. Between 1966 and 1980, personal income receipts rose from ID 12.2 million to ID 55.1 million or 4.5 times. During the same period, GDP increased 17.5 times. It is very clear from these simple indicators that over a period of twenty-five years governments, irrespective of their economic and political orientation, chose to rely increasingly on oil as the primary source of government income. Beyond the diminishing role of taxation, the broader effect of this policy was to discourage national saving and consequently intensify the negative impact on the economy of oil-related external shocks.

Another reason for the lagging of actual expenditure is the political system itself. In addition to violent and constant changes in regimes and cabinets, with their negative impact on plan integrity, formulation, and implementation, there was another important but unquantifiable effect. With minor qualifications, it can be said that ever since its establishment in 1921 the political system in Iraq has been authoritarian. This meant that for all intents and purposes development has been dictated from above. In the absence of democratic institutions and political parties or independent professional and social organizations, Iraq lacked the necessary mechanisms and modalities for the mobilization of popular support for the plans. Ordinary citizens were reduced to the role of spectators while members of the political class and the military carried out their coups and personal struggles for power—all in the name of the masses, of course.

It is important to stress that development spending under various plans and programs was only a fraction of total investment in the economy. There are two other sources of investment.

First, there is investment spending by government- or state-owned enterprises (SOEs) whose activities were lumped under what at times was called the socialist sector. The SOEs were engaged in a wide range of economic activities, producing a vast array of goods and services in all sectors of the economy. The SOEs had their own budgets, independent of the state ordinary budget and the budgets of the economic development plans. Available data on SOEs for the period 1969–81 show that their combined annual appropriations exceeded appropriations under the ordinary budget or the annual allocations under development plans.[24]

Second, public-sector investment – development plans and SOEs – was augmented by private-sector investment, which during the period 1957–70 amounted to 46 percent of total investment. Taking the three sources of investment together, it was found that investment spending represented between 15.5 percent and 27.7 percent of Iraq's GNP during 1957–70.[25] It should be added that private-sector investment as a ratio of public-sector investment declined in the 1970s as the state expanded the scope of its economic activities and as oil revenue fueled public-sector investment.

DEVELOPMENT PROBLEMS, 1980–1993

Iraq's last formal published development plan was the 1970–74 national development plan. The details of this plan are dealt with in Chapter 4. Two important features of the plan and the period bear repeating.

First, the plan was drafted and approved on the eve of major changes in the oil sector. These include the emergence of a national oil industry, the Tehran price agreement which increased per-barrel revenue, the 1972 nationalization of the IPC which further increased oil revenue, and the OPEC-led sharp oil price increases of 1973.

Second, although the plan was approved with total allocations of ID 537 million, such allocations were repeatedly revised to reach ID 1.9 billion, with actual spending reaching ID 1.2 billion. For purposes of comparison, development allocation and spending during the previous two decades, 1951–69, amounted to ID 1.7 billion and ID 954 million respectively.

But the sharp rise in development spending in 1970–74 must be qualified on two counts. First, inflation rates, which had been rather stable in the 1960s, began to move upward in the 1970s. And during the plan period, the consumer price index in Iraq increased by more than 26 percent. Second, the major increase in allocation, ID 580 million out of ID 995 million, was not earmarked to the four traditional sectors—agriculture, industry, transport, and building. Instead, it was allocated to "other" projects. By the same token, actual spending on other projects accounted for nearly 25 percent of total spending, ID 293 million, more than was actually spent on any other sector except industry.

The manner in which these changes were introduced confirms one more time how decisions are made without reference to economic planning or to existing plans. Suffice it that the 1970–74 increment in allocations, ID 1.4 billion, was 81 percent of what had been allocated for development over the period 1951–69 and certainly more than the ID 954 million actually spent during the same period. The point at issue is how could any economy, especially one like Iraq's, expand its absorptive capacity to such an extent as to absorb these disproportionate increases in spending without wasteful and distortive consequences.

The other point, which the decisions confirm, was that development spending was not planned according to a well-informed set of relationships between goals and the financial requirements necessary to attain these goals. Instead, planned spending was made in accordance with government's most optimistic anticipation of oil revenue. In other words, oil revenue (in government calculations) was governed by the euphoria that surrounded the 1973 price hikes rather than serious projections of oil market realities. This contention is supported by the way the government decided on its development allocations for the 1976–80 planning period.

The data in Tables 5.1 and 7.1 (pp. 82 and 142) show that allocations for this period were set at ID 15.7 billion, with ID 4.3 billion under the heading of other projects. The ID 15.7 billion allocation was 8.3 times that of the 1970–74 plan and 13.3 times its actual spending. Again, given the history of development spending in Iraq, such a sharp increase in allocation was very clearly beyond the absorptive capacity of the economy. Another unrealistic dimension of planning in the 1976–80 period relates to the availability of revenue to finance such planned expenditure. As in years past, most of the funding was to be provided by oil revenue. Thus, if we were to assume that development spending continued to receive 50 percent of oil revenue, then this level of allocation implies ID 31.4 billion of revenue, $106.3 billion. But actual oil revenue for the years 1976–80 amounted to $77.4 billion, yielding a deficit of $28.9 billion. It should be noted that the deficit would have been much larger had it not been for the unexpected sharp rise in oil prices due to the 1979 Iranian revolution and the Iran–Iraq war, which erupted in 1980. Given these problems, it can safely be concluded that both allocations and projected revenue in the 1976–80 planning period were unrelated to the realities of Iraq's economy or its oil revenue.

Starting in 1978, the government chose not to publish sources of development funds. Instead, the revenue equivalent of spending was simply decreed. Thus the 1978 law that decreed that ID 2.8 billion was allocated to meet the expenditures of the investment plan in that year also decreed that the revenues of the investment program for the year 1978 would be estimated at ID 2.8 billion.[26]

Following the start of the war with Iran in 1980, development spending was initially accelerated; but had to be subordinated to the goals of the war. In 1982, however, development was drastically curtailed as Iraq lost much of its oil export and revenue and the government was forced to introduce austerity measures throughout the economy. With this turn of events, development spending as it had been known in Iraq ceased to be a priority of the state. The uninterest of the Baath in development planning was further underscored by the Baath regime when it decided in 1987 to abolish the Planning Board and replace it with a unit called the Planning Body within the Ministry of Planning.

The newly established body was to be headed by the minister of planning with members representing the office of the presidency and the ministries of trade and finance and three other senior civil servants. The law specified that the planning body shall act in a consultative capacity to the council of ministers.[27]

Iraq emerged from the war worrying more about inflation, the consequences of the war, and how to deal with its new status as a country overwhelmed with foreign debt than with how to restore its development structures and mechanisms. Less than two years after the end of the war with Iran, the Baath regime plunged the country into another catastrophe when it decided to invade Kuwait.

NOTES

1. William Stivers, *Supremacy and Oil: Iraq, Turkey, and the Anglo-American World Order, 1918-1930* (Ithaca: Cornell University Press, 1982), p. 83.

2. Ibid.

3. See Hanna Batatu, *The Old Social Classes and the Revolutionary Movements of Iraq: A Study of Iraq's Old Landed and Commercial Classes and of Its Communists, Ba'thists, and Free Officers* (Princeton: Princeton University Press, 1982), pp. 29-31.

4. Ibid. The three uprisings, which left hundreds of civilians killed, had their origin in the imbalance in the distribution of income, wealth, and power in favor of tribal and urban elites who tied their fortunes to the crown and the English. Yet each uprising had a different immediate cause. In the case of the 1948 uprising, or *al-Wathba*, the immediate spark was the Portsmouth agreement with England which sought to replace the 1932 agreement without changing its core function. The 1952 uprising, or *Intifadha*, was sparked by

rising inflation and deteriorating living conditions. The 1956 uprising was sparked by the attack on Egypt by Britain, France, and Israel in October of that year.

5. For an extensive study of the Arab League and the issues involved in Arab economic unity, see Muhammad L. Shuqair, *Arab Economic Unity: Its Experiences and Expectations,* 2 vols. (in Arabic) (Beirut: Centre for Arab Unity Studies, 1986).

6. For a detailed study of these issues, see Mahmoud Al-Homsi, *Arab Economic Plans and Their Complementary and Conflicting Tendencies,* 3rd ed. (in Arabic) (Beirut: Centre for Arab Unity Studies, 1984).

7. International Bank for Reconstruction and Development, *The Economic Development of Iraq* (Baltimore: Johns Hopkins University Press, 1952), p. 277.

8. Government of Iraq, *The July 14 Revolution in Its First Year* (in Arabic) (Baghdad, no date), pp. 69–101.

9. Government of Iraq, *The July 14 Revolution in Its Second Year* (in Arabic) (Baghdad, 1960), pp. 125–126.

10. See Batatu, *The Old Social Classes,* pp. 1012–1020.

11. For the texts of these decrees, see Central Bank of Iraq, *Annual Report 1964* (Baghdad, 1964), pp. 169–194.

12. See Abdul Munim Said Ali, "The Role of the State in Economic Activity," in *The Role of the State in Economic Activity in the Arab World,* ed. A. Nassar (in Arabic) (Kuwait: Arab Planning Institute, 1991), pp. 137–141.

13. Ibid.

14. Ibid.

15. Mohammad Salman Hasan, *Studies in the Iraqi Economy* (in Arabic) (Beirut: Dar al-Taliaa, 1966), pp. 305–308.

16. Cited in Y. A. Sayigh, *The Economies of the Arab World: Development since 1945* (New York: St. Martin's Press, 1978), pp. 27–28.

17. Doreen Warriner, *Land Reform and Development in the Middle East: A Study of Egypt, Syria and Iraq* (London: Royal Institute of International Affairs, 1957), pp. 119–137. See also Sayigh, *The Economies of the Arab World,* pp. 28–29.

18. Ian Seymour, *OPEC: An Instrument of Change* (London: The Macmillan Press, 1980), pp. 218–223.

19. For a more detailed review of the development machinery see Khair el Din Haseeb, "Plan Implementation in Iraq, 1951–1967," in United Nations, *Studies on Selected Development Problems in Various Countries in the Middle East, 1969* (New York, 1969), pp. 1–3.

20. Ibid.

21. See A. Al-Ameen, "Investment Allocations and Plan Implementation: Iraq's Absorptive Capacity, 1950–1980," *The Journal of Energy and Development* 6 (2): 265–267; Government of Iraq, *Law No. 89 of 1977.*

22. Haseeb, "Plan Implementation," p. 10.

23. Ibid.

24. See *Law No. 38 of 1969, Law No. 82 of 1971, Law No. 39 of 1974, Law No. 49 of 1976, Law No. 165 of 1977, Law No. 6 of 1978, Law No. 10 of 1979, Law No. 3 of 1981.*

25. See Jawad Hashem, *Capital Formation in Iraq 1957/1970* (in Arabic) (Beirut: Arab Organization for Studies and Publishing, 1975), pp. 122-124.

26. See *Law No. 6 of 1978.*

27. See Revolutionary Command Council, *Resolution No. 455 of June 29, 1987.*

—————— CHAPTER 8 ——————

What Economic Future
for Iraq?

Simply stated, Iraq's economic problem in the coming decades is this: In 1960, Iraq's gross domestic product, measured in 1980 prices, was about $8.7 billion. It increased steadily for the next two decades until it peaked at $54 billion in 1979. Starting in 1980, Iraq's GDP reversed its historical trend and declined to $10 billion in 1993. This was a throwback to the GDP of 1961. In other words, more than three decades of growth were erased. But that is not all.

The 1961 GDP supported a population of 7 million, while the 1993 GDP had to support a population of nearly 21 million. Relating GDP to population, we find that in 1961 per capita GDP was $1400; in 1979, $4219; but in 1993, only $485, as shown in Table 8.1 (p. 152). Indeed one must look back to the 1940s to find a similar per capita GDP. This drastic fall meant the nullification of nearly fifty years of growth and improvement in the living standards of most Iraqi citizens. This, in the final analysis, is the price the average Iraqi had to pay for the economic mismanagement and wars of the last fifteen years.

SANCTIONS, REPARATIONS, DEBT,
AND RECONSTRUCTION

The sanctions the United Nations Security Council (UNSC) imposed against Iraq in the aftermath of its invasion of Kuwait in 1990 are still in effect in 1994. Any attempt to deal with the future of the Iraqi economy is constrained by this fact—the government is effectively paralyzed so long as the sanctions remain in effect. The following analysis, therefore, must assume a normal state of economic interaction between Iraq and the rest of the world.

Table 8.1
Gross Domestic Product and GDP per Capita in Constant 1980 Prices,
1950-1993 (U.S. Dollars)

Year	Population (Million)	GDP ($ Billion)	Per Capita GDP ($)
1950	5.2	3.4	654
1955	5.9	6.4	1085
1960	6.9	8.7	1261
1965	8.1	12.7	1568
1970	9.4	16.4	1745
1975	11.1	30.0	2703
1979	12.8	54.0	4219
1980	13.2	53.9	4083
1982	14.1	42.8	3035
1984	15.4	35.1	2279
1986	16.5	29.1	1764
1988	17.6	30.9	1756
1989	18.3	26.9	1470
1990	18.9	16.4	868
1991	19.6	12.3	627
1992	20.0	11.1	555
1993	20.6	10.0	485

Sources: Derived from United Nations, *National Account Statistics;* International Monetary Fund, *International Financial Statistics;* Arab Monetary Fund et al., *Joint Arab Economic Report;* World Bank, *World Tables;* A. M. S. Ali and H. A. J. Al-Ganabi, "Political Economy of Inflation in Iraq, 1988-1992," *Arab Economic Journal* (in Arabic) 1 (Autumn 1992): 99-109.
Note: Data for 1990-1993 are author's estimates. Other analysts estimated that Iraq's GNP declined by 50 percent in the two years following the invasion of Kuwait. See *MEED*, June 26, 1992, p. 24.

Iraq faces an economic task of extraordinary proportions. It is difficult to see how the country can regain the initiative to chart its economic future under present conditions. If we assume that Iraq will soon be able to export oil at its prewar capacity, a dubious assumption at best, its income from oil at current prices could conceivably be in the vicinity of $20 billion per year. Against this level of income, the following claims must be considered.

First, according to the *Joint Arab Economic Report,* the value of destroyed infrastructure and other economic assets which can be attributed to the 1991 Gulf war was an estimated $232 billion.[1] It is safe to assume that the replacement cost of these assets is bound to be higher than this figure.

Second, Iraq had neither the resources nor the time to replace or repair assets destroyed or damaged in the course of the Iran-Iraq war of 1980-88. The value of such assets was estimated to be $67 billion.[2]

Third, Iraq will have to face the payment of reparations to Iran to compensate for economic losses Iran suffered in the 1980-88 Iran-Iraq war. Although there is no agreement on the precise dollar figure of such damages, a 1991 UNSC report placed the value of the damage at $97 billion.[3]

Fourth, UNSC resolution 687 of April 1991, the ceasefire resolution which Iraq accepted, created a United Nations-administered compensation fund to which 30 percent of Iraq's oil revenue is to be earmarked for the purpose of paying compensation for damage claims against Iraq as a result of its invasion of Kuwait. Claims to be settled through this agency have been estimated at $100 billion.[4]

Fifth, Iraq's foreign debt has been estimated to have reached $86 billion by the end of 1990. The Iraqi government, however, maintained that its foreign debt was $42.1 billion, excluding interest, but $75.1 billion with interest.[5]

THE $586-BILLION QUESTION

Adding up the five items listed yields a total of $586 billion, nearly sixty times Iraq's 1993 real GDP. Simply stated, this is the essence of Iraq's economic problem. Indeed, this figure underestimates the extent of the squandering of the country's scarce resources if we add to it other losses, such as the exhaustion of foreign reserves, lost oil revenue, depletion of commodity stocks and military goods, lost output, lost growth, lost manpower, and brain drain.

Regardless of the figure used, the task of bringing the Iraqi economy back to its 1980 level, or even to that of 1968, the year the present regime seized power, any time soon, is beyond the resources of the country, not to mention the capacity of the present regime.

Any attempt to speculate about Iraq's prospects for economic reconstruction, recovery, and growth must recognize that such prospects are externally determined and beyond the reach of this regime. This is so because Iraq's prospects for economic recovery will be shaped by four factors. These are (1) oil revenue, (2) foreign debt, (3) war reparations, and (4) duration of the U.N.-imposed economic sanctions.

AN ESTIMATE OF OIL REVENUE TO 2010

Iraq, like all other OPEC member countries, must sell its oil to survive. The war with Iran and the invasion of Kuwait have shown how vulnerable Iraq is to any interruption of the flow of its oil exports. As noted earlier, the decline in oil revenue in the aftermath of the war with Iran ultimately pushed Iraq to invade Kuwait.

Iraq's oil exports are intimately tied to OPEC exports, which are determined by the state of the world demand for energy and oil. Since most OPEC oil exports (between 73 percent and 80 percent in the period 1971–91) found their way to the markets of the industrialized countries, it follows that such exports will continue to remain a function of the policies and the state of the economies of these importing countries.

A review of world oil consumption over the period 1971–91 shows clearly that both world oil consumption and OPEC exports entered a period of stagnation in 1980. World oil consumption was 49.3 MBD in 1971 and increased to 64.1 MBD in 1979. Since then, its historical trend reversed and declined in the following six years to 58.6 MBD in 1985. Not until 1992 did consumption reach 65.4 MBD. Another indicator of changing international oil market conditions was the behavior of OPEC oil exports within the total world oil exports. In 1971, OPEC exported 22 MBD, or 87 percent of the world exports. By 1977, OPEC exports peaked at 27.6 MBD, or 84 percent of the world total; but by 1991, OPEC exports had declined to 17 MBD, or 62 percent of the world total. Looking at oil exports from a different perspective shows that non-OPEC oil exports increased from 3.4 MBD in 1971 to 10.6 MBD in 1991.[6]

What about the future demand for oil? Obviously the demand for OPEC oil will continue to be a function of the prospects for economic growth of the world economy, especially of those countries in the Organization of Economic Cooperation and Development (OECD). OPEC's own assessment of a significant increase in the demand for its oil is not very optimistic in the medium term.

The picture, according to OPEC's and other studies, however, looks brighter in the long term. These forecasts estimate that world economic growth will be in the range of 2.3 to 3 percent per year until the year 2010. The impact of such growth on the demand for oil is estimated to raise worldwide consumption to 76 MBD in 2010 from current levels of consumption.[7]

If we assume that OPEC will capture 75 percent of the increment in world demand for oil, this will bring OPEC exports up to 28 MBD by the year 2010 – a level of export OPEC had reached in the mid-1970s.

What will be Iraq's share of this output? The answer to the question will depend on the willingness of other OPEC member countries to reduce their respective shares of the market to make room for Iraq's oil. From Iraq's viewpoint, its share in total OPEC output should be no less than the share it was assigned on the eve of its invasion of Kuwait, 13.96 percent. Assuming that these countries will be willing to relinquish that much of their collective output to Iraq, then the latter's projected output in the year 2010 should reach 3.9 MBD, of which 15 percent will be used for domestic consumption. The balance, 3.3 MBD, will be available for export. Should Iraq succeed in exporting 3.3 MBD by 2010, it will reach the level of export it attained in 1979.[8]

The problem with this scenario is that it is fraught with many imponderables. In the first place, there is no reason to believe that the forecasts will turn out to be correct and that world economic growth rate will be in the range cited above. Nor is there any reason to believe that OPEC will actually capture a 75 percent share of the growth in the demand for oil. Moreover, it is not inconceivable that a combination of energy and environmental technologies will reduce the demand for oil and other conventional sources of energy. Nor is it inconceivable that Iraq's own political instability will be of such magnitude that its oil industry will fail to grow to meet the estimated rise in the demand for oil.

More important, however, is the willingness of OPEC member countries to withdraw from markets where they have established themselves to allow Iraq to reclaim the market position it held prior to the invasion of Kuwait. This problem will not arise, of course, so long as the U.N. sanctions against Iraq are still in effect. This, in turn, means that the reentry of Iraq's oil to the world market is bound in a complex web of regional and international constraints that may not allow such reentry before 1995.[9] According to Walid Khadduri, the politics of sanctions are such that two groups, for an entirely different set of considerations, favor an early resumption of Iraqi oil exports. These groups are composed of U.N. and Iraqi technocrats.

The U.N. technocrats are interested in the resumption because of their interests in diverting some of Iraq's foreign exchange earnings to fund U.N.-sponsored operations in Iraq. Such operations include U.N.-administered humanitarian and security activities; activities of the numerous weapons inspection teams; and the U.N.-created compensation fund, which is supposed to pay war reparation out of that part of Iraqi oil sales diverted to it. The Iraqi technocrats who favor resumption argue that the restrictive UNSC resolutions that allowed limited sale of oil are bound to be relaxed with time and that it would be in the long-term interest of Iraq to reestablish its position in the world oil market. Moreover, the initial oil sales will give a much-needed boost to the faltering economy and the collapsing Iraqi currency. Since these views are not shared by the Iraqi government or the U.S. government, the sanctions are expected to be maintained.[10]

The continuation of the sanctions will serve the interests of all oil-exporting countries in at least two ways. First, sanctions will obviate the need on the part of oil-exporting countries, especially OPEC members, to adjust their sales to allow Iraq's oil to recapture some of its market share. Even if adjustment is made for Iraq's oil to enter the world market again, within the limits of the OPEC quota system, Iraq may not feel bound to respect such a system. Instead, Iraq may decide to export as much as its output capacity and export facilities allow it to do. Under these conditions, Iraq may be able to derive higher revenue through larger volumes at lower prices. More important than any temporary fiscal gain that Iraq may enjoy, this policy may enable Iraq to recapture its traditional share of the market. Once this point is reached, equilibrium between OPEC oil producers and their market shares will be restored to the levels where they were supposed to be just prior to the invasion of Kuwait. The new equilibrium will be reached at a higher level of combined output. It is important to recall that the new high levels of output and exports are projected for 2010.

The scenario that Iraq will recapture its share of pre-August 1990 levels of export is contingent upon the cooperation and willingness of other OPEC members to accommodate Iraq's oil export objectives. To the extent that such cooperation is not forthcoming, Iraq's foreign exchange earnings will have to be scaled down. If, on the other hand, OPEC members choose not to comply with their quotas and decide to increase their output, this act—together with the reentry of Iraq's oil in the world oil market—will undoubtedly undermine the oil price structure and consequently the oil revenues of all member countries. Such an outcome will be similar to what occurred in 1986 when member countries discarded all restraints on output and prices collapsed to such an extent that although output increased by 17 percent between 1985 and 1986 OPEC combined oil revenue declined by 41 percent during the same period.

The level of oil exports is only one of two determinants of Iraqi oil revenue—the other being the price at which oil is sold in the world market. Several elements need to be examined in order to understand the importance of the price of oil for Iraq's oil revenue.

In addition to the usual market conditions of supply and demand, other elements need to be highlighted in the case of oil. The first and most important is the fact that the price of oil and the revenue from oil are expressed in terms of the U.S. dollar. So long as the Bretton Woods system of fixed exchange rates was in effect, oil-producing countries had no reason to be concerned with exchange-rate fluctuations since such fluctuations were confined to a narrow band of 1 percent of official exchange rates. But in 1971 the decision of the U.S. government to suspend convertibility of the dollar into gold and other reserves assets and the subsequent collapse of the Bretton Woods system resulted in floating exchange rates. This phenomenon affected the purchasing power of the U.S. dollar vis-à-vis other currencies. Iraq and other oil-exporting countries stand to benefit when the value of the dollar appreciates but lose purchasing power whenever the dollar depreciates. The linkage between the dollar and the currencies of major European countries was recognized by the oil companies when they agreed to make upward oil price adjustments in 1972 and 1973 to offset currency fluctuations.[11]

Another important element that affects the purchasing power of oil revenue is the rise in imports prices. According to OPEC, the average price for the OPEC basket of crudes in the first nine months of 1992 was $18.35 per barrel, compared with $21 per barrel, the reference price set in 1990. Had this reference price been adjusted to keep its real value, the reference should have been around $25 per barrel. Over the long term, OPEC estimates that the current market price is less than one-half what it was, in real terms, in 1974.[12] Regardless of the precise loss in purchasing power, the long-term decline in the price of oil in real terms over the last twenty years has been very serious; and there is no reason to assume that the control of the oil exporters over the price of their oil will change drastically over the next fifteen years.

What does all this mean to Iraq? If, for the sake of argument, we say that Iraq will be allowed by other OPEC member countries to gradually expand its share of the market to the preinvasion level, then its oil export should be expected to reach 3.3 MBD in 2010. Assuming also a gradual rise in the price to $25 per barrel, then Iraq should expect oil revenue to reach $30 billion in 2010, compared with $14.5 billion in 1989.

In the interim, it will be postulated that the sanctions will be removed effective in 1995 and that Iraq's oil revenue will rise gradually by $1 billion per year from $15 billion in 1995 to $30 billion in 2010. Under these assumptions, Iraq's cumulative oil revenue for the period 1995–2010 will be $360 billion. But this figure must be reduced by 30 percent or $108 billion, that portion of oil revenue the UNSC has earmarked to the compensation fund. The balance, $252 billion, will be, technically speaking, available to the government for spending.

THE BURDEN OF FOREIGN DEBT

Iraq was free of foreign debt from the early 1950s, but in the early phases of the Iran–Iraq war, the country exhausted its accumulated foreign reserves of $35 billion and also incurred heavy foreign debt. Although there are no precise figures on Iraq's foreign obligations or an agreement on what constitutes debt, there are reliable estimates of magnitudes. Thus Iraq's foreign debt was estimated by the end of 1990 to have reached $86 billion – $35 billion to Western governments and banks; $11 billion to the former Soviet Union and Eastern Europe; and $40 billion to other Arab countries.[13]

The Iraqi government has adopted the position that the funds it received from the Gulf states during the war with Iran were a grant. This position was made clear to the United Nations when the government stated that "Iraq's total external debt and obligations" amounted as of December 13, 1990, to ID $13.1 billion, the equivalent of $42.1 billion, excluding interest.[14]

Even if we accept the lower figure as Iraq's actual debt obligation, this still means that if Iraq were to pay its debt within five years it would need to pay a total of $75.1 billion, 126 percent of its net potential oil earnings, for the five-year period 1995–99.

How Iraq's creditors will deal with Iraq's obligations (rescheduling, write off, exchange of debt for equity, etc.) will influence the amount of foreign exchange Iraq will have at its disposal and therefore its prospect for recovery. As indicated earlier, debt payments are like oil revenue in that their levels are externally determined.

THE BURDEN OF WAR REPARATIONS

The third external factor that will have serious impact on the economy's prospects for recovery is the question of war reparations. Kuwait and Iran hold the key. In the case of Kuwait, the value of economic damage to infrastructure and other fixed assets caused by the Gulf war has been estimated at $240 billion. In addition, the U.N. compensation fund estimated that claims against Iraq from individuals, business firms, and other governments adversely affected by the invasion of Kuwait and its consequences could reach $100 billion.[15]

In addition to claims arising from the Gulf war, Iran will undoubtedly press Iraq for payment of reparation for losses it incurred in the course of the Iran–Iraq war, which have been estimated at $97 billion. Iran's claims, however, fall outside the jurisdiction of the compensation fund.

UNITED NATIONS SANCTIONS

The Iraqi government's ability to initiate a modest process of reconstruction and development is a function of its foreign exchange earnings. Since such earnings are blocked by the sanctions the UNSC imposed immediately after Iraq's invasion of Kuwait, it follows that Iraq's economic stagnation and decline will continue so long as these sanctions remain in effect. The list of demands—military, political, economic, and geographic—that Iraq must meet if the sanctions are to be lifted were outlined in many UNSC resolutions, especially resolutions 687, 688, 706, 707, 712, and 715 of 1991.

Such demands are viewed as so stringent that the present regime cannot possibly comply with them and remain in power. The Baath regime seems to have adopted the position that after surviving the war, simultaneous rebellions in two-thirds of the provinces, and three years of sanctions, there is little reason to accept these resolutions now. Instead, the regime hopes for a total removal of sanctions rather than accepting any partial and restricted resumption of oil exports.[16]

Judging by the international politics of sanctions as they have been practiced since they were imposed in 1990, their removal will obviously have to result from a political act. This means that either the U.S. government will change its policy toward the regime of Saddam or the regime of Saddam will have to change its policy toward its compliance with the resolutions. Neither of these changes seems to be imminent. In the meantime, the people of Iraq and their economy have no choice but to continue their downward slide.

OTHER CLAIMS ON SCARCE RESOURCES

It is postulated earlier that if the sanctions are removed in 1995 and Iraq is able to recapture its share of the oil market, its oil revenue will amount to $360 billion by 2010. Since $108 billion of this sum will be earmarked for the compensation fund, the government will be left with $252 billion. Arrayed against the $252 will be Iraq's external debt of $75 billion; Iran's reparation claims of $97 billion; and $299 billion of repair and reconstruction in Iraq due to the Iran-Iraq and Gulf wars — a total of $470 billion. In other words, even before dealing with the questions of imports and development, Iraq will start the postsanctions era with a projected resource gap of $218 billion. To the extent that the government will have to increase imports and reinitiate development above and beyond the mere repair and reconstruction effort, the resource gap will widen. As to imports, it is essential that they be restored to their prewar levels if conditions of impoverishment are to change and if the economy is to function again.

Iraq's per capita nonmilitary imports during the period 1980–89 averaged close to $500. Assuming a population growth rate of 3 percent per year and assuming that Iraq will be able to resume this level of imports in 1995, the import bill will be $11 billion in that year, rising to $13 billion in 2000 and $17 billion in 2010. These imports should be viewed as the lower end of Iraq's requirements since they do not reflect the unavoidable rise in import prices. In other words, these figures imply a reduction in the real value of these imports during this period. It is difficult to see how Iraq can afford to have lower imports, given the present conditions of rampant hyperinflation, idle capacity (85 to 90 percent due to a lack of spare parts and raw materials), malnutrition (which is causing disease and death), high unemployment rates, and collapsing currency.[17]

Another important claim on Iraq's limited resources is the need to allocate resources for development. If the process of reconstruction ever succeeds in stabilizing the Iraqi economy to the point where some form of development spending can be resumed, resources will need to be set aside for that purpose. It goes without saying that growth ratios of the pre-1980 kind are not feasible, given the external claims (debt and reparation payments) that Iraq has to contend with. Moreover, the manner in which these external claims are going to be handled in the years to come will affect the size of the growth rate. In a 1991 study, Sinan Al-Shabibi attempted to project nine different scenarios for GDP growth rate for the year 1995. Depending on the assumptions made, he came up with GDP growth rates ranging from a positive growth rate of 11.2 percent to a negative growth rate of 5.2 percent.[18]

In a report submitted to the United Nations in April 1991 outlining Iraq's dire financial and economic problems, the government indicated that it had planned to invest $92.1 billion (compared with $53.2 billion in 1976–80) for development purposes for the five-year period 1991–95 to attain an average growth rate of 3.4 percent in the nonoil GDP. The foreign exchange component of this sum was estimated to be $55.2 billion, $11 billion per year.[19]

It is pointless to take issue with the government's projected investment in light of its past performance or in light of the absorptive capacity of the economy, since the sanctions are still in place and Iraq's oil is still barred from the world market. But the data are useful in one important respect. By establishing a relationship between a rate of economic growth of 3.4 percent and investment requirements of $92 billion, the data give us an indicator of the magnitude of capital requirements for reconstruction and development. This is so because (with a government-assumed population growth of 2.8 percent) the data inform us that under Iraq's conditions in the period 1991–95, development spending should average $18.4 billion per year (all of Iraq's oil revenue) to achieve a rise of only .6 percent per year in per capita nonoil GDP.

With such heavy investment requirements to achieve such a minuscule rise in per capita GDP, it is not surprising that the government found it necessary to ask the UNSC for a moratorium on war reparations payments since "it is not within the capacity of Iraq alone to restore its economic and social life to that obtaining before the events of 17 January 1991."[20]

In addition to imports and investment requirements, at least two other interrelated problems need mention. The first is the size of the accumulated deficit in the general state budget. The other is the problem of inflation, which both exacerbated and deepened the crisis of the Iraqi economy.

THE CONTINUED CRISIS OF THE ECONOMY

Since the invasion of Kuwait, the economy of Iraq has been virtually cut off from the world economy. UNSC sanctions and embargo measures were imposed in order to force Iraq's withdrawal from Kuwait. Although Iraq was forced to abandon Kuwait, these sanctions are still in effect. Following the ceasefire, UNSC adopted a series of resolutions

intended to regulate the level and the composition of trade – and by extension Iraq's GDP and its growth prospects – that Iraq may engage in.

One of the most serious features of the UNSC sanctions was to require
Iraq to apply to UNSC for permission to engage in trade (i.e., how much
oil it can sell, which exporting terminals such oil may go through, how
much to import, and what to import, etc.). Furthermore, the ceasefire
resolution (Res. 687, April 1991) stipulated that a special U.N.-admin-
istered compensation fund (the Fund) be created, to which 30 percent of
Iraq's oil revenue is to be earmarked to pay compensation for claims
against Iraq for any direct loss, damage (including environmental
damage and depletion of natural resources), and injury to foreign governments, nationals, and corporations as a result of the invasion of
Kuwait. By accepting the resolution, Iraq in effect agreed to mortgage
its oil revenues for a long time to come.

The extent of the control UNSC is exerting over Iraq's economic
future is reflected in the restrictions the August 15, 1991, Security
Council resolution imposed on Iraq. Under the terms of the resolution,
Iraq was allowed a limited one-time sale of $1.6-billion-worth of oil
over a six-month period to fund the purchase of humanitarian items
needed for the Iraqi people, as well as for reparations of war damages.
Although Iraq was to select the buyers, the U.N. Sanctions Committee
approved each contract. The resolution imposed other restrictions.
These include the deposit by the oil purchaser of the full amount of
each purchase into an escrow account set up and administered by the
United Nations and the stipulation that the oil must be exported via
the pipeline through Turkey with U.N. monitors posted along the pipeline and the loading terminal to ensure compliance with the resolution.

Moreover, Iraq was not to have access to the full amount of the sale,
since the resolution stipulated that 30 percent of the proceeds, $480
million, would be placed in the compensation fund and another $186
million would be used to cover the cost of the operations of various
U.N. agencies.[21] The remaining $934 million would be used by Iraq,
with approval of the U.N. Sanctions Committee, to buy food, medicinal
supplies, and other essential civilian needs for distribution in Iraq.
Payments for these purchases were to be approved by the secretary
general from the escrow account mentioned earlier. In other words,
none of the oil money would go through the hands of the Iraqi government. With such restrictions on its freedom of action, it was not inac-
curate on the part of the Iraqi ambassador to the United Nations to
say that the plan would make "a trusteeship of Iraq."[22]

Although the sanctions continue to be in effect, Iraq was able to
generate small amounts of foreign currency from several sources such
as the sale of small quantities of oil to Jordan and Turkey, the sale of
gold by the government, the smuggling of public-sector machinery and

equipment to Iran, the sale of privately-owned gold, liquidation of privately-owned, foreign-held balances to finance trade, and the release of small amounts of frozen assets by certain foreign governments. Such foreign exchange earnings were used by the government and the private sector to import small amounts of food, medicines, and other consumer goods.

The limited access to foreign exchange, together with its own prewar stocks of certain goods and the availability of large numbers of Iraqi professionals and technicians and skilled workers, enabled the country to repair some of the damage inflicted upon the infrastructure during the war. A number of Western newspapers and observers commented positively on the speed with which some of the rebuilding was achieved.[23]

Yet it should be pointed out that the repair was, of necessity, limited in nature. In the first place, most of the repair was concentrated in Baghdad at the expense of other cities. Second, some of the spare parts were removed from one facility to another. Third, there is a limit to what can be done with the limited prewar stockpiles. The process, in other words, is self-limiting.

The limited and discriminatory nature of the regime's effort to repair the infrastructure and other facilities may be seen in what is taking place in Basra, Iraq's second-largest city:

Basra is short of everything. The families drink polluted water, there is not money for spare parts, no possibility, apart from minimal United Nations aid and the voluntary agencies' brave but limited efforts, to rebuild proper sewage and water supply lines, pipes and pumping stations. School children cannot go to the lavatory. There isn't one. Books and pencils are unavailable. They are cheery in Basra, bright, educated, coping, but aggressed on [by] both sides – by the West's imposition on ordinary families, stopping trade and therefore drugs, syringes, medicine, medical equipment, food, spare parts, school books, journals, information and, in the end, hope. And on the other by Himself, in Baghdad, who is happy to have reasserted his power and control yet see the West blamed for a policy of oppression against his people in which he is the arch-collaborator.[24]

Moreover, the government's determination to spend freely on the security organizations and the armed forces and carry out military campaigns in more than one part of the country inevitably diverted the country's scarce resources from the civilian economy to nonproductive and destructive forms of spending.

The continuation of sanctions, the refusal of the Iraqi government to accept UNSC-approved limited sale of oil, and the inability of the regime to generate foreign exchange outside traditional channels considerably slowed the pace of repair and forced further cutbacks in production. These conditions in turn forced local industry almost to grind to a halt leading thousands of factories to close, laying workers off, and causing soaring unemployment in a country that employed three million foreign workers before the Gulf war. Moreover, unemployment conditions were made worse by the mass discharge of soldiers after the end of the war. According to government's own statements, the magnitude of unemployment is unprecedented in Iraq's modern history.[25]

While the change in the American administration gave rise to expectations that U.S. policy toward Iraq under President Clinton might change in such a way that the sanctions are lifted, no such change has taken place. Indeed, there is no reason to expect the sanctions to be lifted any time soon if the Clinton administration continues to insist that Iraq implement all UNSC resolutions, including those that relate to human rights issues.

The combined impact of the war, sanctions, uprising, inflation, unemployment, economic stagnation, social disorganization, and de facto fragmentation led to economic collapse and forced the overwhelming majority of the people to live under severe conditions of poverty, deprivation, malnutrition, premature death, and constantly deteriorating health. Suffice it to say that the sanctions forced hospitals to admit only emergency cases and to slash other operations. The use of X-rays and blood screening decreased by 82 percent in the early part of 1993 because of the acute medical shortages.[26]

It should be noted, however, that certain policies of the regime tended to create different impacts on different groups of the population, as well as on different parts of the country. While the northern part of the country is still subjected to internal embargo, thus aggravating its economic plight, the south was made to suffer through neglect and underdevelopment.

At the same time, preferential treatment was extended to certain privileged groups such as the Baath leadership, the upper strata of the civil service, and the military and security establishments, as well as those who were engaged in construction and the import trade business.[27] Members of the latter group played an important role in deflecting protests against the regime's failed economic policies by increasing the supply of a wide range of foreign goods. By making these goods available for sale in the open market, they provided a false impression that consumer goods were plentiful. Since only members of a small stratum of the society were able to earn and accumulate considerable wealth, they found it easy to indulge in Western-style conspicuous consumption. As the sanctions continued to affect the economy and as the currency continued to depreciate vis-à-vis the dollar, the ultimate currency of imports, prices continued their upward trend and more segments of the middle class found themselves joining the ranks of the poorer majority—a development the regime could not ignore.

To deflect attention from its failed policies, the regime repressed traders (it executed forty-two merchants in August 1992), banned the import of a wide array of luxury commodities, and prohibited consumers from paying high prices. Such measures proved to be self-defeating. Both inflation and currency depreciation continued their unstoppable march, as is seen in the following section.

THE PROBLEM OF HYPERINFLATION
AND THE EXCHANGE RATE

One of the structural features of an oil-based economy like Iraq's is the lack of symmetry between national income and the composition of national output. The root of the problem is that, while generating between one-half and two-thirds of the GDP, the oil sector absorbs no more than 2 or 3 percent of the labor force. Since the goods-producing sectors, agriculture and industry, contribute less than one-fifth of the national output, it follows that any domestically spent portion of the income generated by the oil sector is bound to exert an upward pressure on domestic prices. Since government development spending to increase national output has failed to show serious results, the only avenue left to policy makers was to increase imports.

But this rising dependence on imports reduced the economy to a mere mechanism that exports oil in exchange for imports. Increases in living standards may be attained, but such increases become a hostage to the availability of imports.

In the case of Iraq, the problem was made even worse by a series of decisions by the ruling Baath party in the 1970s to neglect agriculture and industry and invest heavily in the oil sector, thus perpetuating and deepening the phenomenon of an oil-based economy. The regime could mask its failure and also give the appearance of a growing economy so long as oil revenues were rising and it could finance the cost of imported consumer and other goods.

Unfortunately, the Iraqi government's decision to plunge the country into a devastating war with Iran revealed the basic weakness of the economy with its utter dependence on imported goods, outside help, and foreign loans. The problem was made worse when the abnormal cost of the war was superimposed on the economy at a time when its sole foreign exchange earner, oil, was shrinking. This is more or less what happened in Iraq and caused inflation rates to jump beyond control.

It can be said that the period 1960–73 was one of relative price stability as the consumer prices increased at an average rate of 5 to 6 percent per year. The picture, however, changed drastically after 1973. With 1973 as the base year, prices increased between 19 percent and 68 percent between 1975 and 1979. Inflationary conditions worsened during the eight-year war with Iran as larger portions of the national output, imports, and manpower were diverted to the war. In order to finance its war-caused budget deficit, the government borrowed heavily from the central bank and commercial banks, thus expanding the monetary base of the economy and causing the rate of inflation to accelerate. This is reflected in the fact that inflation rates jumped sharply from 95 percent in 1980 to nearly 400 percent in 1989.[28] These high rates of inflation turned out to be mild in comparison to the hyperinflation rates that dominated the Iraqi economy in the aftermath of Iraq's invasion of Kuwait.

The destruction of the Iraqi economy, the decline in its domestic output, and the tight system of sanctions were among the forces that caused severe shortages of all kinds of goods, thus forcing their prices up. The government, for its part, made matters worse by printing, indeed even photocopying, money to pay for its ordinary budget expenditure. Given this chaotic situation, it is no wonder that inflation rates reached unprecedented levels rising to more than 1000 percent per year.[29]

If not curbed, such structural inflation tends to create its own spiral. Unless the government curbs its own spending, it will be forced to increase the supply of money to meet its expenditures targets. Since the supply of goods and services cannot be increased under the present conditions, this increase in the money supply will be translated into higher prices, setting the stage for another round of increased money supply and higher prices and so on. Since only few people (top party and government officials, importers, contractors, etc.) can expect to see their incomes rise at the same rate as inflation (and even higher), it follows that the burden of inflation in the form of further loss in purchasing power and living standards will be endured by the overwhelming majority of the population.

Aside from its impact on living standards, this type of inflation has other effects. As the value of the currency declines, people tend to convert their liquid assets, such as currency and deposits, into other assets – such as land, buildings, goods, and gold – whose real values tend to increase in times of inflation. Another way to protect the value of one's wealth is to convert it into foreign currency and deposit it abroad, giving rise to what is known as capital flight.

Regardless of whether holders of wealth convert their monetary assets (dinar balances) into real assets in Iraq or into foreign assets abroad, the dinar loses its function as a store of value and, in many cases, as a medium of exchange. This simply means that the people have lost confidence in the dinar and prefer to conduct their transactions in another currency, which in Iraq happens to be the American dollar.

The loss of confidence in the dinar is one of the explanations for the constant decline in its value against the dollar.[30] There are other factors at work, of course, as is seen from the following paragraphs.

In 1972, the Iraqi dinar was valued at $3. The strength of Iraq's balance of payments made it possible to revalue the dinar to $3.31. Its value was raised again in 1974 to $3.38. When the Iran–Iraq war turned Iraq's balance of payments surplus into deficit and forced it to incur heavy foreign debt, the dinar was devalued in 1983 to $3.21. While in the 1970s there was proximity between the official rates and the market rate of exchange, this was not the case in the 1980s when the open-market rate started to decline under the impact of the war conditions.

One reason for this decline was the war-generated uncertainties that prompted many people to transfer their currency holdings into dollar and (to a lesser extent) nondollar deposits abroad. Another reason was the emigration of those who could do so, which entailed the conversion of their wealth to other currencies. In either case, such acts increased the supply of dinars on the international market and caused its value to decline.

Another factor was the austerity measures of the war which curtailed consumer-goods imports and prompted the smuggling of the currency to neighboring countries to buy such goods for sale in Iraq at exorbitant prices. The increase in the supply of the dinar in these countries forced its value or exchange rate down vis-à-vis these countries' currencies, as well as other currencies. The practice of exporting dinars to import goods for sale at inflated prices in Iraq gained momentum in 1984 when the government removed the licensing requirement for imports, provided that importers use their foreign-held assets. Instead of using these assets, importers resorted to the smuggling of local currency, thus depressing its value abroad.

The decline in the exchange rate in the 1980s proved, in retrospect, to have been mild by comparison to what happened to the value of the dinar in the aftermath of the invasion of Kuwait. The freezing of Iraqi assets, the sanctions, shortages of goods of all kinds, the emigration of large numbers of professionals, high rates of unemployment, the collapse of the economy, the hyperinflation, the feverish speculation in currency, the continued printing of money, and the general fear and uncertainty about the future were among the factors that contributed to the collapse in the value of the dinar to 5 cents or 2 cents or, at one time, to 1 cent – although the official rate is still $3.21 to the dinar.

But the collapse of the dinar is only symptomatic of the underlying crisis that engulfs the Iraqi economy. Simply put, the economy is unable to generate enough foreign exchange to meet the demand. In the absence of exports, the value of the dinar will continue to be determined by speculators outside the country.

In order to shore up the value of the dinar, the government decided, on May 3, 1993, to withdraw from circulation the ID 25 bank note, which had been printed in Britain before the Gulf crisis. The immediate impact of this decision was to render worthless the estimated ID 15 billion held by Jordanians alone, who maintain that they accepted payment in ID for goods shipped to Iraq because these IDs were brought out of Iraq with the approval of the Iraqi authorities.[31]

The problem with this expediency is that while it may work to the advantage of the government in the short term, which it did not, it will not do so in the longer term. The inevitable refusal of foreign exporters to accept IDs in the future will force the government to come up with hard currency for all its purchases abroad. So long as the sanctions are kept, it is difficult to see how the government will be able to do so without selling its gold holdings.

WHAT ECONOMIC FUTURE FOR IRAQ?

Regardless of whether Iraq is free to sell its oil or not, its prospects for economic recovery are remote because of the inevitable huge gap between its potential foreign exchange earnings and its foreign exchange requirements. Oil revenue is not expected to reach prewar levels for some time to come; its new status as a major debtor country will severely narrow its options; and the war claims it will have to pay will overburden the economy in the future. In short, Iraq will have to labor under a vicious cycle of debt and underdevelopment. For the Iraqi economy to grow, it must save in order to invest in its goods-producing sectors. But to generate savings, Iraq must be able to have a level of income that exceeds the total of private and public consumption, not to mention international obligations. Under present conditions, the prospects for doing that are simply nonexistent.

Regardless of how the Iraqi government will attempt to conduct its economic policy in the coming years, its options are very few and very narrow. Suffice it to say that it took Iraq between four and five decades, vast amounts of foreign exchange, and considerable foreign expertise to build the assets destroyed in the forty-three-day bombing campaign in 1991. The combined effects of this war and the Iran-Iraq war resulted not only in the destruction of economic assets but also in the fiscal bankruptcy of the country, impoverishment of the people, underdevelopment of the economy, and deepening of dependency on the West, not to mention the heavier reliance on the oil sector.

The economic legacy with which the policies of the Baath have saddled Iraq for generations to come may be gleaned from what has been stated earlier about the relationship between economic growth and investment requirements. It will be recalled that in 1991 the government estimated that it required $18.4 billion per year to raise GDP by an annual rate of 3.4 percent. The government admitted, and correctly so, that such rate was paltry when account is taken of the annual population growth rate of 2.8 percent. The relationship between these two rates translates into per capita GDP growth rate of .6 percent per year.

It will be recalled also that per capita GDP in real terms has declined to $485 in 1993 from its peak of $4,219 in 1979 or from such levels as $2,703 in 1975, or from the levels of the pre-oil price revolution of 1973–74–years when per capita GDP was $1,745 in 1970, $1,261 in 1960, or $654 in 1950–as shown in Table 8.1 (p. 152). The question that must interest the ordinary citizens of Iraq is simply this: How long will it take the economy to lift per capita GDP from the depth of its present level to that of 1960 or 1970, not to mention 1979? Given the government estimate of the relationship between investment requirements and per capita GDP and assuming availability of funds, it is obvious that ordinary citizens will have to wait for decades to recapture the living standards they "enjoyed" in 1950.

Given the depth of Iraq's multiple crises and the paucity of resources, it is difficult to see how this regime will be able to get the economy moving again. Moreover, with the overwhelming evidence of the failed policies of this regime over the last two decades, it is difficult to see how its policies can succeed in the future. One is compelled to conclude that nothing short of a radical political change will do.

This in short is the economic legacy the Baath is bestowing on Iraq. It will be decades before the country can regain the economic initiative it once had.

The economic future of Iraq looks bleak indeed.[32]

NOTES

1. See Arab Monetary Fund et al., *Joint Arab Economic Report 1992* (in Arabic) (Abu Dhabi, 1993), p. 18.

2. K. Mofid, *The Economic Consequences of the Gulf War* (London: Routledge, 1990), p. 128.

3. See United Nations Security Council, "Letter dated 24 December 1991 from the Secretary-General Addressed to the President of the Security Council," p. 15. It should be noted that the Iranian government's estimates of these damages exceed those made by the United Nations.

4. See *Middle East Economic Digest (MEED)*, January 8, 1993.

5. See Keith Bradsher, "War Damages and Old Debts Could Exhaust Iraq's Assets," *The New York Times*, March 1, 1991; *Middle East Economic Survey (MEES)*, May 13, 1991, pp. D6–D9.

6. For more details, see British Petroleum, *BP Statistical Review of World Energy* (annual); OPEC, *Annual Bulletin of Statistics*.

7. See Subroto, "Increased production capacity and its financing in OPEC Member Countries," *OPEC Bulletin,* April 1993, pp. 5–8.

8. For the distribution of output quotas, see OPEC, *Official Resolutions and Press Releases 1960–1990* (Vienna, 1990), pp. 305–308. Data on consumption, export, and output were derived from OPEC, *Annual Statistical Bulletin.*

9. For an excellent analysis of these constraints, see Walid Khadduri, "The Politics of Iraqi Oil Exports," *MEES,* May 24, 1993, pp. A1–A5.

10. Ibid.

11. See Abbas Alnasrawi, "The Petrodollar Energy Crisis: An Overview and Interpretation," *Syracuse Journal of International Law* 3 (2) (1975), pp. 387–388.

12. See Subroto, "Assessing the outlook for oil in the short-, medium- and long-term," *OPEC Bulletin,* January 1993, p. 5.

13. See Bradsher, "War Damages."

14. *MEES,* May 13, 1991, p. D6.

15. Arab Monetary Fund, *Joint Arab Economic Report 1992,* p. 18; *MEED,* January 8, 1993, p. 10.

16. See Walid Khadduri, "The Politics of Iraqi Oil Exports," *MEES,* May 24, 1993, pp. A3–A4.

17. Ibid.

18. See Sinan Al-Shabibi, "Iraq's Financial Obligations Could Cripple Economic Prospects," *MEES,* November 4, 1991, pp. B1–B2.

19. *MEES,* May 13, 1991, pp. D6–D9.

20. Ibid., p. D8. The events of 17 January is a reference, of course, to the start of the Gulf war.

21. For the text of the resolution, see U.S. Department of State, *Dispatch,* September 23, 1991, pp. 696–697.

22. See Jerry Gray, "U.N. Decides to Permit Iraq Oil Sale of $1.6 Billion," *The New York Times,* August 16, 1991, p. A8; Marian Houk, "Plan to Allow Iraqi Oil Sale Puts UN Chief in Charge, and Iraqi Officials Bristle," *The Christian Science Monitor,* August 19, 1991.

23. See, for example, Paul Lewis, "Hussein Rebuilds Iraq's Economy Undeterred by the U.N. Sanctions," *The New York Times,* January 24, 1993.

24. Tim Llewellyn, "Letter from Basra," *Middle East International,* June 25, 1993, p. 24.

25. See *MEED,* April 23, 1993, p. 24.

26. Ibid.

27. For an illustration of the paradox between the plight of the overwhelming majority of the population and the affluence of the few, see Françoise Chipaux, "Saddam Sits Pretty as Iraqi People Suffer," *Manchester Guardian Weekly,* August 11, 1991; idem, "Embargo on Iraq Hits the Wrong Targets," *Manchester Guardian Weekly,* February 21, 1993.

28. See A. M. S. Ali and H. A. J. Al-Ganabi, "Political Economy of Inflation in Iraq 1988–1992," *Arab Economic Journal* (in Arabic) 1 (Autumn 1992): 99–109.

29. Ibid.

30. Ibid.

31. See *Alhayat* (in Arabic), May 6, 1993.

32. The state of Iraq's devastated economy and the grim shortages of food

and medicine led a Food and Agriculture Organization mission to observe that government-supplied food rations offer only 50 percent of a person's nutritional needs and that Iraqis are enduring persistent deprivation, chronic hunger, endemic undernutrition, and widespread human suffering. The mission concluded that those government rations are all that stand between the Iraqi people and catastrophe. See Peter Ford, "UN Sanctions Devastate Iraq's Isolated Economy," *The Christian Science Monitor,* July 21, 1993. See also Paul Lewis, "In Iraq, Hunger Wins: Grim Shortages of Food and Medicines Force Hussein to Accept Surveillance," *The New York Times,* July 21, 1993.

The deteriorating economic and living conditions seem to have forced the government in 1993 to reconsider UNSC conditions for the sale of Iraqi oil, conditions the government had rejected in 1991. See *MEES,* July 5 and 12, 1993.

Selected Bibliography

Abdalla, Ibrahim Saad Eddin. "The Role of the State in Economic Activity in the Arab World." *Al Mustaqbal Al Arabi,* September 1989, (in Arabic).

Abdel-Fadil, Mahmoud. *Arab Economic Thought and Issues of Liberation, Development and Unity.* Beirut: Centre for Arab Unity Studies, 1982 (in Arabic).

Abdel-Malek, Anouar, ed. *Contemporary Arab Political Thought.* London: Zed Books Ltd., 1983.

Abdulghani, J. M. *Iraq and Iran: The Years of Crisis.* Baltimore: Johns Hopkins University Press, 1984.

Adelman, M. A. "Oil Prices in the Long Run (1963-1975)." *The Journal of Business* 37 (April 1964).

——. *The World Petroleum Market.* Baltimore: Johns Hopkins University Press, 1972.

Aflaq, Michel. "Arab Unity Above Socialism." In *Contemporary Arab Political Thought,* ed. Anouar Abdel-Malek. London: Zed Books, Ltd., 1983.

Agarwala, A. N., and Singh, S. P., eds. *The Economics of Underdevelopment.* London: Oxford University Press, 1958.

Akins, James E. "Politics and Saudi Oil Policy." *Middle East Economic Survey,* October 12, 1981.

Al-Ameen, A. "Investment Allocations and Plan Implementation: Iraq's Absorptive Capacity, 1951-1980." *The Journal of Energy and Development* 6: 2 (Spring 1981).

Al-Chalabi, Fadhil J. *OPEC and the International Oil Industry: A Changing Structure.* Oxford: Oxford University Press, 1980.

——. *OPEC at the Crossroads.* Oxford: Pergamon Press, 1989.

Al-Homsi, M. *Arab Economic Plans and Their Complementary and Conflicting Tendencies.* Beirut: Centre for Arab Unity Studies, 1984 (in Arabic).

Al-Husri, Sati. "The Primacy of Arabism." In *Contemporary Arab Political Thought,* ed. Anouar Abdel-Malek. London: Zed Books Ltd., 1983.

Al-Khafaji, I. *The State and Capitalist Development in Iraq 1968-1978.* Cairo: Dar Al-Mustaqbal Al-Arabi, 1983 (in Arabic).

——. "The War and the Iraqi Economy." *Al-Thaqafa Al-Jadida.* June 1989 (in Arabic).

Al-Pachachi, N. *Facts and Figures on Oil Policy.* Baghdad: Al-Shaab Press, 1958.

Al-Roubaie, A., and ElAli, W. "The Impact of Economic Sanctions Against Iraq." Paper presented at the annual meeting of the Middle East Economic Association, Anaheim, Calif., January 1993.

Al-Shabibi, S. "Iraq's Financial Obligations Could Cripple Economic Prospects." *Middle East Economic Survey,* November 4, 1991.

Ali, A. M. S., and Al-Ganabi, H. A. J. "Political Economy of Inflation in Iraq 1988–1992." *Arab Economic Journal* 1 (Autumn 1992) (in Arabic).

Allen, Loring. *OPEC Oil.* Cambridge, Mass.: Oelgeschlager, Gunn & Hain, 1979.

Alnasrawi, Abbas. *Arab Nationalism, Oil and the Political Economy of Dependency.* Westport, Conn.: Greenwood Press, 1991.

——. *Arab Oil and U.S. Energy Requirements.* Belmont, Mass.: AAUG Press, 1982.

——. "Collective Bargaining Power in OPEC." *Journal of World Trade Law* 7: 2 (1973): 188–207.

——. *Financing Economic Development in Iraq.* New York: Praeger, 1967.

——. "Iraq: Economic Consequences of the 1991 Gulf War and Future Outlook." *Third World Quarterly* 13: 2 (1992).

——. *OPEC in a Changing World Economy.* Baltimore: Johns Hopkins University Press, 1985.

Amin, Samir. *The Arab Nation: Nationalism and Class Struggles.* London: Zed Books Ltd., 1978.

Arab Monetary Fund. *The Arab States: Economic Data and Statistics, 1975–1983.* Abu Dhabi, 1985.

——. *National Account of the Arab States, 1972–1983.* Abu Dhabi, 1984.

Arab Monetary Fund et al. *Joint Arab Economic Report* (annual).

Arthur D. Little, Inc. *A Plan for Industrial Development in Iraq.* Cambridge, Mass.: Arthur D. Little, Inc., 1956.

Bain, Joe S. *The Economics of the Pacific Coast Petroleum Industry.* Berkeley and Los Angeles: University of California Press, 1944.

——. *Pricing, Distribution and Employment.* New York: Henry Holt and Co., 1953.

Batatu, Hanna. *The Old Social Classes and the Revolutionary Movements of Iraq: A Study of Iraq's Old Landed and Commercial Classes and of Its Communists, Ba'thists, and Free Officers.* Princeton: Princeton University Press, 1982.

Beblawi, Hazem. "The Rentier State in the Arab World." *Arab Studies Quarterly* 9: 4 (Fall 1987).

Berberoglu, B., ed. *Power and Stability in the Middle East.* London: Zed Books Ltd., 1989.

Bina, Cyrus. "Competition, Control and Price Formation in the International Energy Industry." *Energy Economics* 11: 3 (July 1989).

——. "Limits of OPEC Profits and the Nature of Global Oil Accumulation." *OPEC Review* 14: 1 (Spring 1990).

Blair, John M. *The Control of Oil.* New York: Pantheon Books, 1976.

Bradsher, K. "War Damages and Old Debts Could Exhaust Iraq's Assets." *The New York Times,* March 1, 1991.

Butler, Stuart M., ed. *The Privatization Option: A Strategy to Shrink the Size of Government.* Washington: The Heritage Foundation, 1985.

Campagna, A. S. *The Economic Consequences of the Vietnam War.* New York: Praeger, 1991.

Chandler, L. V. *Central Banking and Economic Development.* Bombay: University of Bombay, 1962.

Chaudhry, K. A. "On the Way to Market: Economic Liberalization and Iraq's Invasion of Kuwait." *Middle East Report* 170 (May/June 1991).

Chenery, H. B. "Comparative Advantage and Development Policy." *American Economic Review* 51 (March 1961).

Chilcote, Ronald H. *Theories of Development and Underdevelopment.* Boulder, Colo.: Westview Press, 1984.

Chipaux, F. "Embargo on Iraq Hits the Wrong Targets." *Manchester Guardian Weekly,* February 21, 1993.

———. "Saddam Sits Pretty as Iraqi People Suffer." *Manchester Guardian Weekly,* August 11, 1991.

Clark, J. M. "Basing Point Methods of Price Quoting." *The Canadian Journal of Economic and Political Science* 4: 4 (1938): 477–489.

Clawson, M. *Natural Resources and International Development.* Baltimore: Johns Hopkins University Press, 1964.

Congressional Budget Office. *Limiting Conventional Arms Exports to the Middle East.* Washington, D.C.: U.S. Government Printing Office, 1992.

Coqueron, F. G. *Capital Investment by the World Petroleum Industry.* New York: Chase Manhattan Bank, 1961.

Dawisha, Adeed. *The Arab Radicals.* New York: Council on Foreign Relations, 1986.

Dos Santos, Theotonio. "The Structure of Dependence." *American Economic Review* 60: 2 (May 1970).

El Azhary, M. S., ed. *Iran–Iraq War: An Historical Analysis.* New York: St. Martin's Press, 1984.

El-Naggar, Said, ed. *Privatization and Structural Adjustment in the Arab Countries.* Washington: International Monetary Fund, 1989.

Engler, Robert. *The Politics of Oil: A Study of the Private Power and Democratic Directions.* Chicago: University of Chicago Press, 1961.

Epstein, Gerald. "The Triple Debt Crisis." *World Policy Journal* 2: 4 (Fall 1988).

Faris, H. A., ed. *Arab Nationalism and the Future of the Arab World.* Belmont, Mass.: AAUG Press, 1987.

Farouk-Sluglett, M., and Sluglett, P. *Iraq since 1958: From Revolution to Dictatorship.* London: KPI, 1987.

Fellner, W. "Collusion and Its Limits under Oligopoly." *American Economic Review,* Proceedings 41 (May 1950).

———. *Competition among the Few.* New York: Augustus M. Kelly, 1960.

Ford, P. "UN Sanctions Devastate Iraq's Isolated Economy." *The Christian Science Monitor,* July 21, 1993.

Frank, Helmut J. *Crude Oil Prices in the Middle East: A Study in Oligopolistic*

Price Behavior. New York: Praeger, 1966.

Frankel, P. H. "American Oil in a Changing World." *Oil Forum,* November 1950.

———. *Oil, The Facts of Life.* London: Weidenfield and Nicolson, 1962.

———. "What Price Oil? The International Structure." *Oil Forum,* November 1948.

Fransen, Herman. "Energy Demand and Supply in the 1980s." *Journal of Energy and Development* 6: 2 (1981): 213–224.

Galenson, W., and Leibenstein, H. "Investment Criteria, Productivity, and Economic Development." *Quarterly Journal of Economics* 69 (August 1955): 343–370.

Gellman, B. "Allied Air War Struck Broadly in Iraq: Officials Acknowledge Strategy Went Beyond Purely Military Targets." *The Washington Post,* June 23, 1991.

General Accounting Office. *The Changing Structure of the International Oil Market.* Washington, D.C.: U.S. Government Printing Office, 1982.

Georgescu-Roegen, Nicholas. *Energy and Economic Myths: Institutional and Analytical Economic Essays.* New York: Pergamon Press, 1976.

Gray, J. "U.N. Decides to Permit Iraq Oil Sale of $1.6 Billion." *The New York Times,* August 16, 1991.

Griffin, James M., and Teece, David J. *OPEC Behavior and World Oil Prices.* London: Allen and Unwin, 1982.

Haider, S. *Economic Development in Iraq.* Baghdad: Iraqi Publication and Printing, 1954 (in Arabic).

Harik, I., and Sullivan, D. J., eds. *Privatization and Liberalization in the Middle East.* Bloomington: Indiana University Press, 1992.

Hartshorn, J. E. "Netbacks and the Price Collapse." *Middle East Economic Survey,* March 17, 1986.

———. *Objectives of the Petroleum Exporting Countries.* Nicosia: Middle East Petroleum and Economic Publications, 1978.

———. *Politics of World Oil Economics.* New York: Frederick A. Praeger, 1962.

Harvard Study Team Report. *Public Health in Iraq after the Gulf War.* Washington, D.C.: Wagner Communications, May 1991.

Hasan, Mohammad Salman. *Studies in the Iraqi Economy.* Beirut: Dar al-Taliaa, 1966 (in Arabic).

Haseeb, K. *The National Income of Iraq 1953–1961.* London: Oxford University Press, 1964.

Hashem, J. *Capital Formation in Iraq 1957/1970.* Beirut: Arab Organization for Studies and Publishing, 1975 (in Arabic).

Haub, C. "A Demographic Disaster." *Manchester Guardian Weekly,* March 10, 1991.

Helms, Christine Moss. *Iraq: The Eastern Flank of the Arab World.* Washington, D.C.: The Brookings Institution, 1984.

Higgins, B. H. *Economic Development Principles, Problems and Policies.* New York: W. W. Norton, 1968.

Hilterman, J. R. "Diverting Water, Displacing Iraq's Marsh People." *Middle East Report* 181 (March/April 1993).

Hiro, D. *Desert Shield to Desert Storm: The Second Gulf War.* New York: Routledge, 1992.

——. *The Longest War: The Iran–Iraq Military Conflict.* New York: Routledge, 1991.

Hirschman, A. O. *The Strategy of Economic Development.* New Haven: Yale University Press, 1958.

Hirst, D. *Oil and Public Opinion in the Middle East.* New York: Praeger, 1966.

Houk, M. "Plan to Allow Iraqi Oil Sale Puts UN Chief in Charge, and Iraqi Officials Bristle." *The Christian Science Monitor,* August 19, 1991.

Hourani, Albert. *Arabic Thought in the Liberal Age, 1798–1939.* London: Oxford University Press, 1962.

Ibrahim, I., ed. *The Gulf Crisis: Background and Consequences.* Washington, D.C.: Georgetown University, 1992.

International Bank for Reconstruction and Development. *The Economic Development of Iraq.* Baltimore: Johns Hopkins University Press, 1952.

International Energy Agency. *Energy Policies and Programs of IEA Countries, 1977 Review.* Paris: The Agency, 1978.

——. *World Energy Outlook.* Paris: The Agency, 1982.

International Study Team. *Health and Welfare in Iraq after the Gulf Crisis: An In-Depth Assessment.* October 1991 (no place of publication indicated).

Iraq, Government of. *The July 14 Revolution in Its First Year.* Baghdad, 1959 (in Arabic).

——. *The July 14 Revolution in Its Second Year.* Baghdad, 1960 (in Arabic).

Iraq Advisory Council. *Proceedings of Iraqi-Egyptian Dialogue.* Vienna, 1991 (in Arabic).

Iraq Development Board. *Annual Report for the Fiscal Year 1954.* Baghdad, 1957 (in Arabic).

——. *Annual Report 1954–1955.* Baghdad, 1957 (in Arabic).

——. *Annual Report 1956–1957.* Baghdad, 1958 (in Arabic).

——. *Development of Iraq.* Baghdad, 1956 (in Arabic).

——. *Great Irrigation Projects.* Baghdad, 1954 (in Arabic).

Iraq Ministry of Agrarian Reform. *Agrarian Reform.* Baghdad, 1961 (in Arabic).

——. *Agrarian Reform in Six Years.* Baghdad, 1964 (in Arabic).

Iraq Ministry of Guidance. *Provisional Economic Plan.* Baghdad, 1959.

Iraq Ministry of Planning. *The Agricultural Sector.* Baghdad, 1971 (in Arabic).

——. *The Agricultural Sector in the Five-Year Plan 1965–1969.* Baghdad, (in Arabic).

——. *Analysis of the Iraqi Economy to the Base Year 1969.* Baghdad, 1970 (in Arabic).

——. *Buildings and Services Sector.* Baghdad, 1971 (in Arabic).

——. *Collection of Laws and Regulations Relating to the Formation of Planning Systems in Iraq and Laws of Development Programs and Economic Plans 1950–1970.* Baghdad, 1971 (in Arabic).

——. *Detailed Framework of the Five-Year Plan for 1965–1969.* Baghdad, 1969 (in Arabic).

——. *Detailed Objectives of the Components of the National Development Plan, 1970–1974.* Baghdad, 1971 (in Arabic).

——. *Evaluation of the Five-Year Economic Plan, 1965–1969.* Baghdad, 1971 (in Arabic).

——. *Explanatory Memorandum for Provisional Economic Plan* Baghdad,

1959 (in Arabic).

——. *Follow-Up Annual Report on the Implementation of the Five-Year Plan in the Fiscal Year 1968/1969.* Baghdad, 1971 (in Arabic).

——. *General Summary of Central Goverment Investment Allocations and Self-Financed Investment in the Public Sector and Non-Sectoral Investment Allocations.* Baghdad, 1971 (in Arabic).

——. *Guide to the National Development Plan, 1970–1974.* Baghdad, 1971 (in Arabic).

——. *The Industrial Sector.* Baghdad, 1971 (in Arabic).

——. *Law of National Development Plan for the Fiscal Years 1970–1974 and the Explanatory Memorandum.* Baghdad, 1970 (in Arabic).

——. *Law of National Development Plan 1970–1974 and the General Objectives of the Plan.* Baghdad, 1971 (in Arabic).

——. *National Income Accounts and Sectoral Accounts of Capital Formation and Its Financing, 1969 and 1974.* Baghdad, 1971 (in Arabic).

——. *Progress in the Shadow of Planning.* Baghdad, 1971 (in Arabic).

——. *Progress in the Shadow of Planning.* Baghdad, 1972 (in Arabic).

——. *Progress in the Shadow of Planning.* Baghdad, 1973 (in Arabic).

——. *Progress in the Shadow of Planning.* Baghdad, 1974 (in Arabic).

——. *Progress under Planning.* Baghdad, 1974.

——. *Report of the Implementation of the Objectives of the Third Year of the Plan, 1967/1968.* Baghdad, n.d. (in Arabic).

——. *Sources of Finance in Central Government Sector.* Baghdad, 1971 (in Arabic).

——. *Synopses of Planning in Iraq.* Baghdad, 1969 (in Arabic).

——. *Transportation, Communication and Storage Sector.* Baghdad, 1971 (in Arabic).

Iraq National Oil Company. *Iraq National Oil Company and Direct Exploitation of Oil in Iraq.* Baghdad, 1973.

——. *Oil in Iraq: From Concessions to Direct National Investment, 1912–1972.* Baghdad, 1973 (in Arabic).

Issawi, Charles. *An Economic History of the Middle East and North Africa.* New York: Columbia University Press, 1982.

Issawi, Charles, and Yeganeh, Mohammed. *The Economics of Middle Eastern Oil.* New York: Frederick A. Praeger, 1962.

Iversen, C. *Monetary Policy in Iraq.* Baghdad: National Bank of Iraq, 1954.

Kaysen, Carl. "Basing Point Pricing and Public Policy." *Quarterly Journal of Economics* 62: 3 (1949).

Kazeeha, Walid. "Arab Nationalism in the Stage between the Two World Wars." *Al Mustaqbal Al Arabi* 5 (January 1979) (in Arabic).

——. "The Concept of Arab Unity in Early Twentieth Century." *Al Mustaqbal Al Arabi* 4 (November 1978) (in Arabic).

——. "The Social-Political Foundations of the Growth of Contemporary Nationalist Movement in the Arab East." *Al Mustaqbal Al Arabi* 6 (March 1979) (in Arabic).

Khadduri, Walid. "Arab Oil Decisions for the Years 1973–1974: A Study of Arab Decision Making." In *How Decisions Are Made in the Arab Nation.* Beirut: Centre for Arab Unity Studies, 1985 (in Arabic).

——. "The Politics of Iraqi Oil Exports." *Middle East Economic Survey*, May 24, 1993.

Kubba, I. *Feudalism in Iraq between Nuri Al-Said and the "Free World" Experts.* Baghdad: Al-Maarif Press, 1967 (in Arabic).

——. *This Is the Path of July 14: Defense before the Revolution's Court.* Beirut: Dar al-Taliaa, 1969 (in Arabic).

Langley, K. M. *The Industrialization of Iraq.* Cambridge: Harvard University Press, 1962.

——. "Iraq: Some Aspects of the Economic Scene." *The Middle East Journal* 18 (Spring 1964).

League of Arab States. *Specialized Arab Organizations: Basic Information and Founding Documents.* Tunis, 1984 (in Arabic).

Leeman, Wayne A. *The Price of Middle East Oil: An Essay in Political Economy.* Ithaca: Cornell University Press, 1962.

Levy, W. J. "World Oil in Transition." *The Economist*, August 19, 1961.

Lewis, P. "In Iraq, Hunger Wins: Grim Shortages of Food and Medications Force Hussein to Accept Surveillance." *The New York Times*, July 21, 1993.

Lewis, W. A. *The Theory of Economic Growth.* London: George Allen & Unwin, 1955.

Loftus, J. A. "Middle East Oil: The Pattern of Control." *The Middle East Journal* 2 (January 1948): 17–32.

Longrigg, S. H. *Oil in the Middle East.* Oxford: Royal Institute of International Affairs, 1961.

Lubell, H. *The Soviet Oil Offensive and Interbloc Economic Competition.* Santa Monica: The Rand Corporation, 1961.

McLean, J. G., and Haigh, R. W. *The Growth in Integrated Oil Companies.* Boston: Harvard University, Graduate School of Business Administration, 1954.

Mead, Walter J. "An Economic Analysis of Crude Oil Price Behavior in the 1970s." *Journal of Energy and Development* 4: 2 (1979): 212–228.

Meier, G. M. *Leading Issues in Development Economics.* New York: Oxford University Press, 1964.

Melmaid, Alexander. "Geography of World Petroleum Price Structure." *Economic Geography* 38: 4 (1962): 283–298.

Meyer, A. J. "Economic Modernization." In *The United States and the Middle East.* New York: American Assembly, Columbia University, 1964.

——. *Middle Eastern Capitalism.* Cambridge: Harvard University Press, 1959.

Mikesell, R. F., ed. *Foreign Investment in the Petroleum and Mineral Industries.* Baltimore: Johns Hopkins University Press, 1971.

Miller, J. "Displaced in the Gulf: 5 Million Refugees." *The New York Times*, June 16, 1991.

Mofid, K. *The Economic Consequences of the Gulf War.* London: Routledge, 1990.

Murphy, C. "Iraqi Death Toll Remains Clouded." *The Washington Post*, June 23, 1991.

Mutawali, H. *The Economy of Iraq.* Damascus: Center for Economic Studies, 1964 (in Arabic).

Nassar, A., ed. *The Role of the State in Economic Activity in the Arab World.* Kuwait: Arab Planning Institute, 1991 (in Arabic).

Neil, Jacoby H. *Multinational Oil.* New York: Macmillan, 1974.

Noreng, Oystein. *Oil Politics in the 1980s: Patterns of International Cooperation.* New York: McGraw Hill Book Co., 1978.

Nurkse, R. *Problems of Capital Formation in Underdeveloped Countries.* Oxford: Basil Blackwell, 1953.

Odell, P. R. *Oil and World Power.* Harmondsworth, England: Penguin Books, 1979.

Oman, C. P., and Wignaraja, G. *The Postwar Evolution of Development Thinking.* New York: St. Martin's Press, 1991.

Organization for Economic Cooperation and Development. *Energy Prospects to 1985.* 2 vols. Paris: The Organization, 1974.

——. *Export Cartels.* Paris: The Organization, 1974.

——. *World Energy Outlook.* Paris: The Organization, 1977.

Organization of Petroleum Exporting Countries. *Annual Bulletin of Statistics.* Vienna: The Organization, annual.

——. *From Concessions to Contracts.* Geneva: The Organization, 1965.

——. *Monthly Bulletin.*

——. *The Oil Industry's Organization in the Middle East and Some of Its Fiscal Consequences.* Geneva: The Organization, 1963.

——. *OPEC and the Oil Industry in the Middle East.* Geneva: The Organization, 1962.

——. *OPEC Official Resolutions and Press Releases 1960–1990.* Vienna: The Organization, 1990.

——. *Radical Changes in the International Oil Industry during the Past Decade.* Geneva: The Organization, 1963.

——. "Report of OPEC's Ministerial Committee on Long Term Strategy." *International Currency Review,* July 1980.

——. *Taxation Economics in Crude Production.* Geneva: The Organization, 1965.

Owen, Roger. *The Middle East in the World Economy, 1800–1914.* New York: Methuen, 1981.

Pachachi, N. "The Development of Concession Arrangements in the Middle East." *Middle East Economic Survey,* March 29, 1968.

Penrose, Edith. *The Growth of the Firms, Middle East Oil, and Other Essays.* London: Frank Cass & Co., 1971.

——. *The Large International Firm in Developing Countries: The International Petroleum Industry.* London: Allen & Unwin, 1968.

Penrose, E. "Middle East Oil: The International Distribution of Profits and Income Tax." *Economica* 27 (August 1960).

——. "Profit Sharing between Producing Countries and Oil Companies in the Middle East." *Economic Journal* 49 (June 1959).

Pindyck, Robert S. *Advances in the Economics of Energy and Resources.* 2 vols. Greenwich, Conn.: JAI Press, 1979.

——. *The Structure of World Energy Demand.* Cambridge, Mass.: MIT Press, 1979.

Powelson, John O. P. "The Oil Price Increase: Impacts on Industrial and Less-Developed Countries." *Journal of Energy and Development* 3: 1 (1977): 10–25.

Rodinson, Maxime. *The Arabs*. Chicago: University of Chicago Press, 1981.

———. *Marxism and the Muslim World*. New York: Monthly Review Press, 1981.

Rouhani, Fuad. *A History of O.P.E.C.* New York: Praeger Publishers, 1971.

Sadowski, Yahha. "Patronage and the Ba'th: Corruption and Control in Contemporary Syria." *Arab Studies Quarterly* 9: 4 (Fall 1987).

———. *Scuds or Butter: The Political Economy of Arms Control*. Washington, D.C.: The Brookings Institution, 1993.

Salinger, P., and Laurant, E. *Secret Dossier: The Hidden Agenda behind the Gulf War*. London: Penguin Books, 1991.

Salman, R. "Iraq's Oil Policy." *Middle East Economic Survey*, March 12, 1990.

Sayigh, Yezid. *Arab Military Industry*. Beirut: Centre for Arab Unity Studies, 1992 (in Arabic).

Sayigh, Y. A. *The Economies of the Arab World: Development since 1945*. New York: St. Martin's Press, 1978.

———. *Elusive Development: From Dependence to Self-Reliance in the Arab Region*. London: Routledge, 1991.

Sayigh, Yusif A. "Arab Economic Integration and the Pretext of National Sovereignty." *Al Mustaqbal Al Arabi* 6 (March 1979) (in Arabic).

Seymour, Ian. *OPEC: An Instrument of Change*. London: Macmillan Press, 1980.

Shahin, M. "Surviving Sanction." *Middle East International*, June 25, 1993.

Shell Briefing Service. *Energy Profile*. London: Shell Briefing Service, 1980.

———. *The OPEC Allowances*. London: Shell Briefing Service, 1969.

Shell International Petroleum Company. *Current International Oil Pricing Problems*. London, 1963.

Shuqair, Muhammad L. *Arab Economic Unity: Its Experiences and Expectations*. 2 vols. Beirut: Centre for Arab Unity Studies, 1986 (in Arabic).

Sifry, M. L., and Cerf, C., eds. *The Gulf War Reader: History, Documents, Opinions*. New York: Random House, 1991.

Smithies, A. "Aspects of the Basing Point System." *American Economic Review* 32 (December 1942).

———. "Economic Consequences of the Basing Point Decisions." *Harvard Law Review* 62: (1949).

Solow, R. M. "The Economics of Resources or the Resources of Economics." *American Economic Review*, May 1974, p. 1014.

Springborg, R. "Infitah, Agrarian Transformation, and the Elite Consolidation in Contemporary Iraq." *The Middle East Journal* 40: 1 (Winter 1986).

Stauffer, T. R. "Economic Warfare in the Gulf." *American-Arab Affairs* 14 (Fall 1985).

Stavrianos, L. S. *Global Rift: The Third World Comes of Age*. New York: Morrow, 1981.

Stigler, George J. *The Theory of Price*. 3rd ed. New York: Macmillan Co., 1966.

Stivers, William. *Supremacy and Oil: Iraq, Turkey, and the Anglo-American World Order, 1918–1930*. Ithaca: Cornell University Press, 1982.

Stocking, George W. *Middle East Oil: A Study in Political and Economic Controversy.* Nashville: Vanderbilt University Press, 1970.

Stork, Joe, and Jim Paul. "Arms Sales and the Militarization of the Middle East." *MERIP Reports,* February 1983.

Subroto. "Energy into the 21st Century: An OPEC View." *OPEC Bulletin,* May 1990.

———. "How OPEC Sees the Crucial Energy Issues of the 1990s." *OPEC Bulletin,* April 1990.

Sweezy, P. M. "Demand under Conditions of Oligopoly." *Journal of Political Economy* 47 (August 1939).

Tibi, Bassam. *Arab Nationalism: A Critical Enquiry.* New York: St. Martin's Press, 1981.

UNICEF. *Details of the UNICEF Component of the United Nations Inter-Agency Programme for Iraq, Kuwait and the Iraq/Turkey and Iraq/Iran Border Areas.* New York: UNICEF, 1991.

UNICEF et al. *Vitamin A Deficiency and Malnutrition in Southern Iraq: Rapid Assessment Report 14-26 May 1991.* New York: UNICEF, 1991.

United Nations. *Economic Developments in the Middle East 1945-1954.* New York: United Nations, 1955.

———. *Economic Developments in the Middle East 1955-1956.* New York: United Nations, 1957.

———. *Economic Developments in the Middle East 1956-1957.* New York: United Nations, 1958.

———. *Economic Developments in the Middle East 1957-1958.* New York: United Nations, 1959.

———. *Economic Developments in the Middle East 1958-1959.* New York: United Nations, 1960.

———. *Economic Developments in the Middle East 1959-1960.* New York: United Nations, 1962.

———. *Economic Developments in the Middle East 1961-1963.* New York: United Nations, 1964.

———. *Letter Dated 20 March 1991 from the Secretary General Addressed to the President of the Security Council.* New York.

———. *National Accounts Statistics: Analysis of Main Aggregates, 1988-1989.* New York: United Nations, 1991.

———. *Report to the Secretary General on Humanitarian Needs in Iraq by a Mission Led by Sadruddin Aga Khan, Executive Delegate of the Secretary General, dated 15 July 1991.* New York: United Nations, 1991.

United Nations Economic Commission for Europe. *The Price of Oil in Western Europe.* Geneva: United Nations, 1955.

United Nations Food and Agricultural Organization Mediterranean Development Project. *Iraq, Country Report.* Rome, 1959.

United States. Arms Control and Disarmament Agency. *World Military Expenditures and Arms Transfers.* Washington, D.C., annual.

United States Congress. House. Armed Services Committee. *A Defense for a New Era: Lessons of the Persian Gulf War.* Washington, D.C.: U.S. Government Printing Office, 1992.

United States Congress. Senate. Committee on Energy and Natural Resources. *Access to Oil—The United States' Relationships with Saudi Arabia and Iran.* Washington, D.C.: U.S. Government Printing Office, 1977.

——. *The Geopolitics of Oil.* Washington, D.C.: U.S. Government Printing Office, 1980.

United States Congress. Senate. Committee on Foreign Relations. Subcommittee on Multinational Corporations. *Multinational Oil Corporations and U.S. Foreign Policy.* Washington, D.C.: U.S. Government Printing Office, 1975.

United States Congress. Senate. Select Committee on Small Business. *The International Petroleum Cartel.* Washington, D.C.: U.S. Government Printing Office, 1952.

Vernon, Raymond, ed. *The Promise of Privatization: A Challenge for American Policy.* New York: Council on Foreign Relations, 1988.

Vickers, John, and Yarrow, George. *Privatization: An Economic Analysis.* Cambridge, Mass.: MIT Press, 1988.

Warriner, Doreen. *Land Reform and Development in the Middle East: A Study of Egypt, Syria and Iraq.* London: Royal Institute of International Affairs, 1957.

Waterbury, John. *The Egypt of Nasser and Sadat: The Political Economy of Two Regimes.* Princeton: Princeton University Press, 1983.

Weisberg, Richard C. *The Politics of Crude Oil Pricing in the Middle East, 1970–1975.* Berkeley, Calif.: Institute of International Studies, 1977.

Willet, Thomas D. *The Oil-Transfer Problem and International Economic Stability.* Princeton: Princeton University Press, 1975.

World Bank. *World Development Report.* Annual.

——. *World Tables.* 3rd ed. Baltimore: Johns Hopkins University Press, 1983.

Zalzala, Abdel Hasan. "The Challenges Facing Arab Economic Integration." *Al Mustaqbal Al Arabi* 21 (November 10, 1980) (in Arabic).

——. "The Economic Role of the League of Arab States." *Al Mustaqbal Al Arabi* 42, 43, and 44 (August–October 1982) (in Arabic).

Index

ABOUT THE AUTHOR

ABBAS ALNASRAWI is Professor of Economics at the University of Vermont, where he has been a member of the faculty since 1963. Dr. Alnasrawi has written four books, *Arab Nationalism, Oil and the Political Economy of Dependency* (Greenwood Press, 1991); *OPEC in the Changing World Economy; Arab Oil and U.S. Energy Requirements;* and *Financing Economic Development in Iraq* (Praeger, 1967).